TOPICS IN LEARNING AND PERFORMANCE

TOPICS IN LEARNING AND PERFORMANCE

Edited by

RICHARD F. THOMPSON

DEPARTMENT OF PSYCHOBIOLOGY
UNIVERSITY OF CALIFORNIA
IRVINE, CALIFORNIA

JAMES F. VOSS

DEPARTMENT OF PSYCHOLOGY
UNIVERSITY OF PITTSBURGH
PITTSBURGH, PENNSYLVANIA

ACADEMIC PRESS New York and London 1972

ACADEMIC PRESS, INC.
111 Fifth Avenue, New York, New York 10003

United Kingdom Edition published by
ACADEMIC PRESS, INC. (LONDON) LTD.
24/28 Oval Road, London NW1 7DD

LIBRARY OF CONGRESS CATALOG CARD NUMBER: 70-182665

PRINTED IN THE UNITED STATES OF AMERICA

WE DEDICATE THIS BOOK

to Professor W. J. Brogden

CONTENTS

Chapter 3 Population Pressure, Pollution, and the Behavior of Cichlid Fishes

Donald R. Hoffeld

Chapter 4 Incubation of Avoidance Produced by Generalization to Stimuli of the Conditioning Apparatus

Michael Gabriel

Chapter 5 Component Dynamics within Compound Stimuli

Thomas W. Baker

Chapter 6 Sensory Preconditioning

Richard F. Thompson

Chapter 7 Intratask Interference as a Source of Facilitation in Transfer and Retention

William F. Battig

LIST OF CONTRIBUTORS

Numbers in parentheses indicate the pages on which the authors' contributions begin.

THOMAS W. BAKER (85), Department of Psychology, Lawrence University, Appleton, Wisconsin

WILLIAM F. BATTIG (131), Department of Psychology, University of Colorado, Boulder, Colorado

WILLIAM L. BEWLEY (187), Department of Psychology, Lawrence University, Appleton, Wisconsin

GEORGE E. BRIGGS (1), Department of Psychology, The Ohio State University, Columbus, Ohio

MICHAEL GABRIEL (59), Department of Psychology, Pomona College, Claremont, California

DONALD R. HOFFELD (41), Department of Psychology, Louisiana State University, Baton Rouge, Louisiana

DOUGLAS L. NELSON (215), Department of Psychology, University of South Florida, Tampa, Florida

WILLIAM E. SIMPSON (17), Department of Psychology, State University of New York, College at Oswego, New York

CHARLES P. THOMPSON (241), Department of Psychology, Kansas State University, Manhattan, Kansas

RICHARD F. THOMPSON (105), Department of Psychobiology, University of California, Irvine, California

JAMES F. VOSS (161), Department of Psychology, University of Pittsburgh, Pittsburgh, Pennsylvania

PREFACE

The chapters in this volume are all original contributions surveying current topics in learning and performance. The book is planned for use in upper division and graduate courses and seminars.

Chapter 1 deals with fundamental issues in human performance. Chapter 2 relates human sensory processing to performance. Chapter 3 deals with performance in an ecological context. Chapters 4–6 treat fundamental issues in conditioning. In the remainder of the text, Chapters 7–11, basic topics in human verbal learning and memory are discussed.

This book is not meant to be a comprehensive survey of the vast field of learning and performance. Instead, particular topics of current interest are discussed in depth in the various chapters. Consequently, the book can be used as an ancillary text in a variety of courses in the general areas of learning and performance.

RICHARD F. THOMPSON
JAMES F. VOSS

PROFESSOR W. J. BROGDEN—A TRIBUTE

This volume is a tribute to Professor W. J. Brogden, each chapter having been contributed by a student of his. As such, the book itself stands as an expression of the respect and indebtedness which each of Wulf's students has for his mentor.

The nature of gratitude and respect, however, cannot always be sensed from the final product, any more than the thought, time, and energy that go into science can be fully stated in a brief experimental report. Similarly, those who have worked with Wulf share the belief that his most important influence emphasized not only the final product, but even to a greater extent the means.

The term rigorous scientist may be regarded as a cliché, but those who have worked with Professor Brogden have been exposed not to these words but to a model who epitomized these traits. As one of the country's leading experimental psychologists, Professor Brogden's training of students was concerned not only with the importance of initiating, developing, conducting, and communicating significant experimentation, but also with the crucial significance of proper controls. Indeed, the topics discussed in this volume do not reflect a particular theoretical viewpoint or even a limited content area; instead, the common denominator of the individuals trained by Professor Brogden is their appreciation of the nature of sound experimentation in the areas of learning and performance.

In addition to his insistence upon properly designed, controlled, and analyzed experimentation, Professor Brogden not only encouraged but stressed the importance of independence in thesis and dissertation research. His emphasis upon the importance of independent thinking in scientific research is exemplified by his own research career, a career which clearly reflects an unusual generality of interest in a variety of topics, many of which he originated and pursued. Indeed, Professor Brogden's research career is characterized by the systematic and parametric investigation of a number of very significant problems irrespective of whether or not the particular issue was considered a "hot" topic of theoretical interest to other laboratories at the time. He recognizes more than most scientists that scientific knowledge supercedes transient "fads."

While emphasizing independence in thesis and dissertation research, Professor Brogden has also believed in the equality of his collaborators. In research conferences between Professor Brogden and his students, ideas, designs, and procedures were evaluated regardless of their source. In joint or multiple authorship, almost invariably the names of students occur first, with the names of more than one student occurring in alphabetical order.

To fellow psychologists, Wulf Brogden is probably best known for his discovery of sensory preconditioning. However, his contributions cover a much wider range of phenomena. With Lipman and Culler, he conducted an experiment on the comparison of avoidance and classical conditioning which has become one of the most widely cited papers in the conditioning literature. Professor Brogden was also one of the first investigators to use a partial reinforcement technique and, during and following World War II, he, in collaboration with his students, published an extensive series of studies on tracking. Professor Brogden has also pursued research on verbal mazes and serial learning, has investigated the question of the contiguity basis of conditioning, and has studied certain problems in sensory psychology.

We, the contributors to this volume, wish to acknowledge a man who has taught us much about science, about psychology, about research, and, perhaps most important of all, about scientific and human integrity. Indeed, his conduct with respect to his students as well as colleagues has embraced the highest form of professional behavior and respect for the individual. It has been our good fortune to have worked with Professor Brogden in the infancy of our careers, and to him we wish to express our appreciation.

W. J. Brogden was born May 6, 1912, in Sydney, Australia, and he has lived in the United States since 1914. He attended Southern Methodist University from 1929 to 1932, and received B.A. and Ph.D. degrees at the University of Illinois in 1933 and 1936, respectively. He studied at the Pavlovian Laboratory, Johns Hopkins School of Medicine, from 1936 to 1939, working with W. H. Gantt. From 1936 to 1937 he was a postdoctoral fellow of the National Research Council, and from 1937 to 1939 he held a research appointment on funds supplied by the Medical Sciences Division of the Rockefeller Foundation. Except for some time during World War II and for two summer sessions, he has been at the University of Wisconsin, serving as Assistant Professor of Psychology (1939–1943), Associate Professor of Psychology (1944–1946), and Professor of Psychology since 1946. Professor Brogden also served as Assistant Dean (1947–1951) and Associate Dean (1951–1958) of the Graduate School. He was Visiting Lecturer at the University of Rochester during the summer of 1942 and at Harvard University during the summer of 1946. At the University of Wisconsin Professor Brogden has served on a number of departmental and university committees. As chairman of the building committee, he played an important role in the development of Wisconsin's excellent research facilities.

In addition to his university affiliation, Professor Brogden has held a number of professional and governmental posts. During World War II, he was with the National Research Council in the fall of 1942, he was Director of a National Defense Research Committee research project at Brown University in 1943 and Director of several NDRC research projects at the University of Wisconsin from 1944–1945, and in 1947 he was awarded a Presidential Certificate of Appreciation. He has been Secretary-Treasurer and President of the Division of Experimental Psychology of the American Psychological Association, a member of the APA Council of Representatives, and a member of several APA and Division 3 committees. He was elected to membership in the Society of Experimental Psychologists. He was a member of the Founding Committee of the Psychonomics Society, and has served as a member of the Governing Board and as Chairman of the Society. He has been a member of several Panels of the Research and Development Board of the Department of Defense and Chairman of the Panel of

Psychophysiology of the Office of Naval Research. He has been a member of the Division of Anthropology and Psychology of the National Research Council and a member of several of its committees. He was Chairman of the Advisory Committee on Fellowship Selection Research for NSF Fellows in the Office of Scientific Personnel, National Academy of Sciences; he has served on the Research Advisory Committee of this Office and is currently a member of its Advisory Committee.

RICHARD F. THOMPSON
JAMES F. VOSS

BIBLIOGRAPHY

1935

Brogden, W. J., & Culler, E. Experimental extinction of higher-order responses. *American Journal of Psychology,* 1935, **47,** 663–669.

Brogden, W. J., Mettler, F., & Culler, E. Experimentally increased intracranial pressure. *Archives of Otolaryngology,* 1935, **21,** 464–465.

Culler, E., Finch, G., Girden, E., & Brogden, W. Measurements of acuity by the conditioned-response technique. *Journal of General Psychology,* 1935, **12,** 223–227.

1936

Brogden, W. J. Increased auditory acuity in dogs following roentgen radiation of the pituitary body. Doctoral dissertation, University of Illinois, 1936.

Brogden, W. J., & Culler, E. Device for motor conditioning of small animals. *Science,* 1936, **83,** 269–270.

Brogden, W. J., Girden, E., Mettler, F. A., & Culler, E. Acoustic value of the various components of the auditory system in cats. *American Journal of Physiology,* 1936, **116,** 252–261.

1937

Brogden, W. J., & Culler, E. Increased acoustic sensitivity in dogs following roentgen radiation of the hypophysis. *American Journal of Physiology,* 1937, **119,** 13–23.

Brogden, W. J., & Gantt, W. H. Cerebellar conditioned reflexes. *American Journal of Physiology,* 1937, **119,** 227–278.

1938

Brogden, W. J., Lipman, E. E., & Culler, E. The role of incentive in conditioning and extinction. *American Journal of Psychology,* 1938, **51,** 109–118.

1939

Brogden, W. J. Unconditioned stimulus substitution in the conditioning process. *American Journal of Psychology,* 1939, **52,** 46–55.

Brogden, W. J. Higher order conditioning. *American Journal of Psychology,* 1939, **52,** 579–591.

Brogden, W. J. The effect of frequency of reinforcement upon the level of conditioning. *Journal of Experimental Psychology,* 1939, **24,** 419–431.

Brogden, W. J. Sensory pre-conditioning. *Journal of Experimental Psychology,* 1939, **25,** 323–332.

1940

Brogden, W. J. Retention of conditioned responses tested by experimental extinction. *American Journal of Psychology,* 1940, **53,** 285–288.

Brogden, W. J. Lateral cerebral dominance in the dog tested by the conditioning and extinction of forelimb flexion. *Journal of General Psychology,* 1940, **23,** 387–392.

Brogden, W. J. Conditioned flexion responses in dogs re-established and maintained with change of locus in the application of the unconditioned stimulus. *Journal of Experimental Psychology,* 1940, **27,** 583–600.

1941

Brogden, W. J. The effect of change in time of reinforcement in the maintenance of conditioned flexion responses in dogs. *Journal of Experimental Psychology,* 1941, **29,** 49–57.

1942

Brogden, W. J. Imitation and social facilitation in the social conditioning of forelimb flexion in dogs. *American Journal of Psychology,* 1942, **55,** 77–83.

Brogden, W. J. Non-alimentary components in the food-reinforcement of conditioned forelimb-flexion in food-satiated dogs. *Journal of Experimental Psychology,* 1942, **30,** 326–335.

Brogden, W. J. Tests of sensory pre-conditioning with human subjects. *Journal of Experimental Psychology,* 1942, **31,** 505–517.

Brogden, W. J., & Gantt, W. H. Intraneural conditioning. *Archives of Neurology and Psychiatry,* 1942, **48,** 437–455.

1943

Roessler, R. L., & Brogden, W. J. Conditioned differentiation of vasoconstriction to subvocal stimuli. *American Journal of Psychology,* 1943, **56,** 78–86.

1947

Brogden, W. J. Sensory pre-conditioning of human subjects. *Journal of Experimental Psychology,* 1947, **37,** 527–539.

Brogden, W. J., & Miller, G. A. Physiological noise generated under earphone cushions. *Journal of the Acoustical Society of America,* 1947, **19,** 620–623.

1948

Corrigan R, E., & Brogden, W. J. The effect of angle upon precision of linear pursuit movements. *American Journal of Psychology,* 1948, **61,** 502–510.

Kloehn, N. W., & Brogden, W. J. The alkaline taste: A comparison of absolute thresholds for sodium hydroxide on the tip and mid-dorsal surfaces of the tongue. *American Journal of Psychology,* 1948, **61,** 90–93.

1949

Brogden, W. J. Acquisition and extinction of a conditioned avoidance response in dogs. *Journal of Comparative and Physiological Psychology,* 1949, **42,** 296–302.

Chernikoff, R., & Brogden, W. J. The effect of instructions upon sensory pre-conditioning of human subjects. *Journal of Experimental Psychology,* 1949, **39**, 200–207.

Cherinkoff, R., & Brogden, W. J. The effect of response termination of the stimulus upon reaction time. *Journal of Comparative and Physiological Psychology,* 1949, **42**, 357–364.

Corrigan, R. E., & Brogden, W. J. The trigonometric relationship of precision and angle of linear pursuit movements. *American Journal of Psychology,* 1949, **62**, 90–98.

1950

Brogden, W. J. Sensory conditioning measured by the facilitation of auditory acuity. *Journal of Experimental Psychology,* 1950, **40**, 512–519.

Chernikoff, R., Gregg, L., & Brogden, W. J. The effect of fixed duration stimulus magnitude upon reaction time to a response terminated stimulus. *Journal of Comparative and Physiological Psychology,* 1950, **43**, 123–128.

Gregg, L. W., & Brogden, W. J. The relation between duration and reaction time difference to fixed duration and response terminated stimuli. *Journal of Comparative and Physiological Psychology,* 1950, **43**, 329–337.

Gregg, L. W., & Brogden, W. J. The relation between reaction time and the duration of the auditory stimulus. *Journal of Comparative and Physiological Psychology,* 1950, **43**, 389–395.

1951

Brogden, W. J. Some theoretical considerations of learning. *Psychological Review,* 1951, **58**, 224–229.

Brogden, W. J. Animal studies of learning. S. S. Stevens (ed.) . In *Handbook of experimental psychology*. New York: Wiley, 1951. pp. 568–612.

Brogden, W. J., & Gregg, L. W. Studies of sensory conditioning measured by the facilitation of auditory acuity. *Journal of Experimental Psychology,* 1951, **42**, 384–389.

1952

Gregg, L. W., & Brogden, W. J. The effect of simultaneous visual stimulation on absolute auditory sensitivity. *Journal of Experimental Psychology,* 1952, **43**, 179–186.

1953

Briggs, G. E., & Brogden, W. J. Bilateral aspects of the trigonometric relationship of precision and angle of linear pursuit movements. *American Journal of Psychology,* 1953, **66**, 472–478.

Brogden, W. J. The trigonometric relationship of precision and angle of linear pursuit movements as a function of practice. *American Journal of Psychology,* 1953, **66**, 45–56.

1954

Battig, W. F., Gregg, L. W., Nagel, E. H., Small, A. M., Jr., & Brogden, W. J. Tracking and frequency of target intermittence. *Journal of Experimental Psychology,* 1954, **47**, 309–314.

Brogden, W. J., & Schmidt, R. E. Effects of number of choices per unit of verbal maze on learning and serial position errors. *Journal of Experimental Psychology,* 1954, **47**, 235–240.

Briggs, G. E., & Brogden, W. J. The effect of component practice on performance of a lever positioning skill. *Journal of Experimental Psychology,* 1954, **48,** 375–380.

Briggs, G. E., Thompson, R. F., & Brogden, W. J. The effect of angle of tilt upon the trigonometric relationship of precision and angle of linear pursuit movements. *American Journal of Psychology,* 1954, **67,** 475–483.

Briggs, G. E., Thompson, R. F., & Brogden, W. J. Retention functions in reproductive inhibition. *Journal of Experimental Psychology,* 1954, **48,** 419–423.

Brogden, W. J., & Schmidt, R. E. Acquisition of a 24-unit verbal maze as a function of number of alternate choices per unit. *Journal of Experimental Psychology,* 1954, **48,** 335–338.

1955

Battig, W. F., Nagel, E. H., & Brogden, W. J. The effects of errormagnification and marker-size on bi-dimensional compensatory tracking. *American Journal of Psychology,* 1955, **68,** 585–594.

Battig, W. F., Voss, J. F., & Brogden, W. J. The effect of frequency of target intermittence upon tracking. *Journal of Experimental Psychology,* 1955, **49,** 244–248.

Thompson, R. F., & Brogden, W. J. The effect of angle of slant upon the trigonometric relationship of precision and angle of linear pursuit movements. *American Journal of Psychology,* 1955, **68,** 615–623.

1956

Thompson, R. F., Voss, J. F., & Brogden, W. J. The effect of target-velocity upon the trigonometric relationship of precision and angle of linear pursuit movements. *American Journal of Psychology,* 1956, **69,** 258–263.

1957

Battig, W. F., Hoffeld, D. R., Seidenstein, S., & Brogden, W. J. Supplementary report: Effect of verbal pretraining on the acquisition of a complex motor skill. *Journal of Experimental Psychology,* 1957, **54,** 375–376.

Battig, W. F., Nagel, E. H., Voss, J. F., & Brogden, W. J. Transfer and retention of bidimensional compensatory tracking after extended practice. *American Journal of Psychology,* 1957, **70,** 75–80.

Battig, W. F., Voss, J. F., & Brogden, W. J. The effect of frequency of intermittence upon perceived brightness. *Journal of Comparative and Physiological Psychology,* 1957, **50,** 61–64.

Thompson, R. F., Voss, J. F., & Brogden, W. J. Effect of pattern variation upon verbal maze learning. *Journal of Experimental Psychology,* 1957, **54,** 253–258.

1958

Hoffeld, D. R., Thompson, R. F., & Brogden, W. J. Effect of stimuli time relations during preconditioning training upon the magnitude of sensory preconditioning. *Journal of Experimental Psychology,* 1958, **56,** 437–442.

Thompson, R. F., & Brogden, W. J. Acquisition of a verbal maze as a function of method of correction and number of alternate choices per unit. *Journal of Experimental Psychology,* 1958, **56,** 501–506.

Thompson, R. F., Voss, J. F., & Brogden, W. J. Effect of brightness of simultaneous visual stimulation on absolute auditory sensitivity. *Journal of Experimental Psychology,* 1958, **55,** 45–50.

1960

Ernst, R. L., Hoffeld, D. R., Seidenstein, S., & Brogden, W. J. Relation of serial-position errors to doublet and split-doublet location in verbal maze pattern. *Journal of Experimental Psychology,* 1960, **59,** 94–103.

Hoffeld, D. R., Kendall, S. B., Thompson, R. F., & Brogden, W. J. Effect of amount of preconditioning training upon the magnitude of sensory preconditioning. *Journal of Experimental Psychology,* 1960, **59,** 198–204.

Namikas, G., & Brogden, W. J. Effect of sequential patterns upon serial position errors and acquisition of a verbal maze. *Journal of Experimental Psychology,* 1960, **60,** 50–56.

Namikas, G., Thompson, C. P., & Brogden, W. J. Effect of triplet and quadruplicate location in verbal maze patterns upon serial position errors. *Journal of Experimental Psychology,* 1960, **59,** 383–390.

1961

Brogden, W. J. Conditioning and "voluntary" control. *Psychological Reports,* 1961, **8,** 351–352.

Hoffeld, D. R., Seidenstein, S., & Brogden, W. J. Proficiency in finger tracking as a function of number of fingers. *American Journal of Psychology,* 1961, **64,** 36–44.

1962

Brogden, W. J. The experimenter as a factor in animal conditioning. *Psychological Reports,* 1962, **11,** 239–242.

Brogden, W. J. Contiguous conditioning. *Journal of Experimental Psychology,* 1962, **64,** 172–176.

Brogden, W. J. A book review of G. A. Kimble, (ed.), *Hilgard and Marquis' conditioning and learning.* New York: Appleton, 1961. In *Contemporary Psychology,* 1962, **7,** 78–79.

Brogden, W. J. Elmer Augustine Kurtz Culler: 1889–1961. *American Journal of Psychology,* 1962, **75,** 155–160.

Ernst, R. L., Thompson, C. P., & Brogden, W. J. Effect of pattern and pleonasm location in serial lists upon acquisition and serial position errors. *Journal of Experimental Psychology,* 1962, **64,** 151–157.

Wynne, J. D., & Brogden, W. J. Supplementary report: Effect upon sensory preconditioning of backward, forward, and trace preconditioning training. *Journal of Experimental Psychology,* 1962, **64,** 422–423.

1965

Schoeninger, D. W., Simpson, W. E., & Brogden, W. J. General and local effects of limited trials of shock US on maintenance of an avoidance CR. *Journal of Comparative and Psysiological Psychology,* 1965, **59,** 25–30.

1966

Nelson, D. L., Simpson, W. E., & Brogden, W. J. Simultaneous practice, number and locus of identical items in acquisition of two serial lists. *Journal of Experimental Psychology,* 1966, **72,** 714–721.

1967

Gabriel, M., Sterner, R. T., & Brogden, W. J. Effects of limited classical trials on acquisition, maintenance, and extinction of an avoidance CR. *Journal of Comparative and Physiological Psychology,* 1967, **63,** 270–276.

1968

Bewley, W. L., Nelson, D. L., & Brogden, W. J. Single, alternate, and successive practice in the acquisition of two and three serial lists. *Journal of Experimental Psychology,* 1968, **76**, 376–386.

Brogden, W. J. Classical conditioning. In *International encyclopedia of the social sciences,* New York: Crowell-Collier, 1968.

Brogden, W. J. Motor conditioning of the albino rabbit: Apparatus and procedures for acquisition of the CR. *Conditional Reflex,* 1968, **3**, 269–277.

Brogden, W. J. Effect of change in duration of CS upon extinction of an avoidance CR. *Journal of Comparative and Physiological Psychology,* 1968, **66**, 22–24.

Brogden, W. J. General and local maintenance effects of adjacent classical trials during extinction of an avoidance CR. *Journal of Comparative and Physiological Psychology,* 1968, **66**, 203–207.

Brogden, W. J. *Pavlov to Teplov to Gray.* A review of J. A. Gray (ed.), *Pavlov's typology: Recent theoretical and experimental developments from the laboratory of B. M. Teplov.* Oxford: Pergamon, 1964. In *Contemporary Psychology,* 1968, **13**, 459–460.

1969

Bewley, W. L., Nelson, D. L., & Brogden, W. J. Effect of cue alteration for ordinal position upon acquisition and serial position curve form. *Journal of Experimental Psychology,* 1969, **79**, 445–451.

Brogden, W. J. The acquisition of a conditioned avoidance response by cats, dogs and rabbits. *Journal of Comparative and Physiological Psychology,* 1969, **68**, 343–347.

Gilbert, R. M., & Brogden, W. J. Effects of multiple adjacent classical trials during extinction of an avoidance CR. *Journal of Comparative and Physiological Psychology,* 1969, **69**, 232–237.

1970

Brogden, W. J. Locus effects of single classical trials during extinction of avoidance CRs in rabbits (*Oryctolagus cuniculus*). *Journal of Comparative and Physiological Psychology,* 1970, **70**, 270–275.

Fingeret, A. L., & Brogden, W. J. Part versus whole practice in the acquisition of serial lists as a function of class and organization of material. *Journal of Experimental Psychology,* 1970, **83**, 406–414.

CHAPTER 1

THE ADDITIVITY PRINCIPLE IN CHOICE REACTION TIME—A FUNCTIONALIST APPROACH TO MENTAL PROCESSES[1]

George E. Briggs

In 1868 the Dutch physiologist Frans C. Donders published his now-classic research on the timing of mental processes. Koster (1969) has provided a translation as part of the centenary observation of Donders'

[1] Support for the preparation of this manuscript and for that research cited herein by the author and his graduate students was provided in part by the National Science Foundation through Grant GN-534.1 from the Office of Scientific Information Service to the Computer and Information Science Research Center, Ohio State University.

contribution to our understanding of human information processing. Donders identified two mental processes as being of particular interest: stimulus discrimination and response selection. He then designed three qualitatively different reaction time tasks, one of which he felt involved neither process (the a-reaction), one involving both processes (the b-reaction), and one presumably with only the stimulus discrimination process (the c-reaction). Thus Donders assumed that a c-reaction task was the a-reaction task with discrimination inserted; it follows that one should be able to estimate the time required to carry out that mental process by subtracting the average a-reaction time from that obtained in the c-reaction task. Likewise, an estimate of the time required to select a response should be available from the difference in the b- and the c-reaction times. Donders reported his own average reaction times of 201, 284, and 237 msec for the a-, b-, and c-reaction tasks, respectively. From these averages, then, Donders estimated that stimulus discrimination required 36 msec while response selection added another comparable component (37 msec) to the total reaction time.

Only rarely can one find subsequent attempts to utilize the insertion assumption to estimate the time durations of inferred mental processes. Woodworth (1938) described an attempt by Wundt to improve upon the Donders c-reaction, and Taylor (1966) provides a modern-day attempt to utilize the assumption by rerunning the a-, b-, and c-reactions plus variations on the b- and the c-reactions. Most researchers have been unwilling to adopt the insertion assumption, although the concept of additivity of reaction time components has recurred especially in the past twenty years.

The classic research by Hick (1952) marked the occasion of a renewed interest in the concept of additivity in reaction time. Basically, Hick repeated an earlier experiment by Merkel (see Woodworth, 1938, pp. 332–333), and he found that choice reaction time (RT) was a linear function of stimulus uncertainty (H_s) in an information-conservation task:

$$RT = a + b(H_s) \tag{1}$$

In a subsequent experiment Hick noted an even more important relationship by showing that reaction time is a linear function of accuracy, the latter as expressed by the information transmitted (H_t) metric:

$$RT = a + b(H_t) \tag{2}$$

Equation (2) describes the speed/accuracy tradeoff now known as Hick's law.

Bricker (1955) was one of the first to note that Eq. (2) is the more fundamental relationship, Eq. (1) being a parsimonious statement only when the observer responds with little or no error. Later, Swanson and Briggs (1969) argued that Eq. (2) itself is less fundamental than is the following additivity statement:

$$RT|H_t = a + b(H_c) \tag{3}$$

where H_c is central processing uncertainty and is determined by the number of stimulus classification or identification alternatives present in a particular choice reaction task. When Eq. (3) was applied to data from an information-reduction task, Swanson and Briggs found that reaction time, given a level of accuracy, was a linear function of central processing uncertainty, and they showed that the intercept constant a itself was a linear function of H_t:

$$a = c + d(H_t) \tag{4}$$

Therefore, Swanson and Briggs provided a more extensive statement of additivity of reaction time which represents a substitution of Eq. (4) into Eq. (3):

$$RT = c + d(H_t) + b(H_c) \tag{5}$$

As fitted to the data, the constants of Eq. (5) took the values

$$RT = .243 + .157(H_t) + .108(H_c)$$

Eq. (5) was generated for data collected under a reaction time methodology that did not utilize qualitatively different tasks as in the Donders approach. Thus one can avoid the questionable insertion assumption and still obtain apparent additivity of reaction time. The methodology was first enunciated by Saul Sternberg (1966) at the 1963 meeting of the Eastern Psychological Association. The original version of this task utilizes two possible responses: "Yes" that stimulus matches one being held in memory (it is a positive set stimulus) or "no" there is no match (the stimulus is a member of the negative set). From trial to trial or from one block of trials to the next the experimenter requires that the observer utilize different numbers of stimuli in the positive set, say 1, 2, or 4 stimuli. As such, this methodology involves a systematic variation in memory load. As indicated by Swanson and Briggs (1969), memory load is the primary determinant of H_c.

Briggs and Blaha (1969) had shown that there was a linear relationship between reaction time and memory load (M):

$$RT = a + b(M) \tag{6}$$

rather than a logarithmic relationship as in Eq. (3). Parenthetically, this probably resulted from the particular stimuli (random figures) selected as stimuli for the three different levels of memory load, $M = 1$, 2, and 4 figures. In this study, display load (D) also was varied systematically over three levels. $D = 1$, 2, or 4 figures appeared simultaneously on the display; any one, but no more than one, displayed item could match an item in the positive set. Items in a particular positive set, say the two figures in $M = 2$, never appeared as members of either the $M = 1$, the $M = 4$, or the negative sets.

Briggs and Blaha found that the slope constant b of Eq. (6) was a linear function of display load

$$b = e + f(D) \tag{7}$$

so that for their data, a more complete statement of additivity involves substituting Eq. (7) into Eq. (6):

$$RT = a + e(M) + f(M \times D) \tag{8}$$

The data for the correct positive responses from a block of trials providing experience comparable to that of the Swanson and Briggs (1969) observers (Block 2 of Table 1, p. 397) was fit by Eq. (8) with the result

$$RT = a + .011(M) + .023\,(M \times D)$$

The intercept a assumed values of 447, 469, and 506 msec for the $D = 1$, 2, and 4 conditions, respectively, an average of 474 msec.

At this point in time the empirical contribution was that Briggs and his students had shown that the Sternberg information-reduction task methodology was capable of providing additive components from an overall reaction time: Both the intercept and the slope constants of Eq. (3) [or (6)] could be fractionated into components by the use of appropriate independent variables (accuracy and display load, respectively). This is an example of the Sternberg (1969) additive factor method. How might we interpret these functional relationships?

Donders attempted to measure two mental processes. Equations (5) and (8) suggest that more than two processes can be inferred from the modern data, at least four being apparent at this point of analysis. In order to identify these processes, it is necessary to consider a recent model of human information processing, the four-stage model provided by Smith (1968), and recent interpretations of Eq. (3) [or (6)]. In his thorough review of the choice reaction time literature, Smith suggested that there are four sequential stages between physical stimulus and overt response: stage 1 or stimulus encoding, stage 2 or central processing whereby stimulus classification or identification is achieved, stage 3 or response decoding, and the stage-4 activities involved in response execution. A reaction time begins with stimulus onset and is terminated by the initial part of stage 4; therefore, Eq. (3) deals primarily with the processes in stages 1, 2, and 3.

The slope constant b has been interpreted as central processing time (here identified as stage 2) ever since Hick (1952). More recently, the intercept constant a has been interpreted (see Sternberg, 1967) as the time required for all activities other than those involving memory (other than stage 2); therefore, we may consider that in Eq. (3) [or (6)] the intercept a is the total of the times required to carry out both the stimulus encoding and the response decoding functions. The reciprocal of the constant b would be an estimate of the speed of central processing.

Given the Smith model and the interpretation just presented, consider again Eq. (5) from Swanson and Briggs (1969): The terms c and d originally were embedded within the intercept a [see Eq. (4)]; therefore, one can presume that c and d represent process times within stages 1 and/or 3 of the model. Theory (see Stone, 1960) and subsequent data (see later discussion) suggest that $d(H_t)$ represents the amount of time required to sample and preprocess stimulus information, logically a stage-1 activity; therefore, c would be the time required to carry out all other processes in stages 1 and 3.

By reference to research and modeling by Sperling (1960, 1963, 1967), one can interpret stage 1 as follows: Upon stimulus onset more information than will be utilized is loaded into a short-term visual store, and then that information is sampled as by the Sperling SCAN operator. Presumably, the output of SCAN would be loaded into a buffer memory within stage 1 to permit formating and any pre- (central) processing analysis required prior to being transferred to stage 2 for central processing. Gross features such as stimulus familiarity apparently can be assessed via preprocessing (see Briggs & Swanson, 1969).

The term $d(H_t)$, then, may be interpreted as the time per bit of accuracy to carry out the stimulus sampling function of the Sperling SCAN operation. The reciprocal of this time constant, 6.4 bit/sec, may be interpreted as the rate of gain of information across SCAN. This leads to two interesting conclusions: (1) Stage 1 appears to be the locus of Hick's law (1952) [see Eq. (2)], and (2) apparently, the observer can exert some control over the stimulus sampling process. Further, since the reciprocal of b in the Swanson and Briggs data was 9.2 bit/sec, one can conclude that the stimulus classification functions of stage 2 are carried out at a faster rate than are the input functions of stage 1.

Turning now to the results of the Briggs and Blaha (1969) study, it is clear that both display load and memory load influence stage-2 processes since their interaction was statistically significant [see Eq. (7)]. How then can we interpret Eq. (8)? It would appear logical that when stage 1 receives, samples, and preprocesses stimulus information, part of the result of such preprocessing would be the keying of an appropriate ensemble of information from long-term memory. This information could then be retrieved from long-term memory and placed in a working or active memory wherein encoded and sampled stimulus information is tested against memorial information for purposes of stimulus classification. On this interpretation one would expect two component times: memory retrieval time and the time per test to carry out stimulus classification. This would be the time constants e and f, respectively, of Eq. (8), and the reciprocals of these two constants provide an estimate of 91 items/sec as the memory retrieval rate, while the central testing of stimulus against memorial information presumably was carried out at a somewhat slower speed of 43 comparisons/sec. One can transform these rates to a scale of bits per second by noting that for correct positive responses, there was an average of .37 bits of uncertainty per comparison and an average of .43 bits of uncertainty per item in memory. Thus a memory retrieval rate of .43 × 91 or 39 bits/sec was observed while central testing occurred at a rate of .37 × 43 or 16 bits/sec.

It follows that empirical data from the Sternberg choice reaction time methodology and the data and theory developed from this and other methodologies suggest that it is possible to measure the time durations of the following mental processes: (1) stimulus sampling plus preprocessing speed, 6.4 bits/sec (Swanson & Briggs, 1969); (2) memory retrieval rate from long-term to active memory, 39 bits/sec for random figures (Briggs & Blaha, 1969); and (3) central stimulus classification testing, 16 bits/sec (Briggs & Blaha, 1969).

Briggs and Swanson (1970) sought to verify and extend the data and conclusions just presented. The research of both Briggs and Blaha (1969) and Swanson and Briggs (1969) had utilized eight-sided random figures as stimuli. The Briggs and Swanson (1970) research employed letters of the alphabet, and in addition to manipulating memory load and display load, both performance accuracy and response load were varied systematically across two experiments. As in the earlier research, it was expected that accuracy, expressed as information transmitted, would reveal the time duration of the stage-1 stimulus sampling/processing functions, while an interaction of memory load by display load should provide stage-2 estimates of the retrieval rate from long-term memory plus an estimate of the speed of a working memory. The new variable, response load, was expected to influence stage 3 or response decoding. It also was expected to help validate the H_c scale developed by Swanson and Briggs (1969) as the predictor variable in the basic statement of additivity, Eq. (3). Response load refers to the number of possible responses from which the observer is required to select that one response on each trial to express the outcome of the stage-2 processing. Response load took on values of $R = 2$, 3, and 4 in the first of the two experiments reported, while loads of $R = 2$, 4, and 8 were used in the second study.

The results obtained by Briggs and Swanson (1970) were gratifying in their replication and extension of the previous data. In the first experiment memory load, display load, and response load were varied over three levels each. The results of fitting Eq. (3) to the data are summarized in the upper half of Table 1. From those results it may be noted that, as expected, the slope constant b (actually the average across response load) is a linear function of display load [Eq. (7)]:

$$\begin{aligned}\bar{b} &= e + f(D) \\ &= .020 + .050(D)\end{aligned}$$

and the intercept constant a (actually, an average a within response load but across display load) is a linear function of response load:

$$\begin{aligned}\bar{a} &= g + h(R) \\ &= .242 + .084(R) \qquad (9)\end{aligned}$$

Therefore, the more complete statement of additivity for these data is

$$\begin{aligned}RT &= g + h(R) + e(H_c) + f(H_c \times D) \\ &= .242 + .084(R) + .020(H_c) + .050(H_c \times D) \qquad (10)\end{aligned}$$

Based on the interpretations developed for the earlier research, Eq. (10) suggests the following: (1) A stimulus appeared on the display; (2) information was encoded into a short-term visual store, scanned, and loaded into a buffer memory, all of which occupied approximately 242 msec on the average; (3) the necessary information for stimulus classification was retrieved at a rate of 50 bits/sec and was utilized in the working memory of the central processing stage at an average rate of 20 bits/sec; (4) following stimulus classification as to membership in either the positive or the negative set, the stage-3 process of response decoding (selection) occurred at a rate of about 12 responses/sec; and (5) the selected response was executed. Since there was an average uncertainty of 0.51 bits/response, the response decoding rate was about 6.1 bits/sec.

In their second experiment Briggs and Swanson (1970) varied both memory load and response load, and they encouraged the observers to make about 10–15% errors by offering a bonus for fast responses. The observers in the first study had averaged about 1% errors in the $D = 1$ condition, the level of display load used in the second experiment.

The results of best fits of Eq. (3) to the data are listed in the bottom half of Table 1. It may be noted that as in the first study, the intercept constant a is a linear function of response load

$$a = .160 + .090(R)$$

which provides the additivity statement

$$RT = .160 + .090(R) + .077(H_c)$$

where 77 msec is the average slope constant from the RT-H_c fits of

TABLE 1

Best-Fit Constants from Eq. (3) Applied to the Briggs and Swanson (1970) Data

Experiment I		
Response load	Display load	$RT = a + b\,(H_c)$
2	1	$RT = .390 + .080\,(H_c)$
—	2	$RT = .403 + .103\,(H_c)$
—	4	$RT = .397 + .195\,(H_c)$
3	1	$RT = .516 + .068\,(H_c)$
—	2	$RT = .521 + .106\,(H_c)$
—	4	$RT = .534 + .231\,(H_c)$
4	1	$RT = .570 + .074\,(H_c)$
—	2	$RT = .547 + .138\,(H_c)$
—	4	$RT = .579 + .243\,(H_c)$

Experiment II	
Response load	$RT = a + b\,(H_c)$
2	$RT = .347 + .061\,(H_c)$
4	$RT = .506 + .079\,(H_c)$
8	$RT = .881 + .092\,(H_c)$

Table 1. These constants agree well with those obtained in the first experiment for the $D = 1$ condition:

$$RT = .242 + .084(R) + .070(H_c)$$

As expected from Swanson and Briggs (1969), only the intercepts (160 versus 242 msec) differed between the two experiments. This difference was explored further by contrasting the data from comparable conditions in the first and second experiments of Briggs and Swanson (1970) and by utilizing accuracy information as measured by the H_t index.

Starting with Eq. (3)

$$RT = a + b(H_c)$$

it was found that across the two studies a was a linear function of response load, [Eq. (9)],

$$a = g + h(R)$$

and by expressing g of Eq. (9) as a linear function of H_t [Eq. (10)]

$$g = i + j(H_t)$$

one has the more complete statement of additivity

$$RT = i + j(H_t) + h(R) + b(H_c) \tag{11}$$

For these data the constants of best fit are

$$RT = .007 + .149(H_t) + .085(R) + .075(H_c)$$

Again, then, from the previous data, models, and theory the following interpretation appears to be reasonable: (1) More letter stimulus information than would be required was loaded into a short-term visual store; (2) that information was scanned and loaded into a buffer memory at a rate of approximately 6.7 bits/sec (compare to the 1969 estimate by Swanson and Briggs of 6.4 bits/sec for the sampling rate for random figures); (3) the stage-2 functions of stimulus classification occurred at an average rate of 13.5 bits/sec (compare to the slower average rates of 9.2 bits/sec estimated by Swanson and Briggs and 11.0 bits/sec for correct positive response data from Briggs and Blaha); (4) a response was decoded at the rate of approximately 6 bits/sec; and (5) the response selected was executed.

It is interesting to note that despite substantial differences in statistical structure, stimulus material, and response uncertainty, the SCAN rate from the Briggs and Swanson (1970) experiment matched very closely the previous estimate by Swanson and Briggs (1969): 6.7 versus 6.4 bits/sec, although the central processing rate was much faster for the more familiar letters used by Briggs and Swanson (1970) than was that speed estimated by Swanson and Briggs (1969) for processing the less familiar random forms through stage 2 (13.5 versus 9.2 bits/sec). This suggested a conclusion that stimulus sampling but not central processing may be independent of stimulus familiarity.

Lyons (1970) tested this conclusion by utilizing two types of stimulus material (random figures versus letters of the alphabet) and two levels of performance accuracy. There were four groups of observers formed by the four possible combinations of these two factors, and each group experienced the Sternberg task for three consecutive daily sessions. In each session there were 48 trials (test stimulus presentations) under memory loads of $M = 1$, 2, and 4 items. A display load of $D = 1$ was used throughout, as was the $R = 2$ response load condition. As before, per-

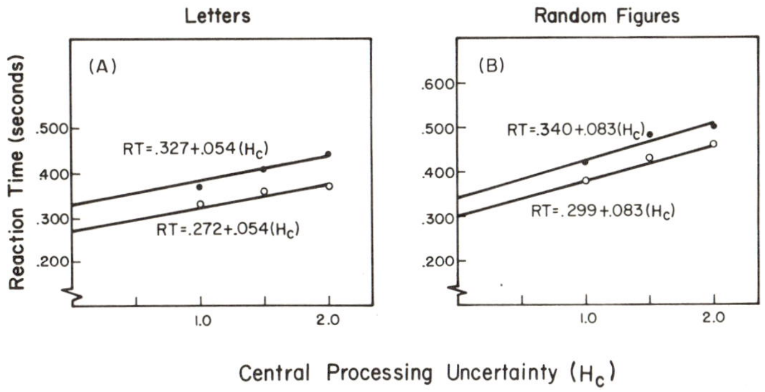

Fig. 1. Parallel fits of Eq. (3) to the letters and to the random figures data of Lyons (1970). Accuracy: (A) ●—● .82 bits, ○—○ .45 bits; (B) ●—● .77 bits, ○—○ .52 bits.

formance accuracy was achieved by a bonus system which utilized response speed criteria.

The results are summarized in Fig. 1, which lists the best fits of Eq. (3). Performance accuracy in terms of H_t is the parameter in each part of Fig. 1. An analysis of variance indicated statistically significant differences ($p < .05$) for each main effect: stimulus material, $F = 29.53$, (1, 40); accuracy, $F = 17.11$ (1,40); and memory load, $F = 75.71$ (2, 40). Most importantly, only the interaction of Stimulus Material by memory load was significant, $F = 3.71$ (2, 40). Thus, whereas the slope constant for letter stimuli (54 msec) was reliably faster than that for the random figures (83 msec), the two slopes within each part of the figure are not different, and so those data were fit by parallel straight lines. The intercepts of Fig. 1 were expressed as a function of H_t, and these data also were fit by parallel straight lines. The result, then, is

$$RT \text{ (figures)} = .220 + .154(H_t) + .083(H_c)$$
$$RT \text{ (letters)} = .202 + .154(H_t) + .054(H_c)$$

It follows that the Lyons thesis confirms the cross-experiment conclusion drawn earlier: The rate of central processing may be faster for more familiar stimulus material (18.5 bits/sec on the average) than for less familiar items (12 bits/sec); however, stimulus sampling speed apparently is not influenced by stimulus familiarity. Remarkably, the latter rate as noted here (6.5 bits/sec) matches very closely those rates obtained earlier by Swanson and Briggs (1969) and by Briggs and Swanson (1970): 6.4 and 6.7 bits/sec, respectively.

It would appear, therefore, that the Sternberg methodology provides replicable data, and, apparently, it provides a means of inferring such mental processes as stimulus sampling and preprocessing, the several central processes of stimulus classification including retrieval from long-term memory and exercising an active memory and the output process of response selection.

Swanson (1970) used the Sternberg methodology in his doctoral dissertation, and he revealed something of the way the central processor carries out the functions of stimulus classification. Thus, this research, unlike the work just described, was not concerned primarily with the identification of a process so much as with how a process is carried out.

Each of 25 observers first spent five daily sessions learning the 16 "names" (two-digit numbers) assigned by the experimenter to 16 eight-sided random figures. Both the forward and backward associations were highly practiced. In the second week, the Sternberg varied-set procedure was employed: The experimenter presented a positive set of $M = 1, 2,$ or 4 items and then the observer responded to a single test item; the ex-

TABLE 2

Reaction Times and Percentage Errors (in Parentheses) from Swanson (1970)

Figure condition	Match condition	Memory load M_1	M_2	M_4
Figure–figure	Match	.953 (0.50)	1.096 (5.50)	1.241 (4.75)
	No match	.974 (2.75)	1.162 (4.25)	1.368 (6.50)
Digit–digit	Match	.819 (3.30)	.878 (3.25)	1.077 (7.75)
	No match	.874 (2.25)	.971 (0.75)	1.141 (3.25)
Figure–digit	Match	.778 (2.25)	.909 (4.00)	1.137 (7.50)
	No match	.890 (1.50)	1.043 (3.50)	1.207 (4.50)
Digit–figure	Match	.985 (3.00)	1.152 (4.00)	1.365 (11.00)
	No match	1.022 (4.25)	1.197 (0.50)	1.433 (7.75)

	$RT = a + b(M)$
Figure–figure	$RT = .881 + .093(M)$
Digit–digit	$RT = .719 + .088(M)$
Figure–digit	$RT = .665 + .118(M)$
Digit–figure	$RT = .880 + .124(M)$

perimenter next presented another positive set of $M = 1, 2,$ or 4 items followed by a single test stimulus, and so on. The response was either "match" or "no match" the $R = 2$ condition of the earlier work. Half the test stimuli should have resulted in a match response while half should have elicited no-match responses.

There were four basic conditions formed by the two possible formats of the positive set (figures or numerals) and the two possible formats of the test stimulus (a figure or a two-digit numeral). Thus, suppose the $M = 2$ condition was to occur. The visual display might appear with 2 of the 16 random figures as the positive set, and then the test stimulus could be either a random figure *or* the two-digit name of a random figure. The next time the $M = 2$ condition occurred, the positive set might be two names (two two-digit numerals) followed by a test stimulus that was either a random figure or a two-digit numeral. It follows that at stage 2 the match responses could have been determined either by the physical identity of a positive set item with the test stimulus (figure–figure or digit–digit) or by associational identity (figure–digit or digit–figure).

Swanson's results are listed in Table 2, which shows the average reaction times in seconds and percent errors for each of the four basic format conditions. As indicated, the data are listed separately for match and no-match responses. In the lower portion of Table 2 are listed best fits of Eq. (6) to the match response data.

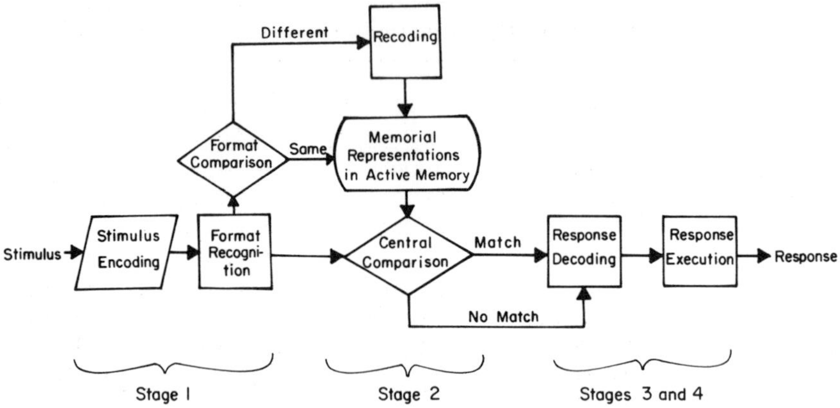

Fig. 2. A flow chart interpretation of the Swanson (1970) results.

The striking observation in Table 2 is that the slope constants are quite similar for those two conditions in which the same format was used when presenting the positive set and the test stimulus ($b = .093$ sec for the figure–figure condition while $b = .088$ sec for the digit–digit condition), and likewise the slopes are quite similar when there was a change in format (.124 and .118 sec for the digit–figure and the figure–digit conditions, respectively). The difference between the two sets of slope constants was significant at $p < .05$, but the constants within each set are not significantly different one from the other. Thus, a significantly longer time constant b occurred when there was a change in format than when both the positive set and the test stimulus were presented in the same format. Based on our earlier interpretation, then, the time per central test of encoded stimulus information against memorial information was faster when no format change occurred.

This leads to the following inferences regarding information processing in this task: under the varied-set procedure the positive set is held in the active memory of stage 2, probably being rehearsed by the observer. When the test stimulus occurs, it is loaded into the short-term visual store, sampled, and held temporarily in a buffer memory, all of these being stage-1 processes. While in buffer memory, the test stimulus information is preprocessed for format information. If the format of the test stimulus is the same as that of the positive set, the test stimulus information can be transmitted to the active memory and testing for a match can occur directly; if, however, the preprocessing indicates that the test stimulus format differs from that of the items being held in active memory, then the *latter* are recoded into the format of the test stimulus prior to the stage-2 process of comparing test against memorial representations. Format presumably is a gross feature which, like familiarity, can be assessed by a preprocessing operation. Figure 2 summarizes these processes and procedures in flow-chart form.

By comparing his data from the no-format-change condition with data obtained earlier by Bashark (1968), the latter in a format certainty version of the same task, Swanson concluded that the preprocessing operation itself required about 280 msec. From the best-fit slope constants of Table 2 he concluded that the recoding process required about 30 msec per item in active memory. The latter estimate is obtained by noting the difference in slope constants for the changed versus no-change format conditions (see Table 2). It follows that the 280-msec preprocessing period is quite slow compared to either the recoding or the other central functions. For example, the 30-msec-per-item estimate of recoding time indicates a total recoding time of 30, 60, and 120 msec for the $M = 1$, 2, and 4 conditions, respectively. $H_c = 1.0$, 1.5, and 2.0 bits, respectively, for these three memory-load conditions; thus, an average recoding rate of 25 bits/sec is noted. While not as fast as the memory retrieval rate either for random figures, 39 bits/sec (Briggs & Blaha, 1969), or letters, 50 bits/sec (Briggs & Swanson, 1970), the central recoding rate is considerably faster than either the estimated rate for the encoding function of stimulus sampling (an average of 6.5 bits/sec) or the apparent rate of response decoding (6 bits/sec).

It is interesting to note that Briggs and Swanson (1969) also attempted to assess preprocessing time. In their study, stimulus familiarity rather than test stimulus format was the information subject to preprocessing, and in the case of familiarity it was estimated that preprocessing required about 180 msec.

Why should recoding, which presumably involves retrieval of information from long-term memory to active memory, occur at a rate substantially slower than the previously given rates of retrieval of information on either random figures or letters (39 and 50 bits/sec, respectively) from long-term memory? Recall that Swanson (1970) imposed his own arbitrary associations of two-digit "names" to the random forms. It is not unreasonable to suppose that this arbitrary set of associations would provide for less efficient indexing to long-term memory than would the highly overlearned associations involving letters of the alphabet or the "natural" coding via verbal descriptors which the human observer himself adopts when dealing with random figures. The latter are quite idiosyncratic and fascinating. When queried after an experiment using random figures without experimenter-assigned "names," each observer has his own verbal label for each figure: "That's the two o'clock shape"; "that is the tilted Z"; etc. This matter speaks to the organization of long-term memory. The Sternberg methodology provides an effective, albeit cumbersome, tool for such analysis.

Concluding Comments

The key to the Sternberg methodology is the use of memory load to differentially influence the central processing functions involved in stimulus classification. One starts his search for additivity from the vantage point of stage 2 in the Smith (1968) model and examines other processes in stages 1, 2, and 3 by the use of other appropriate independent variables made orthogonal to memory load.

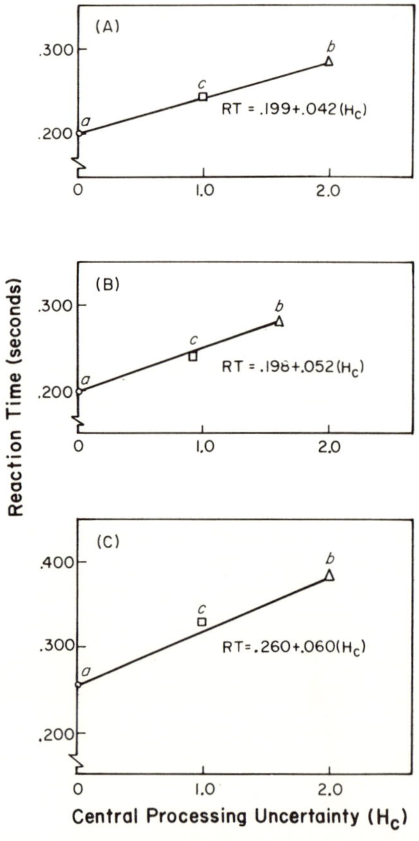

Fig. 3. Equation (3) as applied to Donders' own average reaction times (A and B) and to the average reaction time data of Taylor (1966) (C).

It is possible to view the data provided by Donders in 1868 and more recently by Taylor (1966) in the same way, i.e., to estimate central processing uncertainty for the a-, the b-, and the c-reaction tasks and then use these as the values of the predictor variable for the reaction-time data reported. In the case of Taylor's research this is no problem as he provides sufficient information to indicate that H_c = 0, 1.0, and 2.0 bits for the a-, c-, and b-reaction tasks, respectively. The Donders report is somewhat less informative as to the probabilistic structure of the stimulus sequences in the b- and c-reaction tasks. One can assume that Donders and his assistant, a Mr. Hamer, utilized the key stimulus (the sound "ki") about half the time, or one can take the example of stimulus sequences provided by Donders. If this example was representative, then "ki" occurred more than half the time in both the b- and the c-reaction tasks, thereby reducing H_c for these tasks. Since we cannot resolve this problem at this late date, both sets of values of H_c are shown in Fig. 3 for the Donders data [see panels (A) and (B)]. Panel (C) shows the Taylor data.

The best fits of Eq. (3) are shown in the figure. Donders' methodology may involve the questionable insertion assumption; however, the data do seem lawful when viewed from the vantage point of the central processing unit. Traditionally, the functionalist has stood outside the computer center observing input and output under various conditions. Perhaps he should be so bold as to enter the computer center and make his observations from the room housing the CPU itself.

REFERENCES

Bashark, L. T. High-speed scanning of random figures in human memory. Unpublished Master's thesis, Ohio State University, 1968.

Bricker, P. D. Information measurement and reaction time. In H. Quastler (Ed.), *Information theory in psychology*. Glencoe, Ill.: Free Press, 1955. Pp. 350–359.

Briggs, G. E., & Blaha, J. Memory retrieval and central comparison times in information processing. *Journal of Experimental Psychology,* 1969, **79**, 395–402.

Briggs, G. E., & Swanson, J. M. Retrieval time as a function of memory ensemble size. *Quarterly Journal of Experimental Psychology,* 1969, **21**, 185–191.

Briggs, G. E., & Swanson, J. M. Encoding, decoding, and central functions in human information processing. *Journal of Experimental Psychology,* 1970, **86**, 296–308.

Donders, F. C. Over de snelheid van psychische processen. Onderzoekingen gedann in het Physiologisch Laboratorium der Utrechsche Hoogeschool. *Tweede Reeks,* 1868–1869, **2**, 92–120. (Transl. by W. G. Koster, *Acta Psychologica,* 1969, **30**, 412–431)

Hick, W. E. On the rate of gain of information. *Quarterly Journal of Experimental Psychology,* 1952, **4**, 11–26.

Lyons, J. J. The speed-accuracy tradeoff in processing different classes of material. Master's thesis, Ohio State University, 1970. Also available as Technical Report OSU-CISRC-TR-70-11, Computer and Information Science Research Center, Ohio State University, 1970.

Smith, E. E. Choice reaction time: An analysis of the major theoretical positions. *Psychological Bulletin,* 1968, **69**, 77–110.

Sperling, G. The information available in brief visual presentations. *Psychological Monographs,* 1960, **74** (11 whole No. 498).

Sperling, G. A model for visual memory tasks. *Human Factors,* 1963, **5**, 19–31.

Sperling, G. Successive approximations to a model for short-term memory. *Acta Psychologica,* 1967, **27**, 285–292.

Sternberg, S. High-speed scanning in human memory. *Science,* 1966, **153**, 652–654.

Sternberg, S. Two operations in character recognition: Some evidence from reaction-time measurements. *Perception and Psychophysics,* 1967, **2**, 45–53.

Sternberg, S. The discovery of processing stages: Extensions of Donders' method. *Acta Psychologica,* 1969, **30**, 276–315.

Stone, M. Models for choice reaction time. *Psychometrika,* 1960, **25**, 251–260.

Swanson, J. M. Recoding in a memory search task. Unpublished doctoral dissertation, Ohio State University, 1970.

Swanson, J. M., & Briggs, G. E. Information processing as a function of speed versus accuracy. *Journal of Experimental Psychology,* 1969, **81**, 223–229.

Taylor, D. H. Latency components in two-choice responding. *Journal of Experimental Psychology,* 1966, **72**, 481–487.

Woodworth, R. S. *Experimental psychology.* New York: Holt, 1938.

CHAPTER 2

LOCATING SOURCES OF SOUND

William E. Simpson

Like many questions of interest to students of behavior, there is a great history of attempts to learn how man is able to appreciate where he is located relative to other features in his environment, and the locations of the other features relative to him. Consider yourself, seated in a chair and reading this book. It takes no great effort to make reasonably accurate judgments about your locus in the room, the orientation of your body with respect to vertical, the direction and distance of a window or a table or a television set turned on behind you. In fact such judgments are made so quickly and easily that we generally conceive of such behavior as reflecting relatively direct perception. But apparent simplicity masks what must be very complex processing of information. For example, perceiving where the television is, relative to you, involves specification of its azimuth, elevation, and distance. And such perception can also take into account intensity, size, and shape characteristics of the feature being localized and movement on the part of the feature or of the perceiver. To the extent that you have knowledge about the setting stored in memory and are gathering data through several perceptual systems, the organizational problem of handling all this potential information is truly astounding.

This chapter dissects the perception of space and examines some studies of localizing behavior mediated chiefly by one perceptual system—hearing. A more encompassing review of spatial perception, including visual, haptic, and vestibular systems, has been published by Howard and Templeton (1966).

The traditional label for the collection of questions considered here is auditory localization. Empirical investigations of auditory localization have been sufficiently numerous and their results sufficiently consistent to permit both descriptive and explanatory statements. Although we can study perceptual processes only through overt responses made by the perceiver, it may be instructive to conceive of such processes as including a perceptual component and a response component. Thus errors made in auditory localization experiments probably reflect some real perceptual error plus some error in indicating the perception to the experimenter. The response modes typically employed have been identification (e.g., verbalizing a code name) or pointing (with a finger, stick, or light). Identification of stimuli varying on one dimension (like azimuth) is known to have severe limitations on its accuracy (Miller, 1956). Appreciable error must also occur in kinesthetic pointing. For these reasons, some portion of the error indicated in localization experiments must be attributable to response mechanisms. Present estimates of the accuracy of auditory localization, as perception, may therefore be conservative.

In the following two sections we consider how human observers discriminate the azimuth of a sound source. Emphasis is placed on studies employing the complex stimuli normally encountered in our auditory world, i.e., speech and noise. For simplicity, only "point" sources of sound are considered.

Where in the World It Is and How in the World We Know

The coordinate of localizing sound sources that has been most extensively studied is azimuth. Azimuth refers to direction on a horizontal plane passing through the listener's ears and is specified in degrees relative to straight ahead (0°). Thus a source at 90° would come from *S*'s right side, and 180° azimuth would refer to a source directly behind *S*. In natural listening settings with speech or noise stimuli and where *S* is unencumbered except for the elimination of visual cues (e.g., blindfolded), the accuracy with which he can specify azimuth of the sound source is impressive. The most widely known study of the magnitude of error in localizing sound sources is that of Stevens and Newman (1936). To obtain an echo-free (anechoic) setting, a blindfolded listener was perched atop a pole on the roof of a building. Single clicks or brief bursts of high frequency noise were presented from several azimuths, and *S* named the apparent locus of each stimulus. "The average of the errors of localization was only 8.0° for the click and 5.6° for the hiss" (p. 305). Since the stimulus locations were fixed at 15° intervals and the listeners were Stevens and Newman themselves, the precision and generalizability of the function relating accuracy to azimuth might be questioned. However, similar magnitudes of localization error have been obtained by Thurlow and Runge (1967) from experimentally naive *S*s. In one condition of the Thurlow and Runge experiment, *S*s listened to 5 sec of thermal noise from various locations in an anechoic room. *S*s who were free to move their heads pointed to apparent loci with less than 10° error.

The magnitude of error for discriminating azimuth has long been known to depend upon the stimulus azimuth actually in question. Thus Boring (1942) summarizes evidence reported by Block in 1893 showing that the difference threshold for azimuth (the minimum audible angle) was smallest when the source was in front of *S*, larger when the source was behind, and largest when the source came from the side. This pattern of results has been replicated many times. In the Stevens and Newman study, e.g., localization error for a source straight ahead of *S* was less than a third that obtained with sources at the side. Gardner (1968) has recently reported data on localization accuracy for sources restricted to a 10° arc in front of *S*. The stimuli were speech samples of 7–12 sec duration presented through loudspeakers in an anechoic room. Although the loudspeakers were separated by 2.5° and *S*'s mode of response was not detailed, Gardner reported errors of localization averaging 1.5°. This is quite consistent with values for detecting departure from the median plane reported from studies in other echo-free settings.

While the precision with which *S* can locate a sound source decreases as the sound is moved laterally, a second measure, confusion, describes a complementary function with azimuth. The term confusion has been used to refer to two types of error in localizing sounds: (1) an error in the binary decision of whether the source is in *S*'s right or left auditory field (right–left confusion), and (2) a similar error where *S* perceives a sound in front as coming from behind or the converse (front–back confusion). These confusions were documented in early studies (Boring, 1942) and continue to be reported (Stevens & Newman, 1936; Thurlow & Runge, 1967). Both right–left and front–back confusions are more frequent when the source lies on or near the median plane (the vertical plane passing through the center of *S*'s head and along his line of sight). Right–left confusions are very rare for sounds approaching 90° azimuth, particularly if the stimulus is complex and *S* is allowed to move his head. Thus hemispheric confusions increase as the stimulus moves more medial, but the error in detecting the exact locus of the source decreases. The presence of two functions suggests the operation of two processes and, indeed, hypotheses have been advanced considering the adaptive advantage of a two-process system (Pollack & Rose, 1967). A process that reliably (however imprecisely) specifies whether a source is to the left or the right could start the listener's head moving in that direction and bring the source into position for more precise localization by both auditory and visual perceptual systems. A series of reaction-time papers by Simon and co-workers (Simon, 1969) has provided evidence that observers are indeed biased to respond in the direction of an incoming stimulus.

In a recent investigation of front-back confusions, Hochberg (1966) had Ss point to the apparent locus of speech sources that could come from any of 16 azimuths. About 10% of the responses made in the experiment represented front–back confusions, but all of these confusions were made by only 58% of the *S*s. That is, *S*s could be divided into two groups, those who made no confusion errors and those who did make such errors. Moreover, *S*s who made confusions were also less accurate in localizing all stimuli. Thus, while hemisphere specification (right–left, front–back) and precise azimuth specification appear to be complementary processes, they may not be independent.

The greatest interest of investigators of auditory localization has been in seeking *explanations* for azimuth discrimination. This effort has usually taken the form of determining the necessary and sufficient cues to the locus of a sound source. Contemporary studies of localization cues can be pieced together as a sequence of acoustic and psychophysical experiments. Acoustic experiments measure the potential information in a sound field. For example, by substituting a dummy head with microphone ears in place of a listener, it is possible to measure changes in sound intensity, or differences in arrival time as a function of frequency, azimuth, distance, etc. On the basis of this acoustic information about the cues available, it is then possible to conduct psychophysical experiments selectively eliminating alternatives to discover which cues actually are used. In addition, by comparing an acoustic variable like the difference in arrival time at the two microphones (ears) and a psychophysical variable like minimum audible angle, both as a function of some third variable like azimuth, an estimate can be made of the sufficiency of the acoustic variable to account for the psychophysical variable. Some of the acoustic experiments are summarized by Howard and Templeton (1966). Stevens and Davis (1938) discuss several lines of psychophysical research, and Boring (1942) presents an amusing summary of the early history of this problem.

A wealth of experiments over the last century has resulted in firm support for a "duplicity theory" of azimuth localization (Green & Henning, 1969). The major cues used in specifying azimuth result from the differences in sounds arriving at the two ears. In relatively anechoic settings, binaural differences in intensity of sound transients as they arrive at the two ears inform the listener that the source is on the side of the ear receiving the more intense input. This binaural intensity difference results from the "sound shadow" cast by the head. Audible frequencies above about 2000 Hz are blocked by the head in getting to the farther ear.

The most extensive empirical test of the role of binaural differences in azimuth discrimination is that of Mills (1958, 1960). Mills presented tone stimuli of 1 sec duration from several azimuths between 0° and 90° in an anechoic room. *S*s were required to indicate whether a second tone was to the left or the right of the first. The minimum audible angle increased slowly from 1° to 2° between the median plane and about 60° azimuth. Beyond 60° the increase was more rapid, reaching 10° at an azimuth of 75°. To assess the role of binaural intensity differences in determining the highly precise localization near the median plane, Mills plotted the acoustic difference in intensity at the two ears as a function of stimulus frequency. This curve was then compared with one showing the minimum detectable intensity difference as a function of frequency. The two curves coincided for stimuli between 1500 and 5000 Hz, providing strong evidence of the operation of a binaural intensity difference as the major cue to stimulus locus.

In reverberant settings, like most rooms, reflected sound complicates the listening situation, presumably making the binaural intensity difference less useful as a cue. In addition, acoustic experiments (e.g., Firestone, 1930) suggest that the binaural intensity difference for high frequency sounds does not vary with azimuth in a simple fashion, suggesting that additional cues are probably used to resolve ambiguities about stimulus locus. The sufficiency of binaural intensity differences to cue stimulus locus has also been questioned by Feddersen, Sandel, Teas, and Jeffress (1957).

The second component of the duplicity theory, differences in time of arrival of sounds at the two ears, provides a cue less hampered by normally reverberant settings. There are actually two aspects to the binaural time cue. First, a sound tends to be localized in the direction of the ear first receiving input. The auditory system has been shown to discriminate temporal asynchronies as small as 10 μsec (Klumpp & Eady, 1956), which is close to the binaural acoustic difference occurring with stimuli a few degrees off the median plane. Mills' experiments, cited previously, have implicated this cue for frequencies below 1400 Hz.

The second aspect of the binaural time cue is the precedence effect. According to the precedence effect, the first information arriving at the ears is given greatest weight in source localization. Information arriving subsequent to the first transient is in some manner gated out, and even if this information conflicts with the first transient (by experimental arrangement), it has little influence on the localization decision (Wallach, Newman, & Rosenzweig, 1949). These facts about the binaural time difference cue lead to the idea that it is the arrival (onset) difference of sound to the two ears that determines where the stimulus will be localized. However, the exact way in which the binaural time cue operates is still a matter of debate (Perrott, 1969).

Although the difference in phase of a signal when it arrives at the two ears has long been entertained as a third cue for localization, phase differences are reflected in the auditory nervous system as time differences between impulses. Therefore, statements about phase cues can be translated into statements about binaural time cues and are not given separate consideration here.

Our understanding of the processes involved in localization has been greatly advanced by experiments using earphones rather than sound sources in real space. When presented with diotic stimuli (identical to the two ears) or with dichotic stimuli (different to the two ears) sufficiently close in arrival time (7 msec or less), *S* reports perceiving one stimulus located somewhere on a line between his two ears. This phenomenon is known as lateralization, to distinguish it from real-space localization. Diotic stimuli are lateralized in the center of the line, with minor variation among individuals. By introducing a binaural asymmetry in time or intensity, the apparent stimulus locus will shift toward the ear receiving input leading in time or greater in intensity. Thus lateralization is analagous to localization. Jeffress and Taylor (1961) have in fact argued that these stimuli can reliably be ascribed to external loci, indicating that lateralization and localization differ only in terms of whether *S* is asked to indicate an internal or an external locus. For these reasons, lateralization has been studied extensively as a way of learning about the operation of binaural time and intensity cues.

Two features of the lateralization phenomenon are of particular interest. First, the process provides a method of holding constant normally confounded potential cues (e.g., time differences, head movements) while studying the role of some other cue (e.g., intensity differences). Second, lateralization experiments allow the relative contributions of the different cues to be compared. The major strategy of such experiments has been to study the "time intensity trade." In this procedure, a binaural difference is established with, e.g., the signal to the right ear leading in time. Then a binaural intensity imbalance is introduced with the left ear receiving greater intensity and adjusted until *S* indicates that the sound image is centered. In this way, we obtain values of intensity difference necessary to compensate for given time differences. On the basis of the duplicity theory, we would predict that the time–intensity trade ratio should change as a function of stimulus frequency. It does. Sandel, Teas, Feddersen, and Jeffress (1955) showed that time differences were more potent determinants of the position of a lateralized image of low frequency, but binaural intensity differences had a greater influence for high frequency stimuli. Comparable data have been obtained with narrowband click stimuli (Zerlin, 1969).

Hafter and Jeffress (1968) reported that when a low frequency (500 Hz) tone is presented in a lateralization situation, *S*s can actually distinguish two sound images, one more affected by binaural time differences and the other more affected by binaural intensity differences. This indicates the operation of two mechanisms. Lateralization experiments therefore provide strong support for the duplicity theory.

However, other lateralization experiments have challenged the idea that two functions indicate two processes. Deatherage and Hirsh (1959) suggested that while a duplicity notion may be useful at the acoustic level of analysis, it is not descriptive of events beyond the most peripheral level of the auditory system. They promoted an intensity–time conversion hypothesis which proposed that intensity information is converted to time information somewhere in the cochlea. This would mean that at the level of the central nervous system localization proceeds purely on the basis of differences in timing of impulses in various nerve fibers. More recent studies have presented evidence against the intensity–time conversion hypothesis. Elfner and Perrott (1967) summarized some of this evidence. One strategy has been to fatigue the cochlea of one ear by monaural presentation of noise, thereby increasing the latency of the cochlear response to a signal. According to the intensity–time conversion hypothesis, this should produce a shift in the apparent locus of a normally centered signal. Elfner's group found that signal intensity at the fatigued ear actually had to be decreased more than under control conditions to produce a shift toward the nonfatigued ear. Moreover, the change in binaural intensity difference required for an image shift occurred even for signals at frequencies for which there had been no change in sensitivity as a result of hearing the fatigue stimulus. That is, the effect was so general as to suggest involvement of mechanisms located more centrally than the cochlea. Additional evidence that intensity information is maintained beyond the cochlea is summarized with Elfner and Perrott's demonstration that lateral shift thresholds and intensity difference thresholds both show similar changes as a function of the sound level of the signal being investigated. Finally, physiological studies recording impulses in the inferior colliculi of cats provide evidence of bilateral intensity difference information being maintained at that level (see Elfner & Perrott, 1967). It therefore appears that the contributions of binaural differences in both time and intensity continue beyond the cochlea (see also Babkoff & Sutton, 1969), and the status of the duplicity theory as a meaningful contribution to our understanding of auditory localization is secure.

Lateralization experiments provide important clues to the nature of available mechanisms in localization. However, we normally localize complex sounds in reverberant settings where there also are background noises from which the signals must be discriminated. The particular mix of potential cues that proves adaptive to *S* probably varies considerably with the setting and provides opportunity for a contribution of learning in determining the accuracy of auditory localization.

The Listener as Learner

A mobile and adaptable listener has the possibility of altering the cues available to him in detecting stimulus location. One way in which this has been demonstrated is through studies of the role of head movements in azimuth perception. Wallach (1940) presented an early rationalization for the contribution of head movement in improving azimuth discrimination. Experiments by Thurlow (Thurlow, Mangels, & Runge, 1967; Thurlow & Runge, 1967) have provided strong empirical demonstration that head movement can decrease error of localization. Thurlow and Runge presented 5-sec noise or click stimuli from various locations in an anechoic room. *S*s were fitted to a mechanical linkage which induced head movements of specified direction and speed. *S*'s head was moved during stimulus presentation, and at stimulus offset *S* pointed to the apparent locus with a stick. When *S*'s head was moved in a side-to-side rotation, azimuth localization was significantly more accurate than when *S*'s head was immobile. This was true for high or low frequency noise and for high or low frequency clicks. A pivot movement, moving the ear toward and away from the shoulder, was also helpful in reducing error, but a motion of tipping or nodding the head up and down did not prove helpful. In the latter case it can be observed that the ears move relatively little, the axis of movement being about the same as the interaural axis.

To assess the extent to which *S*s would use such movements without specific inducement, Thurlow *et al.* (1967) made a motion picture analysis of free head movements made in the setting just described. Rotation proved to be the most commonly used motion. There was very little use of the pivot or tip motions except in combination with rotation.

Pollack and Rose (1967) have also demonstrated facilitation of azimuth localization by head movement, but in addition have pointed out that a movement cue is more useful (1) when *S* makes it freely, (2) when the sound is in a lateral location, and (3) when the stimulus is within some optimal range of duration. In the latter instance, head movements were more helpful with 1-sec noise stimuli than with 15-msec clicks or with 3-sec noises.

What is it about head movement that proves helpful? Obviously, moving the head introduces change over time in the binaural time and intensity differences (see Wallach, 1940). Saying this merely compounds the problem, however, for how does a listener use all of this information? In empirical terms, the explanation of the effectiveness of head movement remains a mystery.

A clear example of the role of learning in localization is provided by studies of unilateral signal attenuation (Bauer, Matuzsa, Blackmer, & Glucksberg, 1966; Perrott & Elfner, 1968; Perrott, Elfner, & Homick, 1969). These studies can be considered as analogous to experiments with vision-distorting spectacles and the adaptations that occur under such distortion. The procedure has been to study errors made in azimuth localization while *S* is wearing a plug in one ear. Although such a plug does not eliminate input to the ear, it does provide measurable reduction of sound level and sometimes arrival time (Perrott *et al.*, 1969). The exact effects depend on signal frequency and the composition of the plug. The studies show that, relative to responses made before insertion of the plug, *S*s show large shifts of apparent locus toward the open ear. The error of localization represented by these shifts decreases as *S* wears the plug in his normal daily routine, but the time required for adaptation is of the order of several days. Adaptation time can be reduced to several hours by specific training in the test setting. Perrott and Elfner (1968) showed that *S* can also be taught an incorrect (nonveridical) locus during adaptation to the plug-induced shift. As in the case of vision, when the plug is finally removed, *S* shows errors of localization in the opposite direction, i.e., toward the side of the previously plugged ear, although recovery from this shift is relatively rapid. The Perrott and Elfner (1968) study suggests that *S*s wearing a monaural plug make particular use of changes in intensity which occur as a stimulus is moved from the plugged to the open side. When these intensity differences are eliminated by using sources matched for sensation level (decibels above absolute threshold), localization accuracy is greatly reduced.

Having recognized that *S*s can use head movement to make adaptive adjustment to limited information about stimulus azimuth and that they can learn to use new patterns of perceptual input, we might wonder about the comparative ability for auditory localization shown by two special groups—the blind and the young. G. H. Fisher (1964) reported azimuth discrimination experiments comparing blind and sighted (but blindfolded) *S*s. When asked to indicate which of two bursts of noise was located more lateral or to turn their head to face the sound source, the performances of blind and sighted *S*s were indiscriminable. However, equivalent accuracy does not necessarily mean identical processing. Blind and sighted *S*s may achieve equal accuracy by different weightings of available cues. There is a very old notion that the blind are able to compensate for their blindness by developing greater precision in nonvisual perceptual systems. Rice (1969) summarizes a number of studies similar to Fisher's which contradict this compensation notion by showing equivalent performance by sighted and blind *S*s.

Rice (1967, 1969) has performed an informative series of studies on human auditory echo locating of objects in the environment. In Rice's experiments, *S*s were asked to emit sounds (e.g., clicks, hisses) that would echo off a target varying in location, size, or shape, and then to make a response about the nature of the stimulus. Congenitally blind *S*s performed with greater accuracy than late-blind or sighted *S*s, although the performances of the three groups ranged over the same values. This, in addition to some experiments where *S*s were trained to improve their performance, suggests that observed differences in performance reflect the extent to which *S* has learned to use available cues rather than inherent differences in available mechanisms.

Studies of auditory localization in children are not numerous. This is understandable if one's interest is merely in plotting the accuracy of localization as a function of age. It is difficult to communicate to a young child the need for maximally precise responding, and therefore curves relating minimum audible angle to age would be difficult to interpret. Wertheimer (1961) tested a newborn immediately following delivery and observed eye movements in the direction of a lateral click. Developmentally, this is the earliest evidence of azimuth discrimination, although these data badly need replication. There is greater promise of information in studies which examine the operation of a particular variable in localization at different age levels. A good example is a collection of studies indicating that visual factors play a role in auditory localization (G. H. Fisher, 1964; Jackson, 1953; Witkin, Wapner, & Leventhal, 1952). The first point made by these studies is that we do not process auditory information independently of simultaneous *or past* information from other perceptual systems. The more detailed intent of these studies is to specify the nature of such intermodal interaction and its change with development.

Studies measuring localization accuracy for various perceptual modalities have shown vision to produce the smallest difference thresholds, constant errors, and variability. Such evidence has led many writers to refer to vision as our principle spatial sense. This unique role played by the visual modality has recently been explored by Warren (1970). In a creative series of experiments Warren demonstrated not only the greater reliability of visual localization but visual facilitation of auditory localization as well.

Warren had *S*s point with their hand at the apparent locus of an auditory target (a train of clicks) presented from behind a screen. The apparatus allowed a comfortable but precise method of responding, with responses measured to the nearest degree. Localization accuracy was quantified in terms of response variability with auditory targets relative to response variability when localizing a visual target. For adult *S*s, Warren found that having the eyes open facilitated localization even through *S*s could see neither the sound source nor the hand with which they were responding. Providing only a visual point referent at 0° in an otherwise dark environment was sufficient to produce the facilitation of auditory localization. Warren also made separate estimates of the role of vision on perception and on response. This was done by having *S*s listen with eyes open or closed and then, following stimulus cessation, point with eyes open or closed. Both portions of the task were facilitated by visual input, though the perceptual component benefited more. This was corroborated in a threshold study using the method of constant stimuli, in which a motor response was not involved.

Warren also studied second-grade and sixth-grade *S*s and found that, at these developmental levels, the trend toward visual facilitation was not statistically significant. Specific instructions to look in the direction of the sound before pointing did not increase visual facilitation for the children, although a trend toward facilitation was again present.

Thus Warren's research indicates that auditory azimuth discrimination is improved by some form of visual input, but this input need not involve anything as specific as eye movements toward the source. Of course, the fact that congenitally blind *S*s can perform many spatial tasks as well as sighted *S*s (G. H. Fisher, 1964; Rice, 1969) indicates that the visual contribution is only typical, not necessary. There is support for this in Warren's data; with practice on auditory localization, the visual facilitation effect decreased.

A second body of research on intermodal localization effects concerns the "capture" bias of information in one modality by that in another (Pick, Warren, & Hay, 1969; D. H. Warren & Pick, 1970). Such experiments involve presentation of conflicting information about the location of an object through the intrusion of various distorting devices. For example, *S* might listen to a visible sound source through pseudophones. Pseudophones are artificial ears which introduce some form of distortion of the signal to the real ears, e.g., feeding right-ear input into the left ear. In the present instance, the pseudophones were small microphones set in artificial pinnae and mounted just above *S*'s head. The signals picked up by the microphones were fed to *S*'s ears through headphones. The interaural axis of the pseudophone was rotated slightly, which shifted the apparent locus of the sound (eyes closed) by several degrees. With eyes open, auditory and visual cues were therefore discrepant. But regardless of whether *S* was asked where he heard the sound to be or where he saw the source to be, his response was primarily determined by the visual information. That is, vision biased audition. Although such studies have revealed some reciprocity in capture phenomena, it can be stated generally that the visual system is the strongest "captor."

Weerts and Thurlow (1971) have implicated eye *position* in the visual bias of auditory localization. Having *S*s turn their eyes 20° to the side induced a shift in the apparent locus of a sound source. The shift was in the direction the eyes were turned, but was only a few degrees in magnitude. This effect was intensified when *S* was also led to *expect* that the source was located where he was looking. However, simply inducing the expectation, without accompanying eye positioning, had no effect.

Perceiving Sound Source Elevation

Elementary textbooks usually dismiss perception of the vertical dimension of sound locus as being very poor. This may be more a reflection of a lack of studies of elevation discrimination than a reflection of the behavior capacity of listeners. However, there may be some adaptive rationale for relatively inferior discrimination of sound elevation. At least for the long period between man-in-tree and man-in-aircraft, most sounds in our world have emanated from sources within a few degrees of vertical angle. There has thus been little reason or time for selective advantage to those individuals who are more capable of discriminating elevation of auditory stimuli. Yet, however inferior a process it may be relative to azimuth discrimination, vertical localization is both possible, as indicated by the following studies, and natural, as indicated by the observation that *S*s frequently ascribe different vertical components to sources which are actually on the same horizontal plane.

In a study involving pure tones of several frequencies (Pedley & Harper, 1959) *S*s localized higher frequencies at higher elevations. But the important aspect of frequency was its relative position in the context of the experiment. For example, a 900-Hz signal presented in the context of stimuli ranging from 100 to 1400 Hz was localized at a higher elevation than when it was presented in a 900- to 12,500-Hz context. In Pedley and Harper's experiment, the vertical positions of the stimuli never actually changed. *S*s were merely led to believe that different positions were being used. Such a procedure, in which stimulus variation is relatively improverished but *S* is told otherwise, probably tells us less about perceptual processing than it does about the resourcefulness of *S* in either finding a normally minimal cue or in acquiescing to the experimenter.

Clearly, the most thorough investigation of elevation perception is the work of Roffler and Butler (1968a, 1968b). Stimuli were presented from a 33° vertical array of four loudspeakers located behind a cloth panel. The panel was marked off into 13 numbered sections for *S* to use in identifying apparent locus. Stimuli were tones ranging from 250 to 7200 Hz or noise pulses covering several frequency ranges and were presented for as long a duration as *S* needed. Tones and low frequency noise were poorly localized. Accuracy increased greatly for noise with components of 8000 Hz or higher.

Testing both blind and sighted *S*s, Roffler and Butler (1968b) found that higher frequency tones were ascribed to higher locations, thus corroborating Pedley and Harper, and that blind *S*s perceived a shorter range of apparent loci than did sighted *S*s. This suggests some role of vision in elevation perception, and this was supported further by additional experiments. For example, by increasing the distance of *S* from the stimulus panel but keeping the speakers at the same angle of elevation with respect to *S*, it was found that perceived locus was influenced by the visual angle of expanse of the panel. Roffler and Butler's interpretation was that a given signal appeared to come from a given place on the panel regardless of distance, rather than from a given angle of elevation. By altering *S*'s body position (i.e., having *S* lie on his back or his side) and the configuration of the panel, Roffler and Butler demonstrated that it was not objective vertical but vertical relative to *S*'s head and line of sight that determined where a tone would be localized.

One might question whether the ascription of higher frequencies to higher loci is merely the result of some semantic generalization or confusion. Perhaps, given the ambiguity of the experimental setting, *S*s who are accustomed to distinguishing pitches by "high"–"low" labels simply continue to use these labels with regard to location. This possibility now seems unlikely. Roffler and Butler (1968b) tested 4- and 5-year-old children, who showed the differential vertical localization as a function of frequency. When questioned following the localization task, these children gave no evidence of having yet learned to associate the words low and high with stimulus pitch. Butler (1971) interprets data from *S*s listening monaurally to pure tones as further evidence against a semantic explanation for the frequency effect. Butler's *S*s ascribed different frequency tones to consistent locations, but the locations were neither "correct" nor a simple function of frequency.

The external ear, or pinna, has long been thought to be involved in elevation detection (H. G. Fisher & Freedman, 1967). Roffler and Butler (1968a) presented both broad-band and high frequency noise to *S*s while they were wearing a Plexiglas headband which covered the pinnae. Sound entered the ears through two small holes in the headband. The headband interfered with discrimination of elevation but not discrimination of azimuth. It is known that the pinnae select in favor of high frequencies in an incoming stimulus, which leads to the hypothesis that the pinnae may function like a high frequency band-pass filter in facilitating elevation perception. Roffler and Butler tested this hypothesis by increasing the sound level of the high frequency noise, but found that their pinnaeless *S*s did not improve their performance. The pinnae must influence perception by some means other than merely increasing the level of high frequency stimulus components.

One perplexing aspect of the Roffler and Butler studies is that they found no better elevation discrimination when *S*s were allowed free head movement than when they were not. In the experiment by Thurlow and Runge (1967) cited previously, induced head movements consisting of rotating the head about its vertical axis or pivoting it from side to side reduced error in vertical localization of noise pulses, although such facilitation did not occur for clicks. It has generally been assumed that head movement cues are particularly useful in those settings where discrimination is otherwise poor, e.g., localization in the median plane and localization of elevation. Wallach (1940) implicated some process in which auditory input is correlated with vestibular or, better, visual input. Wallach suggested that binaural differences (intensity, time) are entered into this correlational process. For example, there will be a considerable shift in the binaural intensity difference from a sound on the horizon when the head is rotated about its vertical axis. The magnitude of this shift will decrease and finally cease as the sound source approaches a zenith (overhead) position. Further progress in understanding the process of elevation discrimination therefore seems to await additional studies of the role of head movements, information about how the input from the two ears is combined, and information about the correlation of auditory and nonauditory input.

Perceiving the Distance of a Sound Source

Information about discrimination of the distance of an auditory stimulus is slightly more plentiful than it is for elevation. In early studies (Shutt, 1898; Starch & Crawford, 1909) various noisemakers were employed as stimuli to determine whether or not distance judgments would vary as a function of stimulus azimuth. The original motivation of this quest was probably a rather naive curiosity, though there is now acoustic evidence that stimuli at 90° azimuth offer more potential cues to their distance (Coleman, 1963). Shutt (1898) required *S*s to judge distance in feet and found a tendency to overestimate distances less than 35 feet, to underestimate further distances, and to judge more accurately when the stimulus was from a lateral azimuth than when it was in front of *S*. Starch and Crawford (1909) measured the difference threshold for distance with stimuli located at various azimuths 1 meter from *S*. No azimuth effect was found. Both studies were conducted in settings with complex acoustic characteristics. Perhaps the conflicting results regarding azimuth were obtained because of the different cue settings. At least such early studies demonstrate that reliable distance perception is possible.

A detailed review of possible cues for detecting auditory distance (Coleman, 1963) shows that the major cue is apparently the decrease in loudness of sound reaching the listener as distance increases. In a free-field setting sound level drops off by 6 dB with each doubling of distance. One way to test the sufficiency of loudness to account for apparent distance would be to compare difference thresholds for loudness and distance as a function of distance. Both Starch and Crawford (1909) and

Edwards (1955) tried to do this, but there are in the literature no satisfactory estimates of how such thresholds change with distance.

There is support for a loudness–distance relationship from a different approach. Judgments of half-loudness and double-distance are equivalent under a number of circumstances (Stevens & Guirao, 1962; R. M. Warren, Sersen, & Pores, 1958). While Stevens and Guirao used such evidence to implicate loudness as the cue to distance, Warren *et al.* presented the reverse argument, that a listener learns to use his knowledge of distance and how a sound varies with distance to judge loudness. At the risk of raising a hoary view of the nativism–empiricism ghost, such an argument might benefit from developmental research.

The great role of loudness in distance perception is shown by the demonstrations just presented that loudness and apparent distance vary in complementary fashion under given stimulus changes. Studies attempting to demonstrate the role of other factors have produced much more meager evidence. For example, as distance is increased beyond a few feet, higher frequencies are known to be more attenuated than lower frequencies (Coleman, 1963). But studies attempting to show that *S*s either can or normally do use such a cue as change in frequency spectrum have produced no strong evidence. Similarly, since binaural differences and changes in these differences with head movement have been shown to be influential in azimuth and elevation detection, a comparable role might be expected in distance discrimination. The binaural intensity difference has been shown to change regularly as a function of azimuth, frequency, and distance within about 15 feet (Coleman, 1963). Head movements should, of course, make these differences potentially even more informative. The case is similar for binaural differences in time of arrival. Yet this rich array of potential cues is apparently used very little. Wightman and Firestone (1930) failed to demonstrate a contribution of binaural cues.

Studies by the author have also been unsuccessful at showing any significant role played by binaural cues. Encouraged by the success of Stevens (1962) in describing perceptual responses by power functions, Cochran, Throop, and Simpson (1968) had *S*s make magnitude estimates of from 5 to 9 distances from which a speech stimulus was presented. In one experiment, conducted in a relatively anechoic outdoor setting, stimuli were presented from 5 azimuths and head movements were either prevented or encouraged. Neither azimuth nor head movement had any effect on responses. Near distances tended to be overestimated and farther distances underestimated, though much of this effect seemed to reflect a response process inasmuch as over- and underestima-

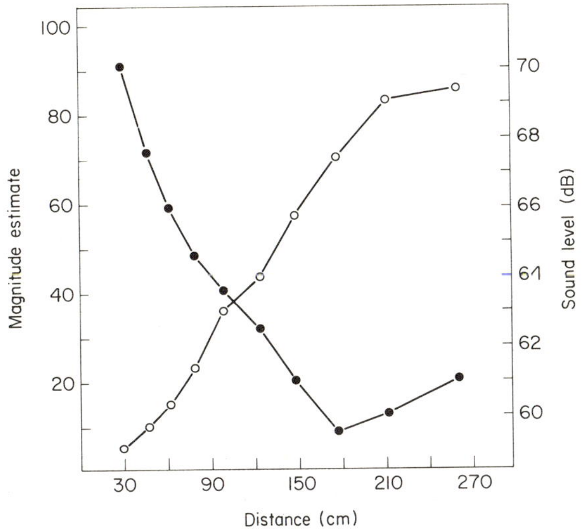

Fig. 1. Mean magnitude estimates (○) and corresponding sound levels (●) as a function of stimulus distance.

tion could be manipulated by varying the standard distance (reference) being used by *S*. Magnitude estimates as a function of stimulus distance were well-described by a power function. However, when the task was presented in a reverberant indoor setting, there was poor discrimination of far distances and the power law was inadequate at describing the data.

In a more recent study [1] evidence for head movement cues was also sought in distance perception. In this study, 3 groups of *S*s were either prevented, encouraged, or required to make head movements during presentation of a train of clicks. The clicks were formed from an 800-Hz signal and presented at a rate of 10/sec for 4 sec. Head movement groups were given demonstrations of the head movements described by Thurlow *et al.* (1967) and told that such head movement would be advantageous. All stimuli were presented from 0° azimuth. Ten distances were studied, ranging from 30 to 266 cm. The experiment was conducted in a room with Fiberglas baffles on the walls, which reduced but did not eliminate echoes. Sound level at the position of *S*'s head is presented in Fig. 1 as a function of distance. There was a regular decrease in sound level as the source was moved through 180 cm., with a slight increase in sound level over the remaining distances. *S*s made magnitude estimates

[1] Unpublished work with Lee Stanton.

relative to a standard ("100") at the farthest distance, 266 cm. Each *S*'s median estimate at each distance was entered into an analysis of variance. There was no difference in response among the 3 groups and therefore no evidence of any use of cues related to head movement. Mean response for all 36 *Ss* is shown in Fig. 1. Other than the fact that responses were quite consistent with values objectively appropriate to the actual distances, the most interesting aspect of this function is the fact that judgments of the three farthest distances did not follow changes in stimulus intensity. This suggests that *Ss* were using some cue other than loudness to discriminate these distances. Apparently, the cue (s) was monaural since head movements were ineffective. A likely possibility is change in stimulus frequency spectrum with changing distance (see Coleman, 1963).

Perhaps binaural cues and monaural cues other than loudness are pressed into service when loudness is unavailable. Holt and Thurlow (1969) recently tried presenting noise bursts for distance judgments in an outdoor setting. Ten bursts were presented at a rate of 1/sec. Intensity was varied to produce a constant sound level at *S*'s ear regardless of distance. Stimulus distances were not discriminated when the sound was presented from 0° azimuth. But with lateral presentation (90°) discrimination did occur; the rank order of judgments agreed with actual distances, although accuracy was not great. Better performance with the lateral stimuli suggests that binaural cues are being used.

One of the most novel attempts to find a relatively echo-free setting is Coleman's (1962) experiment conducted on the surface of a frozen lake. *Ss* indicated which of fourteen loudspeakers, at distances from 5 to 31 feet in the median plane, appeared to be the source of a 1-sec burst of wide-band noise. Coleman found that *Ss*' judgments on trial 1 were unrelated to actual distance but that both discrimination among the various distances and accuracy of judgment improved rapidly with practice. For comparable judgments of stimulus azimuth, Coleman found no such practice effect. Coleman's results indicate that perception of stimulus distance is very much a matter of making a relative judgment, in which *S* takes into account both the set of stimuli being used and the "reasonable" alternatives for response (see also Gardner, 1969).

Taken together, the studies measuring accuracy of distance perception suggest that, given familiarity with the stimuli, *Ss* can make reliable discriminations as a function of distance. The limits of discriminability are unknown. Given the improved experimental techniques now available, it would be interesting to repeat the earlier attempts to measure difference thresholds as a function of distance. In terms of how distance perception occurs, it is clear that *Ss'* responses are determined primarily by the loudness of a stimulus. Additional cues are available, but apparently are used only infrequently, perhaps when loudness is ambiguous or uninformative.

Looking Backward and Forward

The literature on auditory localization is massive. This review has been highly selective and the attention to any one study necessarily superficial. In examining the perception of stimulus azimuth, binaural differences in time and intensity emerged as prime determinants of response accuracy. Head movements were shown to be of great benefit, demonstrating the advantage of an active perceptual system. It was further demonstrated that the auditory system does not operate alone in localization—visual input is also involved, even nonspecific input which provides no information about the source itself. Such contributions suggest the importance of learning to localize.

In the case of specification of stimulus elevation, the major role seemed to be played by the cue of stimulus frequency. Although head movements should also provide help in this dimension, their role is not clear. Regarding perception of the distance of a sound source, head movements and binaural differences appear to be of little value. Monaural changes in loudness indicate distance, and rapid learning occurs, allowing the perceiver to adjust to continuously changing sound fields. Thus unique but overlapping complexes of cues seem to account for the three dimensions of localization.

For convenience, I have dealt separately with three coordinates of stimulus localization. The research which has been summarized has itself been similarly analytic. Investigators have addressed themselves to one dimension or even to the operation of one cue. This is a profitable approach which should eventually yield a rich collection of principles useful in describing and explaining the processes involved. However, it is perhaps of equal import in planning future research to remember that what we perceive is object location. We do not have three perceptions. We do not make separate analyses or decisions about azimuth, elevation, and distance. Each component process seems complicated enough. How is it done in a piece?

Virtually all studies of localization have involved measurement of response accuracy, but there are other characteristics of stimulus localization that might profitably be explored. For example, an index of the time required for localization should be informative. In a series of unpublished experiments, I have compared the times required to decide whether a stimulus is on one's left or right. Both auditory and visual stimuli have been used. Auditory stimuli were sometimes tones but usually noise bursts. Stimulus duration was 50 msec, too short for head movement cues to occur. In control conditions, *Ss* performed a simple reaction-time task by making an arbitrary response to stimulus onset, regardless of the particular stimulus presented. Simple reaction times in these experiments were about 40 msec shorter for auditory than for visual stimuli (see Table 1). This difference has long been known (Woodworth & Schlosberg, 1954), although its limits are now being explored (Kohfeld, 1971). When the task was changed to localization, and *S* was asked to verbalize "left" or "right" depending on stimulus locus, the auditory–visual difference was eliminated, and in some experiments reversed. While the best interpretation of such data is not yet clear, the data are consistent with the hypothesis that vision is a superior modality for localization. This pattern of results has held for stimuli at azimuths of 30° and 60°. Although the visual and auditory stimuli were usually cross-modality matched for subjective intensity, the relatively faster localization of a light has also occurred with auditory stimuli 10 db above the matched level. Thus the indicated difference in localization processing time does not seem to be the result of some fortuitous choice of stimuli.

TABLE 1

Mean Reaction Times from Several Experiments [a]

Single stimulus ("right–left")	Reaction time (msec)			
	Simple [b]		Localization	
	A	V	A	V
Adults	405	445	623	617
Fourth graders	618	655	1073	1018
First graders	736	808	1677	1568
Comparison ("same–different")	**Onset–onset interval (msec)**			
	150		50	
	Naive adults		Naive	Practiced
Visual–visual	499		644	396
Auditory–visual	540		662	416
Visual–auditory	547		678	421
Auditory–auditory	529		715	430

[a] Upper and lower halves of the tables are not comparable because of differences in apparatus.

[b] A, auditory; V, visual.

When children were run in this type of reaction-time experiment, the same pattern of differences resulted. First graders, in fact, showed greater modality differences than fourth graders in both the simple and the localization tasks (Table 1).

A more complex localization reaction-time task also has been studied. In several experiments, *S*s were presented with pairs of stimuli and asked to say whether the members of a pair were located on the "same" side or "different" sides. Data were collected for stimuli presented simultaneously or successively with interstimulus onset intervals up to half a second. All possible combinations of stimulus modality and stimulus location were compared. The adult *S*s were experimentally naive or well-practiced (thirty sessions). The clearest result to emerge from these comparison experiments was evidence that pairs of visual stimuli were localized more quickly than pairs containing one or two auditory stimuli, in spite of the fact that nonlocalization (control) responses were faster to the auditory stimuli. The difference was largest when the stimuli occurred with close temporal contiguity (interstimulus onset intervals zero or 50 msec). Delay in responding seemed to result in part from slower processing of auditory stimuli and in part from having to compare stimuli in different modalities. With unpracticed *S*s intermodal stimulus pairs yielded slower responses than did intramodal pairs. The intermodal portion of the effect held even when members of a stimulus pair were separated by as much as half a second. After much practice with a long interstimulus interval the intermodal portion of the effect disappeared, suggesting some flexibility in processing. In some sessions *S*s were told the modalities of the stimuli beforehand. This foreknowledge produced a slight decrease in response latency but did not otherwise alter processing. This suggests that spatial localization is not flexible to the extent of *S* being able to eliminate the increased processing time required for auditory stimuli.

Thus typical spatial localization processes seem to be more complex for auditory than for visual stimuli and for intermodal pairs of stimuli. Such findings are compatible with previous data on accuracy of localization and can also be used to support the position that vision plays an important role in auditory localization. The modality differences in the time required for localization are large. So are the decrements in time that occur with practice. Perhaps this means that the intermodal differences in spatial localization are "interpretive" in character (see Warren, 1970). It is possible that *S* refers incoming stimuli to some learned frame of reference, normally visual in nature, as part of perceiving stimulus location.

In the future, more precise specification of the processes involved in auditory localization will doubtless be gleaned from additional new measures. One approach toward new understanding might involve application of the reaction-time procedures described by Hohle (1967) to tease apart the components of localization processing. The major components in this pursuit of understanding are, of course, hard work and hard thinking [see Battig's discussion (Chapter 7)]. These components are well-illustrated in the work of the man to whom this volume is dedicated. In response to the announcement of a new daughter in my family, the reply came, "A new infant in the family will have you up early and off to the laboratory."[2] Perhaps that says it all.

REFERENCES

Babkoff, H., & Sutton, S. Binaural interaction of transients: Interaural intensity asymmetry. *Journal of the Acoustical Society of America,* 1969, **46**, 887–892.

Bauer, R. W., Matuzsa, J. L., Blackmer, R. F., & Glucksberg, S. Noise localization after unilateral attenuation. *Journal of the Acoustical Society of America,* 1966, **40**, 441–444.

Boring, E. G. *Sensation and perception in the history of experimental psychology.* New York: Appleton, 1942.

Butler, R. A. The monaural localization of tonal stimuli. *Perception and Psychophysics,* 1971, **9**, 99–101.

Cochran, P., Throop, J., & Simpson, W. E. Estimation of distance of a source of sound. *American Journal of Psychology,* 1968, **81**, 198–206.

Coleman, P. D. Failure to localize the source distance of an unfamiliar sound. *Journal of the Acoustical Society of America,* 1962, **34**, 345–346.

Coleman, P. D. An analysis of cues to auditory depth perception in free space. *Psychological Bulletin,* 1963, **60**, 302–315.

Deatherage, B. H., & Hirsch, I. J. Auditory localization of clicks. *Journal of the Acoustical Society of America,* 1959, **31**, 486–492.

Edwards, A. A. Accuracy of auditory depth perception. *Journal of General Psychology,* 1955, 52, 327–329.

Elfner, L. F., & Perrott, D. R. Lateralization and intensity discrimination. *Journal of the Acoustical Society of America,* 1967, **42**, 441–445.

Feddersen, W. E., Sandel, T. T., Teas, D. C., & Jeffress, L. A. Localization of high-frequency tones. *Journal of the Acoustical Society of America,* 1957, **29**, 988–991.

Firestone, F. A. The phase difference and amplitude ratio at the ears due to a source of pure tone. *Journal of the Acoustical Society of America,* 1930, **2**, 260–270.

Fisher, G. H. Spatial localization by the blind. *American Journal of Psychology,* 1964, **77**, 2–14.

Fisher, H. G., & Freedman, S. J. The role of the pinna in auditory localization. Paper presented to the Eastern Psychological Association, Boston, April 1967.

Gardner, M. B. Lateral localization of 0°- or near-0°-oriented speech signals in anechoic space. *Journal of the Acoustical Society of America,* 1968, **44**, 797–802.

[2] W. J. Brogden, personal communication, 1968.

Gardner, M. B. Distance estimation of 0° or apparent 0°-oriented speech signals in anechoic space. *Journal of the Acoustical Society of America,* 1969, **45**, 47–53.

Green, D. M., & Henning, G. B. Auditon. *Annual Review of Psychology,* 1969, **20**, 105–128.

Hafter, E. R., & Jeffress, L. A. Two-image lateralization of tones and clicks. *Journal of the Acoustical Society of America,* 1968, **44**, 563–569.

Hochberg, I. Median plane localization of speech. *Journal of Auditory Research,* 1966, **6**, 277–281.

Hohle, R. H. Component process latencies in reaction times of children and adults. In L. P. Lipsitt and C. C. Spiker (Eds.), *Advances in child development and behavior.* Vol. 3. New York: Academic Press, 1967. pp. 225–261.

Holt, R. E., & Thurlow, W. R. Subject orientation and judgment of distance of a sound source. *Journal of the Acoustical Society of America,* 1969, **46**, 1584–1585.

Howard, I. P., & Templeton, W. B. *Human spatial orientation.* New York: Wiley, 1966.

Jackson, C. V. Visual factors in auditory localization. *Quarterly Journal of Experimental Psychology,* 1953, **5**, 52–65.

Jeffress, L. A., & Taylor, R. W. Lateralization vs localization. *Journal of the Acoustical Society of America,* 1961, **33**, 482–483.

Klumpp, R. G., & Eady, H. R. Some measurements of interaural time difference thresholds. *Journal of the Acoustical Society of America,* 1956, **28**, 359–360.

Kohfeld, D. L. Simple reaction time as a function of stimulus intensity in decibels of light and sound. *Journal of Experimental Psychology,* 1971, **88**, 251–257.

Miller, G. A. The magical number seven, plus or minus two: Some limits on our capacity for processing information. *Psychological Review,* 1956, **63**, 81–97.

Mills, A. W. On the minimum audible angle. *Journal of the Acoustical Society of America,* 1958, **30**, 237–246.

Mills, A. W. Lateralization of high frequency tones. *Journal of the Acoustical Society of America,* 1960, **32**, 132–134.

Pedley, P. E., & Harper, R. S. Pitch and the vertical localization of sound. *American Journal of Psychology,* 1959, **72**, 447–449.

Perrott, D. R. Role of signal onset in sound localization. *Journal of the Acoustical Society of America,* 1969, **45**, 436–445.

Perrott, D. R., & Elfner, L. F. Monaural localization. *Journal of Auditory Research,* 1968, **8**, 185–193.

Perrott, D. R., Elfner, L. F., & Homick, J. L. Auditory spatial orientation. *Perception and Psychophysics,* 1969, **5**, 189–192.

Pick, H. L., Jr., Warren, D. H., & Hay, J. C. Sensory conflict in judgments of spatial direction. *Perception and Psychophysics,* 1969, **6**, 203–205.

Pollack, I., & Rose, M. Effect of head movement on the localization of sounds in the equatorial plane. *Perception and Psychophysics,* 1967, **2**, 591–596.

Rice, C. E. Human echo perception. *Science,* 1967, **155**, 656–664.

Rice, C. E. Perceptual enhancement in the early blind? *Psychological Record,* 1969, **19**, 1–14.

Roffler, S. K., & Butler, R. A. Factors that influence the localization of sound in the vertical plane. *Journal of the Acoustical Society of America,* 1968, **43**, 1255–1259. (a)

Roffler, S. K., Butler, R. A. Localization of tonal stimuli in the vertical plane. *Journal of the Acoustical Society of America,* 1968, **43**, 1260–1266. (b)

Sandel, T. T., Teas, D. C., Feddersen, W. E., Jeffress, L. A. Localization of sound from single and paired sources. *Journal of the Acoustical Society of America,* 1955, **27,** 842–852.

Shutt, C. E. Experiments in judging the distance of sound. *Kansas University Quarterly,* 1898, **7,** 1–5.

Simon, J. R. Reactions toward the source of stimulation. *Journal of Experimental Psychology,* 1969, **81,** 174–176.

Starch, D., & Crawford, A. L. The perception of the distance of sound. *Psychological Review,* 1909, **16,** 427–430.

Stevens, S. S. The surprising simplicity of sensory metrics. *American Psychologist,* 1962, **17,** 29–39.

Stevens, S. S., & Davis, H. *Hearing: Its psychology and physiology.* New York: Wiley, 1938.

Stevens, S. S., & Guirao, M. Loudness, reciprocality, and partition scales. *Journal of the Acoustical Society of America,* 1962, **34,** 1466–1471.

Stevens, S. S., & Newman, E. B. The localization of actual sources of sound. *American Journal of Psychology,* 1936, **48,** 297–306.

Thurlow, W. R., Mangels, J. W., & Runge, P. S. Head movements during sound localization. *Journal of the Acoustical Society of America,* 1967, **42,** 489–493.

Thurlow, W. R., & Runge, P. S. Effect of induced head movements on localization of direction of sounds. *Journal of the Acoustical Society of America,* 1967, **42,** 480–488.

Wallach, H. The role of head movements and vestibular and visual cues in sound localization. *Journal of Experimental Psychology,* 1940, **27,** 339–368.

Wallach, H., Newman, E. B., & Rosenzweig, M. R. The precedence effect in sound localization. *American Journal of Psychology,* 1949, **62,** 315–336.

Warren, D. H. Intermodality interactions in spatial localization. *Cognitive Psychology,* 1970, **1,** 114–133.

Warren, D. H., & Pick, H. L., Jr. Intermodality relations in localization in blind and sighted people. *Perception and Psychophysics,* 1970, **8,** 430–432.

Warren, R. M., Sersen, E. A., & Pores, E. B. A basis for loudness judgments. *American Journal of Psychology,* 1958, **71,** 700–709.

Weerts, T. C., & Thurlow, W. R. The effects of eye position and expectation on sound localization. *Perception and Psychophysics,* 1971, **9,** 35–39.

Wertheimer, M. Psychomotor coordination of auditory and visual space at birth. *Science,* 1961, **134,** 1692.

Wightman, E. R., & Firestone, F. A. Binaural localization of pure tones. *Journal of the Acoustical Society of America,* 1930, **2,** 271–280.

Witkin, H. A., Wapner, S., & Leventhal, T. Sound localization with conflicting visual and auditory cues. *Journal of Experimental Psychology,* 1952, **43,** 58–67.

Woodworth, R. S., & Schlosberg, H. *Experimental psychology.* New York: Holt, 1954.

Zerlin, S. Time-intensity trading ratios for narrow-band transients. *Journal of the Acoustical Society of America,* 1969, **46,** 125. (Abstract)

CHAPTER 3

POPULATION PRESSURE, POLLUTION, AND THE BEHAVIOR OF CICHLID FISHES[1]

Donald R. Hoffeld

In the past few years, widespread attention has begun to be focused upon two problems, both products of twentieth-century science and technology. These two problems, overpopulation and pollution, probably pose as great a threat to the continued existence of mankind as does atomic warfare, yet the psychologist is forced to admit that generally his

[1] The author is indebted to a number of both graduate and undergraduate students for their help with this project. In particular, this project could not have progressed without the untiring efforts of Bill Rivero and Carol Costelloe, whose work in both data collection and laboratory maintenance has been beyond what could reasonably be expected. This project has been supported in part by funds granted by the Graduate Research Council of Louisiana State University, Baton Rouge.

discipline can offer almost no real knowledge about the effects that either population pressures or increasing pollution might have upon the behavior of man or beast. A few fragmentary observations, mostly incidental or accidental, come largely from zoologists, but there is no real, direct study of the problem. With so much verbiage currently being generated by politicans and would-be politicians about this topic, it might be of some interest to attempt to gather some facts about the subject.

Biologists have devoted considerable effort to the investigation of the conditions regulating the size of various animal populations. At one extreme there are animals, usually living in very harsh, marginal environments, that are essentially at the mercy of those environments. Of much more interest are those animals living in less stringent habitats, existing therefore relatively independently of their physical environment. Under these conditions, the supply of a particular food, mineral, or growth factor may be involved, with only the fittest animals being able to get sufficient nutrients to breed (Wynne-Edwards, 1962). Likewise, population density may be affected by predator and/or parasite (or host) populations. In almost all cases, the concentration of effort has been in the investigation of those factors which *regulate* population density.

The problem, in relation to man, seems to come in quite different terms. For the present time, at least, the factors governing population density in the human appear to be largely cultural in nature, although, in any particular region, climate, disease, and other local conditions may be influential. Fortunately, man is still a discernable distance from the point where shortages of food, water, etc., will be a world-wide problem of sufficient dimension to actually affect the population density appreciably. Man, with his constantly increasing capacity to control his environment and increase his food supply, has a more immediate problem confronting him. It is rather assumed that a person who grows up and lives in a small, rural village is different in many respects from a person who grows up and lives in a megalopolis, and statistics on crime rates, etc., can be furnished to illustrate possible differences. But the difference between Dry Prong, Louisiana, and New York City is certainly far more than simply the population density. There are so many other variables operating in any comparison of this sort that we must conclude that it is not possible at this time to give a factually based answer to the question of whether or not changes in population have any effects on behavior. Obviously, behavior is affected by a change from one person (Adam) to two persons (Adam and Eve). A third and fourth (Cain and Abel) likewise can produce changes in behavior. The exact nature of these changes, particularly as the density increases to an appreciable number of individuals, is not really known, however.

In recent years, ecologists have been increasingly concerned with the problem of pollution and its lethal effects of various animal populations. Young activists have unfurled Rachel Carson's banner and forced politicians to pay at least lip service to the idea of pollution control. But, with notable exceptions, pollution has not generally reached the lethal level, particularly for man. Again, as in the case of the effects of population density, we have virtually no data on the effects of *sublethal* pollution of various types upon the behavior of a species.

There have been a few studies which have reported behavioral effects associated with changes in the population density. Studies of small rodents have indicated (MacArthur & Connell, 1966) that denser populations tend to produce glandular (i.e., adrenal) malfunctions, damaging the offspring, with an apparent increase in aggressive behavior as a result. Along the same lines, the well-known "behavioral sink" phenomenon (Calhoun, 1962) produces higher fetal and neonate death rates, more aggression, and abnormal sexual behavior in laboratory rats. An increase in the population density of the cichlid fish *Aequidens latifrons* (i.e., the drying up of the pools inhabited by them) has been shown to be associated first with an increase in aggressive behavior as the population density increases, followed by a shift to schooling behavior (Breder, 1934). Crowding, carbon dioxide buildup, and adverse temperature changes also produce denser schooling in the sunfish *Lepornis auritus* (Breder and Negrelli, 1935). The minnow *Phoxinus laevis* increases in aggressive behavior as the population density decreases (Holzapfel, 1942), probably indicating the reappearance of sexual behavior suppressed by the overcrowding. Studies of several genera of cichlid fishes (Baerends & Baerends-Van Room, 1950) indicate that the pattern of aggression connected with territorial establishment may vary with the density of the population, but no systematic investigation has been conducted.

In surveying the studies just mentioned specifically, and, generally, all of the relevant studies of population density, it is apparent that the factors of population density and pollution may be confounded. Certainly, increases in the density of the population give, in most cases, more opportunity for pollutions of various types to occur. However, in the most relevant case, that of humans, the two factors do not necessarily have to vary concurrently. Man's capacity to handle pollution as a problem is almost strictly a matter of technology and economics, while his ability to control the population density involves much more complex problems of politics, culture, religion, sociology, etc. The reverse problem is also quite possible since man is ingeniously capable of polluting the environment without any help from increased population density. For this reason it seemed worthwhile to expend some effort in separating out the possible effects of pollution and increased population density from each other. The determination of the separate effects of pollution and population density are particularly important since it seems inevitable that, at some time in the near future, the question of the cost of pollution control or prevention relative to the harmful effects is going to be (or should be) a major factor in decisions made.

Selection of the Animal Population

Although psychologists have been very sparing in their use of any inframammalian species (except pigeons) for behavioral studies, the choice of an aquatic animal for the study of the effects of pollution and population density effects seems to be a very natural one. Fishermen were among the first of the nonscientist groups to become concerned with the effects of pollution since lethal levels have been reached sooner in certain waterways than is the case with the air or soil. In a laboratory setting, the aquarium environment is relatively easy and economical to control and, in the case of a large variety of tropical fishes, will house a large number of animals in a relatively small space, a factor of considerable relavance in studies of the effects of population density. Tropical fish are often easy to breed, economical to purchase and feed, and readily available for local purchase.

CICHLIDS IN GENERAL

The Cichlidae family, from the order Percomorphi (perchlike, spiny ray fishes), offers one of the most interesting groups of small, fresh water fishes for behavioral study. As a family, they tend to be quite territorial and aggressive, although an additional advantage is a considerable range in aggressiveness, from the rather mild *Apistogramma ramireizi* to very aggressive species like *Cichlasoma biocellatum*. They likewise come in a wide range of sizes, from the dwarf cichlids, such as *A. ramireizi* (1½ inches at maturity) to species like *Tilapia mossambica* and *Cichlasoma dowi*, which can grow to substantial size (12 inches and larger) if given proper conditions. Dozens of species have been successfully raised and bred by amateurs, although there is a considerable range of difficulty in attaining successful breeding. Most of the family will live on commercially prepared dried food, although most prefer live food, and the very large species usually need a plentiful supply of minnows at hand, in addition to oversized tanks, for successful breeding to take place.

In addition to a number of behavioral studies, discussed later, there also exists an extensive literature on cichlids, particularly on *Tilapia,* widely used as food fish in Africa and the Far East. A search of the literature for the past 20 years shows over 250 studies. Standard aquarium references (Axelrod, Emmens, Sculthorpe, Vorderwinkler, Socolof, & Pronek, 1962; Innes, 1966; Vorderwinkler, 1958) provide considerable background information, which is supplemented by the *Buntbarsche Bulletin,* the publication of the American Cichlid Association, an organization containing many professional scientists from all over the world as well as hobbyists.

CICHLID BEHAVIOR

One of the most striking features of cichlid behavior, in addition to territoriality and aggression, is the common pattern of elaborate courtship, breeding, and parental care of the young. Upon becoming sexually mature, a male or female may establish a territory, usually by digging a pit in the gravel (preferably in a corner of the aquarium tank) and tearing out any nearby plants. It defends this territory by making various displays and attacks. When a sexually mature member of the opposite sex comes into the territory, both the owner and intruder deliver displays, tail beats, and similar threatening responses. Finally, if the intruder does not leave, they lock their jaws and engage in a wrestling bout which may last up to an hour or more. If neither fish leaves at the end of the mouth fighting, they may settle down as mates and mutually defend the territory against intruders. As the female ripens, the pair clean (using the lower jaw as a scraper) a spot on a rock surface, upon which the female deposits the eggs. The male swims by, fertilizing the eggs, and they settle down to tend the spawning. One usually remains over the eggs, fanning the water with the pectoral fins while the other stands guard over the territory. Upon hatching (3 or 4 days), the young wigglers are picked up in the mouth by the parents and moved to a new pit, an action usually repeated several times in the next few days. When the young have reached the swimming stage, they are closely herded by the adults, who will often deliver violent attacks against even considerably larger fish, human hands, etc., which come too near to the brood. On some occasions they may also devour the entire spawning if its appears to be threatened. With minor deviations, this is the general pattern for most cichlids except the "angel fish" *(Pterophyllum scalare)* and the many species of mouthbreeders. The *P. scalare* are essentially like other cichlids except that they normally live in the heavy grass of the Amazon River, so they lay their eggs on the underside of broad-leaved plants and do not dig territorial pits. The mouthbreeders, upon spawning, pick up and carry the eggs and newly hatched young in their mouths for several weeks, releasing them for short periods but gathering them back at the first sign of danger.

One minor problem in many of the cichlids comes if it is necessary to sex them. Most of the species do not reveal their sex until sexual maturity is reached, at which time it usually shows as a slightly larger dorsal fin on the male. In fact, the fish themselves often seem to have trouble in this respect, and homosexual pairings have been noted in *P. scalare* (Innes, 1966), *T. macrocephala* (Aronson, 1948, 1949), and several other species (Baerends and Baerends-Van Roon, 1950).

PREVIOUS RESEARCH ON CICHLIDS

There have been a number of studies describing and analyzing the behavior of cichlid fishes (Baerends & Baerends-Van Roon, 1950; Myrberg, 1965; Noble & Curtis, 1939), generally from a qualitative standpoint only. Most of the more recent work has, however, concerned itself with specific problems in an experimental setting.

Frequently, the research questions have been formulated in terms of ethological ideas and principles. A number of studies have been concerned with cross-fostering and the conditions required for its success (Aronson, 1948, 1949; Baerends & Baerends-Van Roon, 1950; Collins & Braddock, 1962; Greenberg, 1963a, 1963b, 1963c), with recognition of conspecific fry or mates (Myrberg, 1966; Neil, 1964; Seitz, 1960), and with *releasers* in sexual behavior (Winkler, 1962, 1965).

More traditionally, psychological studies have utilized cichlids in various types of conditioning and discrimination problems (Bitterman & Wodinsky, 1959; Mark & Maxwell, 1969; Weitzmann, 1967), but of more immediate interest to this project is work on aggression in cichlids, defined by Aronson (1949) as nipping, mouthing, chasing, and fighting. Heiligenberg (1965) would add digging to this list, as representing displacement activity when attack is prevented. Color changes, indicative both of sexual maturity and emotional arousal in most cichlids, seem to trigger attack behavior in the cichlid *T. mossambica* (Neil, 1964). Attacks are directed against striped (courting) males' nests, but usually not against black (mated) males' nests. Disruption of the established dominance hierarchy in *C. biocellatum* by either crowding or the introduction of a new fish produces increases in the frequency of aggressive responses (Gottier, 1968), defined in this case as either threat or actual attacking responses.

This previous history of successful research using cichlids, plus the advantages, previously cited, of low cost and maintenance requirements, small size, relative ease of breeding, and relatively easy control of the environment, all gave me additional encouragement in undertaking a large-scale project involving the quantitative study of their social behavior.

Construction of the Behavior Rating Scale

Perhaps the most critical phase of this research was contained in the first stage of the project. The dependent variables of major interest to us, social behaviors, are plentifully described in the literature but only in qualitative terms. No rating scales, quantitative scores, or rater reliability coefficients were generally available, so the first task became the determination of whether or not sufficiently reliable, quantitative measures of these social behaviors could be obtained.

The first step required was the compilation of a descriptive list of the various possible behaviors. Using the results of previous studies (Baerends & Baerends-Van Roon, 1950; Heiligenberg, 1965; Myrberg, 1965) and a series of informal observational sessions in our own laboratory, the following 23 behaviors were selected:

Territorial frontal (Tf)—The adversaries approach each other frontally, usually with the dorsal fin erect. The gill covers are erected, broadening the frontal view of the head.

Territorial chasing (Tc)—The resident fish flattens its fins against its body and pursues the intruder fish with rapid, darting movements.

Territorial bite-butt (Tb)—The fish approaches its adversary rapidly and makes contact, using its head or mouth, with the other fish.

Territorial braking (Too)—The two adversaries narrow the distance between themselves with alternating approach and retreat movements, much in the manner of an approach–avoidance vacillation.

Territorial tail beat (T/)—With gill covers and dorsal fin erect, the fish turns its side to its adversary and thrashes the tail from side to side, sending a flow of water against the other fish.

Territorial Lateral Display (Td)—The fish turns its side toward its adversary, with its dorsal, and usually its anal, fin erected. The caudal fin is usually fully opened.

Territorial tilting (Ti)—The fish lies close to the surface of the water, with the dorsal and anal fins close to the body. The body is tilted at an angle to the water surface, with the head higher or lower than the tail according to the species involved. A submissive response in which the fish declines to make an aggressive reply to an adversary, much in the way a wolf offers its throat to a more dominant wolf.

Territorial circling (To)—Both fish chase each other in a very tight circle.

Territorial mouth fighting (Tm)—The opponents open their mouths, grip each other's jaw, and engage in pulling and twisting movements, often for a protracted period of time.

Courting frontal (Cf), courting chasing (Cc), courting bite-butt (Cb), courting braking (Coo), courting tail beat (C/), courting tilting (Ci), courting circling (Ce)—All these responses are the same as the corresponding responses described as territorial, except that the interaction is between the two members of the territorial pair.

Courting inviting (Cv)—The male fish swims ahead of the female. If she stops, he swims close to the front of her head, making his tail move back and forth slowly.

Pit digging (P)—From an initial horizontal position, the fish turns to a vertical position, approaches the substrate sand with open mouth, takes some sand into the mouth, closes the mouth, swims backward and resumes the horizontal position. It then swims foreward and ejects the sand from the mouth.

Nipping (n)—The fish bites at the substrate sand. If any is taken into the mouth, it is spit out on the spot and is not carried elsewhere.

Jerking (j)—A rapid, snapping-type movement of the body, taking place near the substrate gravel, normally near the territorial pit.

Chafing (K)—From the upper area of the tank, the fish quickly darts to the substrate and skims its flanks over the gravel, then returns to the surface.

Aerating (A)—The fish swims in place immediately above the eggs, parallel to the substrate. Caudal, anal, and pectoral fins are usually all active and the head appears to wobble from side to side.

Following (—)—A pattern of responses in the young fry that tends to keep them close to the parent (s).

Next, four observers were trained in the use of the behavior scale. Each of the observers was paired with each other observer approximately thirteen times, for a total of forty sessions per observer. The data-collection procedure was an adaptation of a system used successfully with primates (Seay, Hansen, & Harlow, 1962), wherein each 15-min session is divided up into sixty 15-sec intervals (the beginning of each interval is signaled by a tape recording). The first time that a particular behavior category occurs in a 15-sec interval, it is recorded, but only the first time during an interval. Each of the behavior categories can therefore occur but once in a 15-sec interval. The total possible occurrences for a particular category during an observational session is therefore 60. The two observers sat approximately 3 feet from the tank, behind a one-way mirror, in a room darkened except for the hood lights in the aquarium tanks. Observations were made from one 20-gallon tank, containing from

8 to 10 mature *C. nigrofasciatum* fish. More complete details of the procedure can be found elsewhere (Costelloe, 1970).

Only those behavior categories observed in 50% or more of the sessions were included in the reliability analysis, a total of 11 of the 23 categories. Pearson product-moment correlation coefficients were computed between each observer and the scores of his partners in the 40 sessions. These coefficients, together with the mean *r* values (computed from Fisher's Z transformation) are shown in Table 1. It was decided, on the basis of the coefficients shown in Table 1, that the scale is sufficiently reliable to permit its use without any further refinements. Those 12 categories which did not occur with sufficient frequency to be included in the reliability analysis were left as a part of the basic scale, on the assumption that they would probably fall within the range of reliability shown by the 11 measures computed. While these untested categories did not occur with sufficient frequency in this case, some will undoubtedly occur with other species and situations, permitting reliability checks at that time. Tilting and courting inviting responses have been informally observed in *T. mossambica* in our laboratory. Aerating and following responses occur naturally only in the special situation where a spawning has taken place, but both are quite easy to recognize.

Research Program Objectives

The basic purpose of the research program is to separate and study the possible effects of population density changes and physical environmental stresses upon the various social behaviors of several species of cichlid fishes. Past studies, as pointed out previously, have tended to confound the two types of effects since physical stresses (decreased food supply, decreased oxygen, increased pollution, etc.) are often associated with increased population density. Hopefully, the use of the following two-phase approach will enable these two major variable classes to be effectively separated.

In the first phase of the experiments, three different population densities of each of the species involved will be studied in a physical arrangement where, so far as is possible, the environmental conditions are the same for all of the population densities.

Upon the conclusion of phase-1 experiments, the social behaviors of the same organisms will be studied as various relevant physical environmental stresses (oxygen shortage, etc.) are systematically manipulated. As a control for both size and experience factors, at least one replication of naive animals of each species will be studied during this second phase.

General Procedure

POPULATION DENSITY DEFINITION

At this point it became apparent that we had to get some sort of definition of what our population densities would consist of. Strictly for general descriptive purposes, we decided to define three levels of population density as light, normal, and overcrowded. The *normal* population density, upon which the other two population density definitions are based, is in no sense of the word intended to imply anything about ecologically or naturalistically normal but is simply the anchoring midpoint of a three-point scale of density. We found that the recommendations of two leading authorities (Axelrod, *et al.,* 1962; Innes, 1966) lead to essentially the same result in making the determination of the *normal* population. Making the assumptions that the oxygen comsumption per square inch of fish surface decreases with increased size of the fish, that the surface area of the tank is the most important determining factor in capacity, and that the tanks are filtered and aerated, the figures given in Table 2 represent the capacity of the given tank size at 80°F, as required for normal health and growth, not simply for sustaining the life of the fish. The length of the fish refers to the average length (estimated) of male fish of the species *at sexual maturity* (excluding caudal fin), not the size of the fish when first separated into their experimental tanks. Since even the normal population density tanks are somewhat crowded by our definition, we decided to make the overcrowded population 1½ times the normal; this seemed to approach the reasonable viability limits. We made the light population 1/2 the normal, yielding a final ratio of 1:2:3.

EXPERIMENTAL ANIMALS

Wherever possible, all of the animals used in these studies are spawned and raised in the laboratory. Where this cannot be achieved, they are obtained from commercial breeders at a size of 1/2 inch or less. The young are separated from the parents at hatching and raised as a group until they are about 1 inch long, at which time they are separated into their appropriate experimental groups as defined in Table 2.

The species being used in this research represent several different degrees of aggressiveness. They all mature at a relatively small size and are commonly found in tropical fish stores. All of the species were originally native to South or Central America, go through the typical breeding procedures described previously, prefer slightly alkaline water (pH 7–7.2) at 75°–80°F, and thrive on commercial dried food. The species presently being used, with a brief description of each, are as follows:

Cichlasoma nigrofasciatum—A relatively small cichlid, maturing at 2½ to 3 inches. The variation used in this research is a pale pink variety and is variously called the pink congo, pink convict, albino congo, etc., by hobbyists. It is not an albino and has, for cichlids, the unusual feature of a slightly more colorful female than a male. Both fish are basically whitish pink, but the female has some golden-yellowish tinge in the area caudal to the pectoral fins. For a cichlid, it is rather mild in disposition and rarely kills its own kind. For this research its *normal* 10-gallon tank population is 16 fish.

Cichlasoma cutteri—A medium-sized cichlid, maturing at about 3½ inches. Its only common name is Cutter's cichlid. It is probably a bit more aggressive than *C. nigrofasciatum.* Its normal population in a 20-gallon tank is 18 fish.

Cichlasoma meeki—A medium-sized cichlid, maturing at about 4 inches. It is commonly called the firemouth cichlid and is reputed to be fairly aggressive, often killing potential mates before a selection is made. Its normal population in a 20-gallon tank is 12.

Cichlasoma biocellatum—A medium-sized to large cichlid, maturing at 4 inches but growing to 7 inches in the aquarium. It is one of the more aggressive of the cichlids, as its common name, Jack Dempsey, suggests. Its normal population in a 20-gallon tank is 12.

The judgment about the aggressiveness of each of the species just listed is based on the aquarium literature and is somewhat suspect since the aggressiveness seems to be a direct function of the size of the fish, leading one to suspect that it is based on how likely the particular cichlid species is to eat smaller members of some other species in the same tank. Our observations certainly seem to indicate that *C. biocellatum* is more aggressive than *C. nigrofasciatum,* but the exact relationships between species will have to await data collection. Several other species, particularly *T. mossambica,* are being considered for research possibilities, but problems in obtaining sufficient healthy offspring have made these other species problematical at the present time.

ENVIRONMENTS

All of the fish live in standard, filtered, aerated aquarium tanks 10, 20, or 50 gallons in size. The 10-gallon tanks will be used for the *C. nigrofasciatum* since they mature at a relatively small size. The remainder of the species will be housed primarily in 20-gallon tanks. Because, in studies of

TABLE 1

Interobserver Correlation Coefficients and Mean Coefficients for those Behavioral Categories Occurring on More Than Half of the Observational Sessions

Behavioral category	Observer	*r*	Mean *r*
Territorial frontal	A	.92	
	B	.82	
	C	.83	
	D	.88	.87
Territorial chase	A	.93	
	B	.89	
	C	.87	
	D	.94	.91
Territorial braking	A	.95	
	B	.69	
	C	.72	
	D	.91	.86
Territorial bite-butt	A	.70	
	B	.65	
	C	.78	
	D	.74	.76
Courting frontal	A	.98	
	B	.81	
	C	.95	
	D	.81	.92
Courting chase	A	.96	
	B	.97	
	C	.95	
	D	.96	.96
Courting bite-butt	A	.80	
	B	.75	
	C	.92	
	D	.89	.85
Courting tail beat	A	.90	
	B	.92	
	C	.90	
	D	.77	.88
Pit digging	A	.98	
	B	.95	
	C	.93	
	D	.97	.96
Nipping	A	.98	
	B	.96	
	C	.93	
	D	.95	.96
Jerking	A	.87	
	B	.67	
	C	.82	
	D	.86	.82

TABLE 2

Population Density Definition of Normal Population

Length of fish (inches)	10-gallon tank (200 inches²)	20-gallon tank (360 inches²)	50-gallon tank (648 inches²)
2.0	32	60	n/a
2.5	20	35	n/a
3.0	n/a	25	45
3.5	n/a	18	32
4.0	n/a	12	22

territorial behavior of cichlids, particularly substrate breeders, it has been pointed out (Baerends & Baerends-Van Roon, 1950) that the number of territories which are possible is a direct function of the size of the tank, as well as a function of the particular species that is involved, it seems advisable to raise some of the *C. nigrofasciatum* in 20-gallon tanks and some of each of the other species in 50-gallon tanks. This will permit a greater number of territories to be formed and will also serve as a control for the effect of the size of the social group, as distinct from the population density.

The physical arrangement is a grouping of tanks into sets of four. Each tank in a set is connected to another tank of the set so that there is complete circulation (driven by a pump, with syphons in all occupied tanks). One of the four tanks (containing the pump) is empty of fish and is used for water changes, etc. The other three tanks contain, respectively, a light, normal, and overcrowded population of one species. Thus, except for the population density, the three environments are essentially identical.

DATA COLLECTION

Upon reaching the size of approximately 1 inch, the young fish are placed in their experimental tanks and observed daily for signs of territorial behavior. When the first sign occurs (normally the occupancy of a corner of the tank, combined with pit digging and territorial defense), regular observations are begun on all fish in that set of tanks.

The basic unit of observation is the territorial fish/pair. Each territorial fish/pair is watched for 5 min daily, as described previously. The observer spends a minimum of 20 min observing each tank, with 5 min devoted to each corner of the tank. If a territorial fish/pair occupies more than one corner, it is observed only in one of the corners. If there is no territorial fish/pair in a corner, no responses are recorded in that 5-

TABLE 3

Mean Responses of Fish/Pairs of C. cutteri, with Mean Reliability Coefficients

	Light	Normal	Overcrowded	Mean *r*
Territorial frontal	3.02	2.55	3.43	.92
Territorial chasing	1.83	1.75	1.94	.88
Territorial braking	1.17	.96	1.71	.95
Territorial bite-butt	.50	.47	.64	.68
Territorial tail beat	.28	.21	.37	.82
Combined courting	1.62	.74	1.49	—
Nipping	5.95	7.23	6.46	.97
Pit digging	.57	1.56	.87	.92
Jerking	.28	1.31	.40	.93
Total fish/tank	9	18	27	—
Mean fish/pairs per tank	1.8	2.6	3.2	—
Mean total fish/pairs observed	5.4	8.8	9.6	—

min period. If there are other territories in addition to those in the corners, each of these is also observed for 5 min. Data collected so far with *C. cutteri* have shown a maximum of six territories in the 20-gallon tanks. The order of observation of corners within a tank and the order of tank observations within a set is balanced in a Latin-square-type design. The exact method of recording responses, etc., is the same as described previously in the discussion of the development of the rating scale.

PHASE 2

While the basic observational method, rating scale, and observational unit will be the same in phase 2 as in the first phase, there will be important procedural changes. When a particular stress is to be applied (e.g., increased carbon dioxide), observations will be taken at frequent intervals throughout the day (e.g., every 2 hr), with monitoring of the environment at the same frequent intervals through use of a pH meter with ion-specific electrodes or an oxygen meter, as appropriate. Hopefully, if major changes in behaviors do take place as a result of the stress agent, we will be able to get some idea (quantitatively) of the approximate concentration required for the change.

Preliminary Results

Although the project is still in its infancy, some preliminary results are available from two species. Observations for 8 weeks on three sets of *C. cutteri* tanks have been tabulated, and those responses occurring with sufficient frequency are shown in Table 3. Note that the courting responses have all been combined into one class. The data shown give the mean number of responses per fish/pair per observational session (20 responses/category is the maximum possible). The fish in the overcrowded tanks give significantly more territorial frontal and braking responses than those in the normal tanks and significantly more braking responses than those in the light tanks. Both light and overcrowded tanks produce more courting responses than the normal tank does. The normal tank produces significantly more nipping, digging, and jerking responses than either of the other two tanks. All differences are significant at the .01 level. It is probably also worthy of note that although the size of the tank undoubtedly controls in part the number of territorial fish/pairs, the total number of fish in the tank (population density) also has an apparent effect (no test of significance).

One set of *C. nigrofasciatum* tanks have also been observed to date, but since a maximum of three fish/pairs per population density condition is involved, no analysis has been attempted. Both qualitative and quantitative observations, however, indicate interspecies differences, with the population density apparently having less effect with *C. nigrofasciatum* than with *C. cutteri*. One qualitative observation of particular interest for phase-2 research occurred when a defective pump resulted in a marked increase in pH (equipment to measure the pollution and oxygen content is not yet available, but it is assumed that these factors also changed). The active territorial behavior ceased and the fish reverted back to schooling behavior. Restoration of normal conditions by a water change resulted in an immediate shift back to territorial behavior, similar to Breder's findings (1934).

Significance of the Project

Whether or not one attributes as much importance to territorial behavior as does Ardrey (1966), it is undoubtedly a major part of the social behavior of most cichlid species, forming the core of their adult social and sexual patterns of behavior. It probably helps to serve both as a breeding selector and population control since only the strongest fish are able to mate if there is any crowding in the environment, while the remainder of the adults form a "bachelor school," much in the manner of English roe deer (Ardrey, 1966) and African antelopes (Buechner, 1961).

There is, of course, considerable doubt as to how the aquarium observations reflect the natural behavior of the species. In nature, cichlids rarely kill each other or do any real harm in their battles since it is possible for the weaker fish to escape from a stronger fish's territory, something not possible on occasion in the relatively cramped quarters of an aquarium. The population densities used are probably not very ecological since it is doubtful if 2½ cubic feet of water would be able to support 25 3-inch cichlids in nature. However, New York City is probably also not very ecological, and the purpose of this project is to study the effects of increased population density and pollution. In fact, the naturalness of both the setting and behavior is probably not particularly important to the purpose of the project since the main concern is to provide a research model that can be controlled and manipulated to a significant degree without any enormous or expensive efforts. There is every reason to believe, from both previous research and our own results to date, that the social behavior of cichlids in an aquarium environment does provide such a model.

While it is certainly true that it is a long way from cichlids to man, it is likewise true that considerable evidence relative to man can be obtained from cichlids. A variety of factors can be directly manipulated and controlled with cichlids in an experimental setting, something not possible with man, for whom indirect, nonexperimental methods offer the only approach now possible.

REFERENCES

Ardrey, R. *The territorial imperative*. New York: Dell, 1966.

Aronson, L. R. Problems in the behavior and physiology of a species of African mouthbreeding fish. *Transactions of the New York Academy of Sciences* [series 2], 1948, **11**, 33–42.

Aronson, L. R. An analysis of reproductive behavior in mouthbreeding cichlid fish, *Tilapia macrocephala* (Bleeker). *Zoologia*, 1949, **34**, 133–158.

Axelrod, H., Emmens, C., Schulthorpe, D., Vorderwinkler, W., Socolof, R., & Pronek, N. *Exotic tropical fishes*. New York: Sterling, 1962.

Baerends, G. P., & Baerends-Van Roon, J. M. An introduction to the study of the ethology of cichlid fishes. *Behaviour*, 1950 *Supplement* **1**, 1–242.

Bitterman, M. E., & Wodinsky, J. Some experiments on learning in *Tilapia*. *Bulletin of the Ecological Society of America*, 1959, **40**, 94.

Breder, C. M. An experimental study of the reproductive habits and life history of the cichlid fish *Aequidens latifrons* (Steindachner). *Zoologica, (New York)*, 1934, **18**, 1–42.

Breder, C. M., & Negrelli, R. F. The influence of temperature and other factors on the winter aggregations of the sunfish *(Lepomis auritus)* with critical remarks on the social behavior of fishes. *Ecology*, 1935, **16**, 33–47.

Buechner, H. Territorial behavior in the Uganda kob. *Science*, 1961, **133**, 698–699.

Calhoun, J. B. A behavioral sink. In E. Bliss (Ed.), *Roots of behavior.* New York: Harper, 1962. Pp. 295–315.

Collins, H. L., & Braddock, J. C. Notes on fostering experiments with cichlid fishes, *Tilapia sparrmani* and *Aequidens portalegrensis. American Zoologist,* 1962, **2**, 400.

Costelloe, Carol. The development of a quantitative scale for the measurement of social behavior of cichlid fish. Unpublished master's thesis, Louisiana State University, 1970.

Gottier, R. F. *The effects of social disorganization in Cichlasoma biocellatum.* Ann Arbor, Mich.: University Microfilms, 1968.

Greenberg, B. Flexibility of the parental cycle in the teleost *Cichlasoma biocellatum. American Zoologist,* 1963, **3**, 519. (a)

Greenberg, B. Parental behavior and imprinting in cichlid fishes. *Behaviour,* 1963, **21**, 127–144. (b)

Greenberg, B. Parental behaviour and recognition of young in *Cichlasoma biocellatum. Animal Behaviour,* 1963, **11**, 578–582. (c)

Heiligenberg, W. A quantitative analysis of digging movements and their relation to aggressive behavior in cichlids. *Animal Behavior,* 1965, **13**, 163–170.

Holzapfel, M. Versuche uber das soziale Verhalten der Elritzen *(Phoxinus laevis* Agass.). *Verhandlungen der Schweizerischen naturforschenden Gesellschaft und Sitten,* 1942, *no volume number applicable,* 134–135.

Innes, W. *Exotic aquarium fishes.* Maywood, N.J.: Metaframe Corp., 1966.

MacArthur, R. H., & Connell, J. *The biology of populations.* New York: Wiley, 1966.

Mark, R. F., & Maxwell, A. Circle size discrimination and transposition behavior in cichlid fish. *Animal Behaviour,* 1969, **17**, 155–158.

Myrberg, A. A descriptive analysis of the behavior of the African cichlid fish, *Pelmatochromis guentheri* (Sauvage). *Animal Behaviour,* 1965, **13**, 311–328.

Myrberg, A. Parental recognition of young cichlid fishes. *Animal Behaviour,* 1966, **14**, 565–571.

Neil, E. H. An analysis of color changes and social behavior of *Tilapia mossambica. University of California, Berkeley, Publications in Zoology,* 1964, **75**, 1–46.

Noble, G. K., & Curtis, B. The social behavior of the jewel fish *Hemichromis bimaculatus* Gill. *Bulletin of the American Museum of Natural History,* 1939, **76**, 1–46.

Seay, B., Hansen, E. & Harlow, H. Mother-infant separation in Monkeys. *Journal of Child Psychology and Psychiatry,* 1962, **3**, 133–132.

Seitz, A. Die Paarbildung bei einigen Cichliden. 1. Die paarbildung bei *Astatotilapia strigigena* Pfeffer. *Zeitschrift für Tierpsychologie,* 1960, **17**, 40–84.

Vorderwinkler, W. *Cichlids: A guide to the identification, care, and breeding of large cichlids.* Jersey City, N.J.: T. F. H. Publications, 1958.

Weitzmann, R. Positional matching in rats and fish *(Tilapia macrocephala). Journal of Comparative and Physiological Psychology,* 1967, **63**, 54–59.

Wickler, W. "Egg-dummies" as natural releasers in mouthbreeding cichlids. *Nature (London),* 1962, **194**, 1092–1093.

Wickler, W. Signal value of the genital tassel in the male *Tilapia macrochir* (pisces: Cichlidae). *Nature (London),* 1965, **208**, 595–596.

Wynne-Edwards, V. C. *Animal dispersion in relation to social behaviour.* Edinburgh: Oliver & Boyd, 1962.

CHAPTER 4

INCUBATION OF AVOIDANCE PRODUCED BY GENERALIZATION TO STIMULI OF THE CONDITIONING APPARATUS

Michael Gabriel[1]

Introduction

DEFINITION OF INCUBATION

When albino rabbits *(Oryctolagus cuniculus)* undergo avoidance conditioning with a shock unconditioned stimulus (US), signaled by a tone

[1] The author is currently on leave of absence at the Department of Psychobiology, University of California, Irvine, California. Research was supported in part by Senior Postdoctoral Fellowship MH-44158 from the National Institute of Mental Health.

conditioned stimulus (CS), and rotation of an activity wheel as conditioned response (CR), they show superior retention after long postconditioning intervals (12–48 hr) relative to that displayed after brief (6 min to 1 hr) intervals. The increase in retention follows a continuous function which attains statistical reliability for intervals as brief as 12 hr. This function continues to an interval directly related to the amount of conditioning (Gabriel, 1968). Also, the function has been observed to reverse direction in studies (Gabriel, 1967; Gabriel & Vogt, 1972) employing a moderate amount of conditioning and a sufficiently long postconditioning interval. The increase in retention will be referred to as incubation of avoidance, in keeping with precedents set in studies involving analogous phenomena (e.g., Kamin, 1957, 1963).

GENERAL THEORETICAL APPROACH

It is the purpose of the present chapter to attempt to offer an explanation for incubation. A "model construct" (Lachman, 1960) explanation will be used in which incubation will be related to a construct (stimulus generalization) which is viewed as more fundamental, though less directly observable, than incubation. Thus, in explaining a phenomenon (incubation) by relating it to a fundamental construct of conditioning (stimulus generalization), I would describe the general theoretical approach as analogous to other familiar approaches (e.g., Amsel, 1962), namely, those which have attempted to explain phenomena (e.g., the frustration effect) by relating them to the fractional anticipatory goal response (r_g–s_g) construct.

AN EXAMPLE OF INCUBATION

A prototype for incubation may be found in the results of the following study (Gabriel, 1967). Rabbits were conditioned to avoid a constant current shock US .2 sec in duration, applied through the grid floor of the rotating wheel apparatus of Brogden and Culler (1936). The response was any rotation of the wheel, the CS was a 1000-cps tone, and the mean ITI was 15 sec and ranged from 5 to 25 sec. Intertrial responses (ITRs) reset the ITI, and responses during the CS terminated that stimulus and prevented shock, otherwise scheduled to occur 4 sec following CS onset. Following attainment of the criterion of 9/10 CRs on any consecutive block of 10 trials, the rabbits were returned to their home cages, where they awaited testing (extinction) of the avoidance CR. Independent groups of rabbits received extinction either .5, 12.0, 24.0, or 48.0 hr after

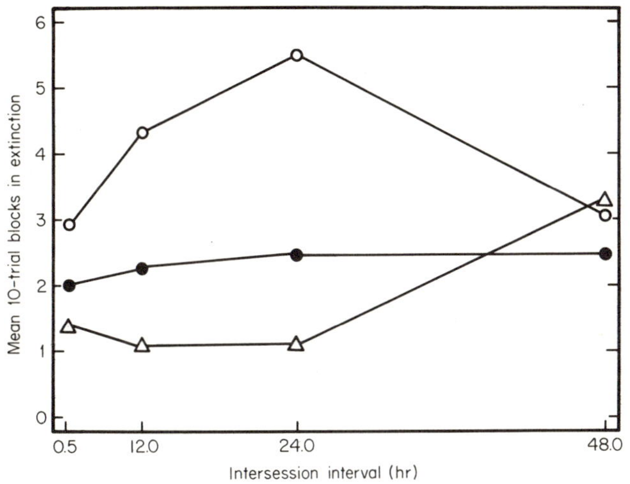

Fig. 1. Mean number of blocks of 10 trials in extinction as a function of ISD, with test stimulus frequency as the parameter (○, 1000 cps; ●, 2000 cps; △, 4000 cps).

the end of conditioning. Each delay condition was further subdivided so that independent subgroups received a 1000-, 2000-, or 4000-cps extinction stimulus within each delay condition. Extinction was carried out to the first consecutive block of 9/10 failures to respond. The results, plotted in Fig. 1, show an incubation function using the means of groups which had the same stimulus (1000 cps) for both conditioning and testing. Specifically, resistance to extinction (in terms of blocks to the extinction criterion) was greater following a 24-hr intersession delay (ISD) than resistance after .5 hr. Resistance at the 12-hr and 48-hr delays was intermediate between the .5- and 24-hr amounts, and did not differ from either. The decrease in resistance obtained at 48 hr compared to 24 hr was typical of extinction results following moderate amounts of conditioning.

It is interesting to note that resistance to extinction showed no change as a function of ISD when the 2000-cps stimulus was used for extinction, and when the 4000-cps stimulus was used; however, a significant increase in resistance was observed at 48 hr compared to the minimal resistance to extinction obtained for the three briefer ISDs. Thus, the incubation function was specific to the original training stimulus. A different function was obtained when different stimuli were used for extinction. More will be made of the stimulus effect later; it is sufficient for present purposes to emphasize the basic phenomenon of incubation obtained with the training stimulus.

ANALOGOUS PHENOMENA

This phenomenon has been replicated in several studies (Gabriel, 1968, 1970; Gabriel & Vogt 1972) using rabbits as subjects, with similar training and test parameters. Additionally, analogous findings have been obtained in studies of discrete-trial active avoidance retention using the shuttlebox (Kamin, 1957, 1963; Webster & Rabedeau, 1964), a 1-trial passive avoidance paradigm (e.g., Zammit-Montebello, Black, & Suboski, 1969), and avoidance of a previously classically conditioned CS (e.g., W. R. McAllister & McAllister, 1965), conditioned suppression of an ongoing operant response (Tarpy, 1966); they have also been obtained for human GSR to a stimulus paired with shock in a classic paradigm (e.g., Golin, 1961). In all of these studies, response frequency, or amplitude, increased as ISD increased. The species investigated include the rabbit, rat, guinea pig, and human.

The question of whether the present explanation of incubation will apply to all of these instances of incubation will not be of concern in the present chapter. It is an explicit intention, however, to make the explanation relevant to incubation of a discrete-trial, well-learned, active avoidance response, i.e., the kind of behavior just described (Gabriel, 1967).

Hypothesis

At first, incubation may seem to represent a passive improvement in learning without practice. Indeed, some authors (Bovet, Bovet-Nitti, & Olivero, 1969; Irwin & Benuazizi, 1966) have chosen to invoke this kind of a hypothesis about incubation, citing the phenomenon as an overt manifestation of consolidation of memory, and as empirical support for the consolidation hypothesis. However, it seems clear that the consolidation hypothesis does not explicitly predict progressive improvement in performance (i.e., incubation) with progressive consolidation of memory. Rather, the hypothesis states that different memory storage mechanisms operate at different time intervals following learning. Performance of the learned response ought to be forthcoming equally from any mechanism of storage, unless explicit provision to the contrary is made. Thus on logical grounds, incubation does not seem to offer evidence of consolidation of memory, and consolidation does not seem a likely "model explanation" for incubation.

The basic hypothesis of the present chapter is something opposite to explaining incubation as a passive improvement in learning. Rather, the hypothesis states that incubation is a performance improvement which results from progressive loss of discrimination. Indeed, many studies have suggested progressive discrimination loss following the learning of aversely motivated behavior at time intervals comparable to those required to produce incubation (Desiderato, Butler, & Meyer, 1966; Gabriel, 1967; W. R. McAllister and McAllister, 1965). These studies each demonstrate a flatter gradient of stimulus generalization (SG) following a long (24–48 hr) ISD compared to the gradients obtained immediately after training. Several authors have chosen to interpret this finding as a manifestation of progressive forgetting of the value of the CS, resulting in confusion of the CS with different stimuli presented in a delayed test for SG. The forgetting and resultant confusion is assumed to operate with respect to those values of the CS and test stimuli which the experimenter presents in an SG test. A point critical for the hypothesis is that forgetting and resultant confusion may also occur with respect to stimuli which the experimenter does not manipulate. Suppose, e.g., that progressive forgetting during ISD results in confusion of the CS with auditory, visual, tactile, kinesthetic, and olfactory, etc., stimuli (i.e., apparatus stimuli) which are present during the inertrial interval. It is this hypothetical process which I am calling SG to apparatus, and my basic hypothesis states that the result of SG to apparatus is that both CS and apparatus stimuli possess control over conditioned responding. Prior to SG, only the CS possesses control. Thus, CS presentation occurs simultaneously with the presence of additional CR-evoking stimuli (apparatus stimuli) following SG to apparatus. Incubation results from stimulus compounding—it is regarded as similar to potentiation of a CR through simultaneous presentation of separately conditioned stimuli (Grings & O'Donnell, 1956; Grings Tadao, & Fiebiger, 1965).

The implicit assertion contained in the hypothesis that SG to apparatus results in increased control by apparatus stimuli may seem paradoxical to the reader. This would be natural enough since the traditional language of SG places increased SG, flat gradients, and loss of stimulus control into one class, whereas decreased SG, sharpened gradients, and increased stimulus control are placed into a separate and essentially opposite class.

The hypothesis does not adhere to all of these distinctions. It is recognized that gradient-slope and stimulus control are negatively related to SG in the case of intramodal SG. However, the hypothesis requires that SG to apparatus, which is essentially intermodal, be positively related to the slopes of SG gradients obtained through postacquisition manipulation of apparatus stimuli. That is, SG to apparatus and stimulus control by apparatus are both assumed to vary directly with the slope of apparatus gradients.

In summary then, it was asserted that intermodal stimulus generalization (i.e., confusion of CS and apparatus stimuli) increases progressively through time following acquisition. This increase is accompanied by increased stimulus control by apparatus stimuli. Incubation is regarded as a heightened level of conditioned responding produced by stimulus control originating from two sources (CS and apparatus stimuli) instead of one (CS alone). Thus incubation may be analogous to potentiation of a CR through stimulus compounding. I will attempt to support this viewpoint by providing evidence that incubation is correlated over time following conditioning with: (a) SG to apparatus stimuli, and; (b) increased control over responding by apparatus stimuli.

Empirical Studies

Empirical documentation of the hypothesis requires examination of the results of six experiments. The methodology and results of the first (Gabriel, 1967) were described previously in this chapter. The remaining five, presented elsewhere (Gabriel, 1968, 1970; Gabriel and Vogt, 1972), while essentially similar in method to the 1967 study, contain in common some significant alterations of the 1967 methods. The following description of these alterations should permit presentation of the remainder of the chapter unhindered by laborious description of methods.

GENERAL METHODOLOGY

The apparatus used in the post-1967 studies was altered such that the definition of a response, the timing of intertrial intervals, and the decision to abort a programmed shock were all automated. All responses (i.e., CRs and ITRs) were recorded automatically in the later studies, whereas in the 1967 study only CRs were manually recorded. The raw frequencies of ITRs were submitted to a normalizing square-root transformation. The CS intensity was increased from 60 to 80 DB SPL, and CS frequency was changed from 1000 to 4000 cps. Both CS and US were response terminated. These alterations resulted in reliable acquisition to a criterion of ten consecutive avoidances in a mean of approximately 30 trials. The percentage of failures to achieve criterion dropped from about 15 to about 6 with the new parameters. Also, all rabbits were trained to criterion in a single experimental session, and in four of the five studies training continued beyond criterion for an additional 100 or 150 trials of overtraining in the same session. It should be noted that performance following criterion in all of the studies which employed overtraining was uniformly high. After criterion, the rabbits in each experiment maintained a mean number of CRs equaling 18 or better in each 20-trial block. In addition, all studies showed slight but statistically significant improvement in the frequency of CR with blocks of overtraining. However, no significant differences over blocks of overtraining were detected for ITRs. Finally, all post-1967 subjects received a fixed number (100) of extinction trials rather than extinction to a criterion.

INCUBATION AND INTERTRIAL RESPONSES

The experimental finding that will be stressed first in providing documentation of the SG hypothesis is the finding that ITRs increase as a function of ISD. Several studies (Gabriel, 1968, 1970; Gabriel & Vogt, 1972) have shown that rabbits make a greater frequency of ITRs during delayed extinction compared to extinction given immediately after acquisition. The ISDs associated with heightened ITRs were also invariably associated with incubation of the avoidance CR. If one is willing to assume that ITRs may be CRs which have generalized to apparatus stimuli, this finding is consistent with the position that confusion of the CS and apparatus stimuli, or SG to apparatus, is an increasing function of time following conditioning. Further, the findings are consistent with the second major assumption of a correlation of incubation with increased control by apparatus stimuli. Increase in responses (i.e., ITRs) in the presence of apparatus stimuli concomitant with incubation is a necessary, though not a sufficient, observation to justify the assertion of increased control by apparatus stimuli. I have tentatively adopted ITR level as an operational definition of SG to apparatus stimuli on the basis of these findings. This view of ITRs is given support by the results of C. P. Thompson, Sachson, and Higgins (1969), who studied the distribution of ITRs in two-way shuttle avoidance acquisition. These authors concluded that ITRs are misplaced avoidance responses resulting from failure to discriminate between danger (CS) and safety (non-CS) periods.

INCUBATION AND THE EFFECTS OF INTERSESSION EXPOSURE TO APPARATUS STIMULI

Additional findings supporting the SG hypothesis have to do with the effects of exposure to the apparatus without the CS or US during ISD. If incubation results from a progressive increase in SG to apparatus stimuli, and if intersession exposure of animals to the apparatus without presentation of the CS or US extinguishes generalized responses to the apparatus, then such exposure should diminish the incubation effect. What should be the expectation regarding the effects of exposure to apparatus on ITRs in extinction? Coupling the foregoing explanation of incubation in terms of SG to apparatus with our operational definition of ITRs as SG to apparatus, clearly, we expect that exposure will reduce ITRs in a delayed extinction test. In addition, we should expect that exposure to apparatus will have a more pronounced effect on ITRs than on CRs. This prediction is arrived at through the assumption that CRs in delayed extinction are controlled by two sources (CS and apparatus stimuli), while ITRs are controlled by only one source (apparatus). Thus the predicted extinction of generalized responses during exposure should be more complete for ITRs than for CRs since all stimuli controlling ITRs are "presented" unpaired with shock during exposure while only a portion of stimuli controlling CRs are presented.

Finally, the SG account predicts a monotonic decline in spontaneous responses over successive periods of exposure. This function would be assumed to reflect the hypothesized extinction during exposure of CRs which have generalized to apparatus stimuli.

Three experiments were carried out to test the predictions about exposure. In all three, the rabbits were given single-session conditioning to a criterion of 10 consecutive avoidances plus 100 additional trials of overtraining. The parameters of training and testing were as described in the section on post-1967 ıevisions of method. In the first experiment, the treatments involved detention in the conditioning apparatus (exposure) under conditions identical to training but with the CS and the US omitted. Four experimental treatments were exposures of 30, 60 (two groups), or 120 min. All exposures were given during some portion of a 120-min interval (experimental interval) beginning 45.9 hr after the end of conditioning. The two 60-min exposures differed in terms of whether exposure occurred during the initial hour (group 60I) or the latter hour (group 60L) of the experimental interval. The rabbits in group 30 received exposure for the initial 30 min of the experimental interval, while exposure of rabbits in group 120 occupied the full interval. Rabbits in these experimental conditions received 100 extinction trials beginning 48 hr after the end of training. The extinction procedure was identical to acquisition but with shock omitted. Three control groups were (a) NISD: extinction immediately after training; (b) NE: 48-hr-delayed extinction with no exposure; (c) 120H: same as (b) but with handling, deprivation, and activity comparable to 120. The rabbits in 120H were detained during the full experimental interval in a large cardboard box. Rabbits were randomly assigned to the seven treatments until the experiment was repli-

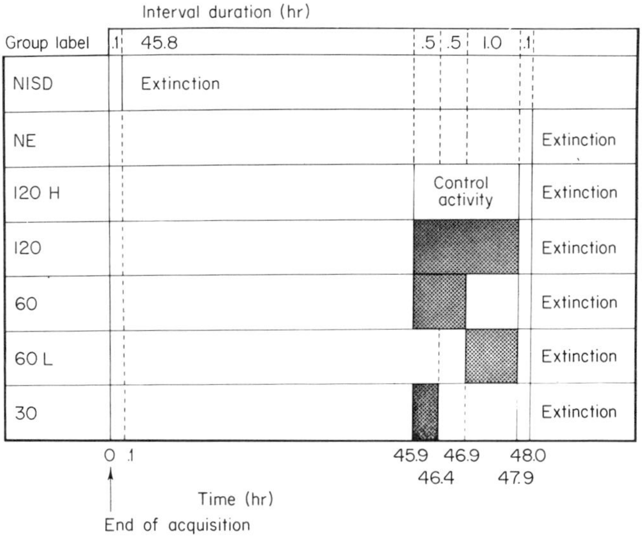

Fig. 2. Treatment labels and intervals for the initial exposure experiment. The upper scale shows interval durations and the lower scale shows cumulative interval boundaries. The shaded portions indicate periods of exposure to the apparatus. [From Gabriel (1970). Copyright (1970) by the American Psychological Association, and reproduced by permission.]

cated ten times. The group labels and time relations which define the treatments are shown in Fig. 2.

The results showed a significant monotonic decline in spontaneous responses over four consecutive 15-min periods of exposure using the data of groups 60L, 60I, and the initial four periods of group 120. The mean overall spontaneous response score for the initial period was significantly greater than the remaining three homogeneous means. This finding was in agreement with the expectations regarding behavior during exposure. Also, exposure did, as expected, systematically reduce ITRs in extinction. Significantly fewer ITRs occurred in 100 extinction trials for all groups receiving exposure except 30, compared to NE.

Contrary to expectations, all groups showed incubation (superiority to NISI) except 60L, whose mean was significantly reduced compared to the exposure controls (NE and 120H). There were no significant differences between the other groups receiving exposure and these controls; thus, 60L was the only exposure associated with a decrement in CRs during the extinction test. Instead of the predicted inverse relation between exposure and CRs in extinction, the results of this experiment suggested a

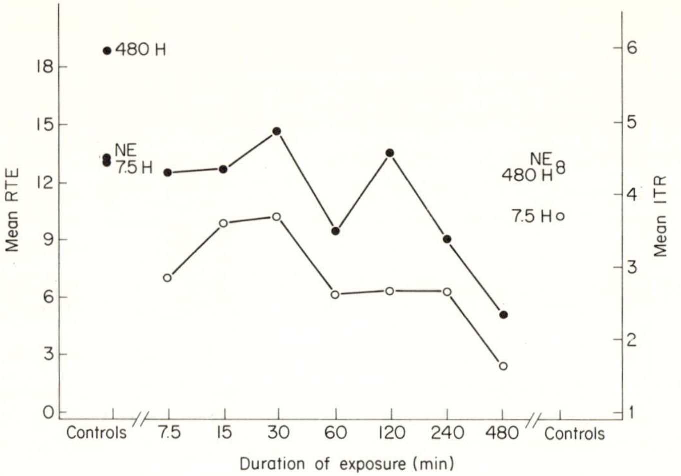

Fig. 3. Resistance to extinction (RTE) and intertrial behavior (ITR) as a function of exposure duration (●, mean frequency of CR averaged over the initial three 20-trial extinction blocks; ○, mean ITRs averaged over five 20-trial extinction blocks). [From Gabriel (1970). Copyright (1970) by The American Psychological Association, and reproduced by permission.]

U-shaped function with the least frequency of CR following a 60-min exposure and performance similar to that of nonexposed controls in groups given 30- and 120-min durations.

The obtained U-shaped relation was completely unexpected and seemed, therefore, to require immediate replication. In addition, the possibility remained that the range of exposures adopted in the first experiment was insufficient to show an overall monotonic negative relation between exposure duration and CRs in extinction. Therefore, a second experiment was run to replicate the findings of the first, and to extend the scale of exposures to briefer and greater durations. In the second study the training and test parameters were identical to those of the first. The treatments involved exposures of 7.5, 15.0, 30.0, 60.0, 120.0, and 480.0 min, all terminating 6 min prior to 48-hr delayed extinction. The results for spontaneous responses in exposure corroborated those of the previous study, showing a significant decline in these responses over the initial 15–20 min of exposure.

The results of the extinction test are plotted in Fig. 3, which shows the mean frequency of CR per block, and the mean ITR scores per block, over 20-trial blocks of extinction. A U-shaped function relating CRs and exposures of 7.5–120.0 min seemed evident from the upper function of the figure, yet this appearance was not borne out. The statistical test (60 < NE) required to replicate the U-shaped function of the first study fell just short of significance. However, when the data of both experiments were combined for those treatments (NE, 60/60L, and 120) which were identical in both, the U-shaped function, defined as a decrement at 60, compared to NE and 120, was verified.

I intend to drop discussion of this effect, at least as far as the present chapter is concerned. Discussion of it would necessitate too large a departure from the present context, especially for a phenomenon whose inferential basis remains somewhat questionable.

The expectation of a negative monotonic relation between CRs in extinction and exposure for durations greater than those of the first study was realized. The mean frequency of CR obtained after 240 min of exposure was significantly smaller than the mean obtained for all briefer durations except 60 min. The mean associated with 480 was significantly smaller than all other exposure means.

Finally, and perhaps most importantly, the second experiment revealed a negative monotonic relation between ITRs and exposure durations for the full scale of durations used in the second study. This effect is por-

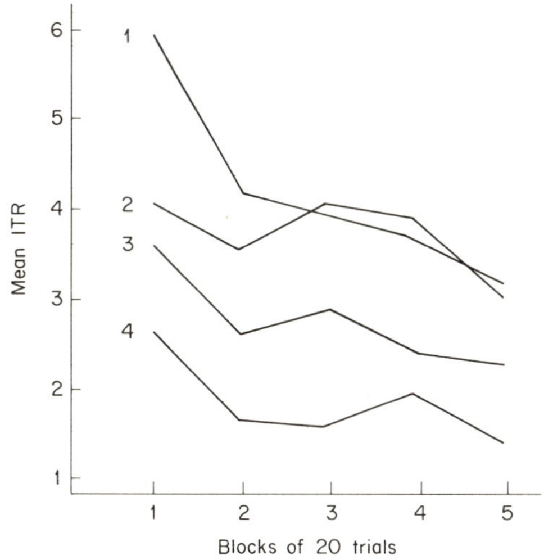

Fig. 4. The treatments X blocks interaction for ITRs in extinction. Each of the four functions represents a set of the treatments which were homogeneous in terms of overall ITRs in extinction (1) NE, 7.5H, 480H; (2) 7.5, 15, 30; (3) 60, 120, 240; (4) 480. [From Gabriel (1970). Copyright (1970) by The American Psychological Association, and reproduced by permission.]

trayed in Fig. 4, in which separate functions relating ITRs and blocks are plotted, with each function representing a set of exposure treatments which were homogeneous in terms of overall ITRs. These data show that even the briefest exposures (7.5, 15, and 30 min) affected ITRs by abolishing the significantly heightened trial block 1 responding obtained in groups receiving no exposure. Also, 60-, 120-, and 240-min exposures reduced ITR scores below those obtained in the nonexposure control groups within all blocks, and the 480-min exposure produced significantly fewer ITRs than the 60- to 240-min periods.

In summary, exposures of 240- and 480-min durations produced a diminution of the incubation effect and a reduction in ITR scores. It was apparent that the ITR measure was more sensitively affected by exposure than the CR measure since brief exposures, which did not affect CRs, produced a significant reduction in ITRs. Finally, spontaneous responses showed a negative monotonic relation to successive periods of exposure.

Before we are able to extract support for the SG hypothesis from these findings, it is necessary to demonstrate that the decrement in CRs and ITRs produced by exposure has substantial persistence. It is possible, e.g., that 240 or 480 min of exposure produced sleep in the rabbits of the previous study, and that this effect persisted into the temporally adjacent extinction period. To rule out this and related possibilities, an experiment was designed which provided for a substantial interval between the end of exposure and the onset of extinction. Also, the experiment was designed to provide information on an additional question raised by the SG hypothesis, namely, what is the effect of the "location" of an exposure within the ISD?

Operationally, we are asking about the effect of exposure-delay on extinction performance obtained following a fixed ISD. The hypothesis presumes minimal SG to apparatus immediately after acquisition since SG increases gradually with time following acquisition. It follows that exposure which is given immediately after acquisition should produce only minimal extinction of generalized responses. However, sufficient SG to apparatus should accumulate 24 hr after acquisition to permit substantial extinction of generalized responses during a 24-hr delayed exposure. In sum, the SG hypothesis requires that exposure given just after acquisition be less effective in reducing CRs and ITRs compared to exposure given 24 hr after acquisition. Finally, spontaneous responses in exposure should increase with exposure delay and decline monotonically as a function of successive periods of exposure.

The following experiment was designed to provide information on the question of the persistence of the exposure-produced decrement, and on the question of the effects of exposure-delay upon responses during exposure and during extinction. All conditions of training and testing were identical to those of the previous exposure studies. The treatments were no exposure (group NE), exposure for 480 min given immediately after the end of acquisition (group IE), or exposure for 480 min delayed until 24 hr after the end of acquisition (group DE). The inevitable confounding of exposure delay with the ISD was controlled experimentally by systematic variation of the ISD. Thus, orthogonal subgroups of each exposure condition were tested either 48 or 72 hr after acquisition.

The results for spontaneous responses were as expected. The overall mean frequency of spontaneous responses in eight 15-min periods of the initial 2 hr of exposure was greater for delayed exposure than for immediate exposure. In addition, exposure delay interacted significantly with periods such that the largest difference between the immediate and delayed conditions occurred for the initial period (see Fig. 5). This difference declined as a function of successive periods following the initial one; however, the difference did not decline monotonically over periods, as is evident from the figure.

In extinction, the mean frequency of CR per block in three 20-trial

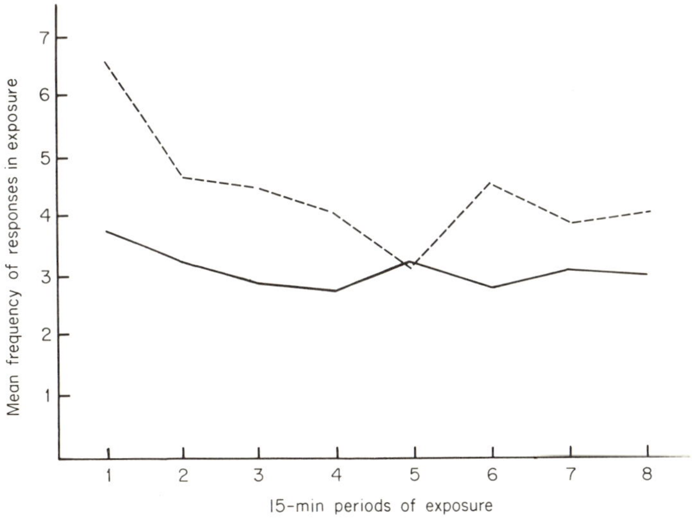

Fig. 5. Mean frequency of spontaneous responses during exposure as a function of eight 15-minute periods of exposure for the immediate (—) and delayed (- - -) exposure conditions.

blocks was 14.35 in group NE, 11.24 in group IE, and 7.25 in group DE. The main source of variation was significant for these conditions, and subsequent tests revealed that the mean for DE was significantly different from the mean for NE. There was no significant difference between the mean for IE and the mean for NE or DE.

The mean ITR score per block, over the initial three extinction blocks, was 6.31 for NE, 4.42 for IE, and 3.72 for DE. Again, the main source of variation was significant. However, unlike the effects on CRs, subsequent tests revealed that the ITR means for IE and DE both differed significantly from NE. There were no effects of the overall acquisition–extinction interval for either CRs or ITRs.

To summarize the results, rabbits given delayed exposure showed a decrement in CRs and ITRs in extinction compared to the extinction of controls given no exposure. Rabbits given immediate exposure showed a decrement in ITRs but not in CRs.

RELATION OF THE HYPOTHESIS TO THE EFFECTS OF EXPOSURE TO APPARATUS STIMULI

The results of the third exposure study demonstrated a persistence of the exposure-produced decrement for as long as 40 hr. Probably, the effects of exposure would show persistence for intervals greater than 40 hr if appropriate studies were run, but the 40-hr persistence that was demonstrated seems sufficient to warrant taking up additional questions raised by the SG hypothesis. It does not seem likely that the "sleep hypothesis" will remain a contender.

The SG hypothesis assumes that exposure to apparatus stimuli results in extinction of responses which have generalized over time to apparatus stimuli. Results from all of the exposure studies reported here seemed compatible with this view.

Spontaneous responses declined monotonically as a function of successive periods of exposure. The decline may be regarded as a gradual extinction of CRs which have generalized to apparatus stimuli.

Exposure diminished the incubation effect and reduced ITRs in extinction. The reduction in ITRs was anticipated on the basis of the assumption that ITRs reflect SG to apparatus. Thus exposure, believed to extinguish SG to apparatus, reduced the behavior (ITRs) assumed to reflect SGs during extinction.

Diminution of the incubation effect follows from the assumptions that: (a) increase over time in SG to apparatus produces stimulus control by a compound stimulus composed of the CS and apparatus stimuli; (b) stimulus control by two sources instead of one (CS only) produces incubation; (c) exposure extinguishes responses controlled by the apparatus component of the compound. The net result is that the frequency of CR occurring in the presence of the CS during delayed extinction is diminished by exposure since exposure tends to reestablish the situation prevailing just after acquisition in which only one stimulus source (the CS) shows control over the CR.

In two instances, exposure produced more pronounced reductions of ITRs than of CRs. In the second experiment, brief exposures which did not affect CRs were sufficient to reduce ITRs. In the third experiment, immediate exposure reduced ITRs in delayed extinction but failed to reduce CRs. The SG account is supported by these results through its provision that CRs in delayed extinction are controlled by two sources (CS and apparatus stimuli), whereas ITRs are controlled by apparatus stimuli alone. Thus the totality of stimuli controlling ITRs undergo extinction through presentation unpaired with shock during exposure; only a portion of the stimuli controlling CRs undergo extinction. Consequently, values of exposure duration ranging from 7.5 to 480 min produce greater extinction of ITRs than of CRs.

The finding of the third exposure study, that delayed exposure diminished the incubation effect but immediate exposure did not, is compatible with the assertion that sufficient time must elapse to permit the development of SG to apparatus if exposure is to be an effective means of diminishing incubation. Failure of the overall ISD to produce significant variation in extinction behavior suggests that the exposure–extinction interval, confounded with exposure delay, was not responsible for the effects of the latter variable.

The fact that ITRs were reduced by immediate exposure as well as by delayed exposure was an unanticipated finding of the third exposure study. This result does not cause embarrassement to the SG hypothesis. Rather, it is a result that might have been anticipated on the basis of the provision that exposure should have more pronounced effects on ITRs than on CRs. The 480-min immediate exposure period employed in the third study may have been sufficiently long to encompass substantial SG to apparatus, and concomitant extinction of generalized responses. Thus, we would expect to observe the originally predicted results in a study which used a briefer (say 240-min) exposure. The monotonic numerical ordering (NE $<$ IE $<$ DE) of the ITR means of the third exposure study suggests that this expectation would be realized in such an experiment, or by increasing the sample size of the original study.

Finally, the increase with exposure delay in spontaneous responses in exposure is compatible with the SG hypothesis. This increase may be presumed to directly reflect increase over time in SG to apparatus stimuli.

INCUBATION AND SG

It was stated previously that incubation results from increase over time in SG to apparatus stimuli and from increase over time in stimulus control by apparatus stimuli. The results from the exposure studies seemed to support both propositions equally in the ways just enumerated, although I have chosen somewhat arbitrarily to emphasize the phrase "SG to apparatus stimuli" in discussing the exposure results.

It may occur to the reader at this point that two phrases, one dealing with increased control and the other dealing with increased SG, may stand for constructs which serve identical purposes. Why not dispense with one construct and use the other exclusively since they seem to be operationally indistinguishable?

In the following sections I hope to provide evidence that the two phrases stand for constructs which are, in fact, operationally distinguishable, and that the denotations of each phrase make a unique contribution to the explanation of the incubation effect. First, I will deal with the unique contribution of the construct denoted by the phrase "SG to apparatus stimuli."

It should be stressed that the intention is to define SG in a purely descriptive sense, implying only by its use that conditioned responses sometimes occur to stimuli which were not used as the CS. I intend no implication of intrinsic theoretical gradients of the Hullian variety (Hull, 1943, p. 183) by this usage. Thus I have no objections to equivocation between "SG" and such phrases as "confusion of stimuli" and "failure of discrimination." In order to inquire whether or not "SG to apparatus stimuli" makes a unique contribution, we may ask whether variables which affect SG affect incubation in a similar fashion. If experiments demonstrate that manipulation of certain variables produces similar quantitative effects on SG and on incubation, then some advantage would seem to be gained by the use of SG in the explanation.

One variable which has been shown to influence SG in several studies (e.g., R. F. Thompson, 1958) is the amount of conditioning. Most investigators have concluded that SG is inversely related to the amount of conditioning, or that steepness of intramodal gradients of SG is directly related to amount of conditioning. The following study was designed to show that incubation, like SG, is inversely related to the amount of conditioning. The parameters of training and testing were identical to those described in the exposure studies except that 150 trials of overtraining were used for the overtrained condition instead of 100. Independent groups of rabbits were given avoidance conditioning to one of three criteria of shock avoidance, four consecutive avoidance CRs (low), ten consecutive avoidance CRs (medium), and ten consecutive CRs plus 150 trials of overtraining (high). Subgroups of 10 rabbits from each conditioning group were given 150 extinction trials following one of six ISDs, 7 min, or 1, 12, 24, 36, or 48 hr. The SG account predicts an inverse relation between amount of conditioning and incubation. In experimental terms, this means that the duration of the ISD associated with maximum resistance to extinction should be directly related to the amount of conditioning.

The results are plotted in Fig. 6, showing mean frequency of CR in extinction as a function of amount of conditioning, ISD, and trial block. In

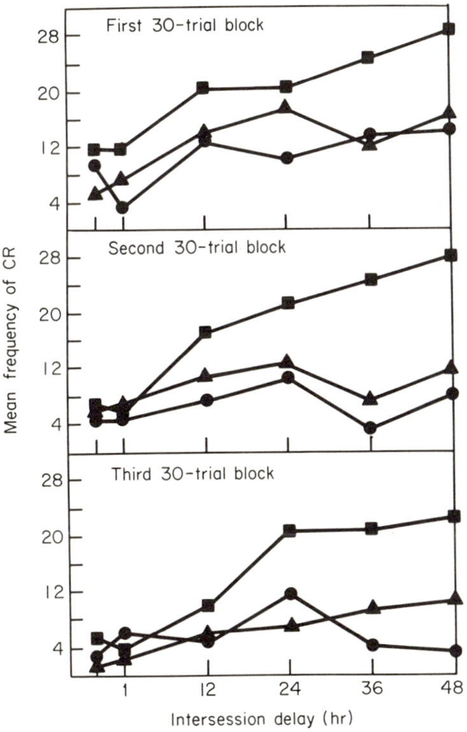

Fig. 6. Mean frequency of CR in extinction as a function of amount of conditioning (OL), ISD, and trial block. Each of the initial three 30-trial blocks is represented in one of the three vertical subsections. Within each subsection, the simple interaction (OL × ISD) is plotted with ISD on the abscissa and OL as the parameter (■, OL 10 + OT; ▲, OL 10; ●, OL 4. [From Gabriel (1968). Copyright (1968) by the American Psychological Association, and reproduced by permission.]

this figure, each of the initial 30-trial extinction blocks is represented in one of the three vertical subsections. Within each subsection the simple interaction (amount of conditioning × ISD) is plotted with ISD on the abscissa and the amount of conditioning as the parameter. The hypothesis was supported by the results of statistical tests on interaction means within the first and second trial blocks. Within the first block maximal mean frequency of CR occurred following 12 hr in the low (OL4 in the figure), 24 hr in the medium (OL10), and 48 hr in the high group (OLOT). These findings support the hypothesis that SG and incubation are related similarly to the amount-of-conditioning variable. It is this evidence which I feel basically justifies the use of an SG construct in the explanation of incubation. It seems reasonable that if incubation were fundamentally the result of SG, or discrimination loss, then increasing the amount of conditioning should delay its onset and decrease its growth rate over time. The experiment just reviewed seems to bear out this line of reasoning.

Additional variables having effects on the slope of an SG gradient (e.g., level of motivation, or presence versus absence of discrimination training) should affect incubation predictably in appropriately designed experiments. Unfortunately, such experiments may prove difficult to implement in the context of an active avoidance conditioning situation due to the rather severe restrictions of conditioning parameters imposed by the necessity of obtaining reliable single-session acquisition.

INCUBATION AND STIMULUS CONTROL

The usefulness of the construct of stimulus control in the explanation may be illustrated by first examining the implications of a denial of its existence. Suppose one were to assert that incubation is accompanied by no change in stimulus control by apparatus stimuli. From all I have shown heretofore, it is possible that responses which define the incubation effect simply occur in the presence of apparatus stimuli but are not controlled by them. This situation might best be elucidated by having reference to the mathematical model of signal detection (Swets, Tanner, & Birdsall, 1961). In so doing, one might postulate that the behaviors which define and accompany incubation (i.e., CRs and ITRs) result from a progressive lowering with time in the criterion for a response. Thus the rabbits may be emitting more responses as time after conditioning passes, with no concomitant change in the stimulating conditions which control the responses. Such behavior might be construed as a kind of optimal strategy, given a progressive loss of retention of many of the properties of the CS, yet one need not postulate any necessary influence on the responses of properties of the conditioning apparatus.

A similar argument results from use of the phrase "incubation of anxiety" in explaining incubation. One might easily imagine that increasing anxiety over time following conditioning could lead, after a sufficient ISD, to a situation in which any phasically presented stimulus would elicit a response resembling the CR.

Thus the "signal detection" and the "anxiety" views of incubation state that responses occur in the presence of apparatus stimuli, while the SG hypothesis emphasizes control of responses by apparatus stimuli. The former hypotheses suggest independence of incubation behavior from stimuli of the conditioning situation, while the latter hypothesis suggests dependence.

A partial resolution of this question has already been referred to in terms of the stimulus effect of the initial experiment described in this chapter. Recall that incubation occurred at the 24-hr ISD in this study, but when a test stimulus different from the CS was presented at various ISDs, no incubation was seen. The rabbits were not simply free-responding after 24 hr, as the signal-detection view requires, nor were they responding to any phasically presented stimulus, as the anxiety view requires. Thus the SG account is supported by default, given these data.

It remains to be demonstrated in a positive fashion that apparatus stimuli manifest stimulus control when incubation is occurring. One criterion of stimulus control is the demonstration that a given stimulus elicits the behavior in question. This criterion will be referred to as control_1. In the experimental context this criterion is only partially fulfilled by the demonstration of increase in the ITRs which accompanies incubation. Since apparatus stimuli cannot conveniently be presented phasically, in the manner of a CS or of a test stimulus, there is no way to be certain that the heightened ITRs which accompanied incubation were actually elicited by apparatus stimuli. It would therefore seem necessary to invoke an additional criterion of stimulus control in order to see whether or not apparatus stimuli control ITRs. In general terms this additional criterion, called control_2, involves the demonstration that change in the stimulus in question is associated with change in the response being measured. More specifically, a stimulus is said to manifest control_2 over behavior along with behavior in the presence of the stimulus; alterations in the properties of the stimulus lead to a significant decrement in the behavior (Baron, 1965; Ganz, 1968). Thus our SG account would gain positive differential support over the signal detection and anxiety views if a significant SG decrement in ITRs to altered apparatus stimuli were observed at ISDs associated with incubation. In the following study (Gabriel & Vogt, 1972) stimulus control by apparatus was assessed at three ISDs (0, 24, and 48 hr) using the frequency of ITRs ($control_1$) and SG gradients of ITRs to altered apparatus stimuli ($control_2$) as criteria of stimulus control. The SG hypothesis requires that incubation and stimulus control by apparatus will covary directly as a function of time following acquisition. Rabbits were trained and tested as in the exposure studies. Extinction was given either immediately, or 24 or 48 hr after conditioning. Orthogonal subgroups of rabbits were extinguished with an apparatus either identical to the conditioning apparatus (group C), with tactile alteration of the apparatus (group T) in which the grid floor of the apparatus was lined with hardware cloth, or with visual plus tactile alteration of the apparatus (group TV) in which the grid floor was lined with hardware cloth and the clear sides of the rotator were lined with black plastic sheeting. The

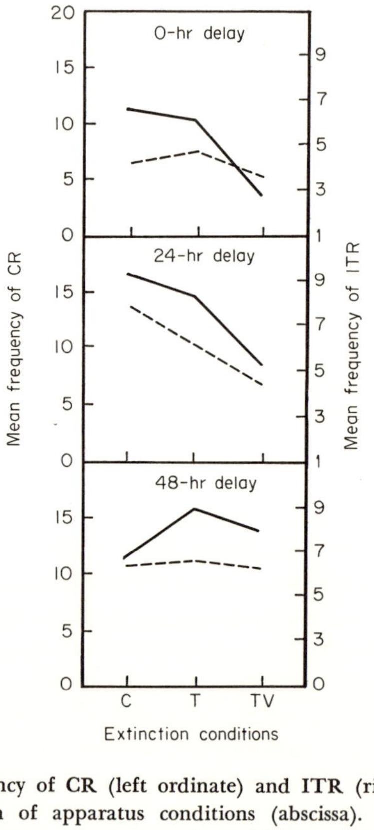

Fig. 7. Mean frequency of CR (left ordinate) and ITR (right ordinate) during extinction as a function of apparatus conditions (abscissa). The vertical subsections represent, from top to bottom, increasing values of ISD (— CR; - - - ITR).

results showed incubation following 24 hr in the control group, i.e., the group which did not have altered apparatus stimuli during extinction. The mean frequency of CR per block for the initial three 20-trial blocks (16.75) was significantly greater for the 24-hr ISD, compared with the 0-hr (11.50) and the 48-hr (11.25) ISDs. In conformity with the CR measure, the 24-hr ISD was associated with a significant increase in ITRs compared to the 0-hr ISD within the control group. Also, the mean ITR score associated with 48 hr did not exceed the 0-hr score. Gradients of SG (Fig. 7) were plotted for CRs and ITRs at each value of the ISD factor. The mean ITR score for condition TV was significantly less than that of condition C within the 24 hr ISD condition, but T and C were not different, and no differences in ITR scores between apparatus conditions were obtained at the 0-hr and 48-hr delays. Thus ITRs in extinction were reduced by combined visual and tactile alterations of apparatus stimuli only following a 24-hr ISD. Differences in ITR frequency between apparatus conditions were not obtained at the 0- and 48-hr delays. To summarize, significant incubation was obtained after 24 hr but not after 48 hr. Twenty-four hours was also the ISD associated with a significant increase in ITRs ($control_1$) compared to 0 hr, and a significant SG decrement in ITRs produced by altering the tactile and visual properties of the apparatus ($control_2$). Neither of the remaining ISDs was associated with both varieties of control by apparatus stimuli. Thus the results of this study satisfied the requirements of the SG hypothesis by showing correspondence between the delay associated with incubation and that associated with control by apparatus stimuli.

It is important to pay close attention to the relationship between CRs and ITRs obtained at the 0-hr ISD in the study just described. A significant SG decrement in CRs was produced by altering apparatus stimuli; significantly fewer mean CRs were observed in the extinction of the group which had visual and tactile alteration of apparatus. Thus apparatus stimuli did show $control_2$ over conditioned responding at the 0-hr ISD. However, the ITR scores of the 0-hr conditions were minimal and no differences in mean ITRs were observed as a function of apparatus conditions. Thus $control_1$ by apparatus was not present in the 0-hr conditions. At the 48-hr ISD, significant responding in the presence of apparatus stimuli was apparent since ITR scores for each apparatus condition were significantly greater at 48 hr, compared to 0 hr. However, at 48 hr, $control_2$ (demonstration of an SG gradient of ITRs to altered apparatus stimuli) was not present. Thus simultaneous satisfaction of both criteria of stimulus control was evidenced only at the 24-hr ISD, the same ISD associated with incubation of the CR.

Some interesting implications follow from these findings. First, it is worth noting that evidence for stimulus $control_2$ by apparatus stimuli seemed to depend upon the presence of the experimental CS at the 0-hr ISD. Alteration of apparatus stimuli reduced only conditioned responding and not ITRs at the brief ISD. It may be that failure of apparatus alterations to reduce ITRs at 0 hr was the result of the low frequency of ITRs (i.e., low $control_1$) prevalent at 0 hr. Thus apparatus stimuli influenced behavior at the brief delay value only when an additional stimulus source (the CS) operated to elicit the behavior. At brief ISDs, apparatus stimuli seem to lack independent behavior-eliciting properties (i.e., $control_1$).

After 24 hr, the dependence of $control_2$ by apparatus on the presence of the CS seemed to disappear since responding in the form of ITRs ($control_1$) occurred in the absence of the CS and $control_2$ over this responding was evidenced through manipulation of apparatus stimuli. It may be that processes which occur through the 24-hr ISD result in a dissociation of apparatus stimuli and the CS, such that each becomes an independent stimulus source controlling the behavior being measured. Furthermore, it would seem that the arrival of independence of these two stimulus sources may be the critical condition for the production of incubation of avoidance. Thus, incubation may be a phenomenon which is analogous to the summation obtained through the compound presentation of independently conditioned CS elements.

The following summary will specify the relevance of the results just described to the SG account of incubation.

Summary of the Hypothesis

The summary will attempt to state the hypothetical static conditions which occur at three ISDs for each of the following variables: (1) CRs; (2) ITRs; (3) CS-SG (confusion of CS with test stimuli); (4) apparatus-SG (confusion of apparatus stimuli); (5) SG to apparatus (confusion between CS and apparatus stimuli); (6) stimulus $control_1$; (7) stimulus $control_2$.

The relations among these variables are also illustrated graphically in Fig. 8. The summary assumes that both $control_1$ and $control_2$ are associated with increased responding to the stimulus in question.

When extinction is presented immediately after conditioning, all three of the varieties of SG (i.e., 3, 4, and 5) are minimal. $Control_1$ and $control_2$ by the CS is maximal. $Control_1$ by apparatus stimuli is mimimal; however, $control_2$ by apparatus stimuli is appreciable. Behaviorally, this combination of circumstances results in an appreciable level of CR due to

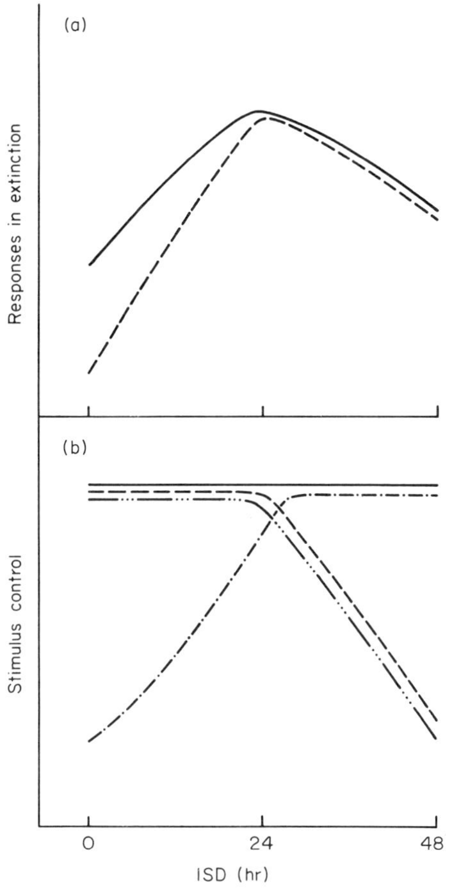

Fig. 8. Graphic representation of the hypothetical relations of seven variables. CS-SG, apparatus-SG, and SG to apparatus are not represented because each is linearly related to one of the functions. For example, CS-SG is an inverse linear function of $control_2$ by the CS; apparatus-SG is an inverse linear function of $control_2$ by apparatus; SG to apparatus is a direct linear function of $control_1$ by apparatus. The abscissa values are arbitrary: A family of incubation functions exists whose parameter, amount of conditioning, is directly related to the ISD associated with incubation. (a) — CR; - - - ITR (b) — $control_1$ by CS; - - - $control_2$ by CS; —•—•— $control_1$ by apparatus; — • • • $control_2$ by apparatus.

the presence of $control_1$ and $control_2$ by the CS; minimal ITR scores also result due to the absence of $control_1$ by apparatus stimuli. However, SG gradients to altered CS and apparatus stimuli will show steep slopes due to the presence of $control_2$ by CS and apparatus stimuli.

When extinction is presented at some moderate ISD (e.g., 24 hr), both varieties of intramodal SG (3 and 4) are minimal; however, SG to apparatus (5) has now attained an appreciable level. Therefore, $control_1$ is added to already existing $control_2$ by apparatus stimuli. Both varieties of control exist for the CS. The behavioral outcome is maximal ITRs and increased CRs (incubation) due to the addition of $control_1$ by apparatus stimuli. SG gradients to altered CS and apparatus stimuli show steep slopes due to the presence of $control_2$ by both stimuli.

After 48 hr, SG to apparatus remains appreciable, but now both varieties of intramodal SG (3 and 4) have also become appreciable. Therefore $control_1$ is present, but $control_2$ by CS and apparatus has declined. Therefore, CRs and ITRs have declined and the SG gradients to altered CS and apparatus stimuli have flattened. It should be clear that the critical hypothetical event producing incubation is increase over time in SG to apparatus, which in turn contributes an increase in $control_1$. The importance of the stimulus control construct for the hypothesis should now be clear.

Incubation and Anxiety

What is the relation between the explanation of the incubation effect and incubation of anxiety, emotionality, or fear, spoken of by some authors (e.g., Golin, 1961)? As we have seen, the anxiety account proposed earlier did not fit very neatly with the facts of one of the studies, but this apparent failure was contingent on the assumption that the anxiety account must predict that subjects showing incubation of anxiety will respond indiscriminately to all phasically presented stimuli. Perhaps proponents of the anxiety interpretation would not be willing to make this rather strong assumption. A moderated position utilizing incubation of anxiety might state simply that following avoidance conditioning, a progressive increase in anxiety occurs, resulting in a heightened level of responsiveness to stimuli of the conditioning situation. This account views the increase in anxiety as axiomatic and the increase in responsiveness as axiomatically related to anxiety increase.

The SG account would seem to have several advantages over this view at present. No studies exist which adequately demonstrate a progressive increase concomitant with an incubation function in physiological indexes typically used in the measurement of anxiety. In addition, the SG account does not preclude a positive correlation of anxiety with incubation. It merely asserts that loss of discrimination, in the form of progressive acquisition of stimulus control by apparatus stimuli, is *fundamentally* responsible for incubation. All of the evidence cited in this chapter supported the fundamental importance of discrimination loss. Whether the loss of discrimination leads to increased anxiety, which in turn produces incubation, or whether increased anxiety as well as incubation result equally and independently from loss of discrimination, or whether some combination of these alternatives actually happens, remain alternatives open to speculation and experimentation. It does, however, seem gratuitous and unparsimonious to simply grant the axiomatic version of the anxiety hypothesis. A more elaborate critique of the view which regards anxiety as axiomatically fundamental to the production of incubation behavior is presented in D. E. McAllister and McAllister (1967).

REFERENCES

Amsel, A. Frustrative nonreward in partial reinforcement and discrimination learning: Some recent history and a theoretical extension. *Psychological Review,* 1962, **69**, 306–328.

Baron, M. R. The stimulus, stimulus control, and stimulus generalization. In D. I. Mostovsky (Ed.), *Stimulus generalization.* Stanford, Calif.: Stanford University Press, 1965. Pp. 62–71.

Bovet, O., Bovet-Nitti, F., & Olivero, A. Genetic aspects of learning and memory in mice. *Science,* 1969, **163**, 139–149.

Brogden, W. J., & Culler, F. A. A device for the motor conditioning of small animals. *Science,* 1936, **56**, 539–545.

Desiderato, O., Butler, B., & Meyer, C. Changes in fear generalization gradients as a function of delayed testing. *Journal of Experimental Psychology,* 1966, **72**, 678–682.

Gabriel, M. Intercession delay and avoidance extinction to training and generalization stimuli. *Psychonomic Science,* 1967, **9**, 243–244.

Gabriel, M. Effects of intersession delay and training level on avoidance extinction and intertrial behavior. *Journal of Comparative and Physiological Psychology,* 1968, **66**, 412–416.

Gabriel, M. Intersession exposure to conditioning apparatus, avoidance extinction and intertrial behavior. *Journal of Comparative and Physiological Psychology,* 1970, **72**, 244–249.

Gabriel, M., & Vogt, J. Incubation of avoidance CRs in the rabbit produced by increase over time in stimulus generalization to apparatus. *Behavioral Biology,* 1972, (in press).

Ganz, L. An analysis of generalization behavior in the stimulus-deprived organism. In G. Newton and S. Levine (Eds.), *Early experience and behavior.* Springfield, Ill: Thomas, 1968. Pp 365–411.

Golin, S. The incubation effect; role of awareness in immediate versus delayed test of conditioned emotionality. *Journal of Abnormal and Social Psychology,* 1961, **63**, 534–539.

Grings, W., & O'Donnell, D. Magnitude of response to Compounds of discriminated stimuli. *Journal of Experimental Psychology,* 1956, **52**, 354–358.

Grings, W., Tadao, U., & Fiebiger, J. Component to compound stimulus transfer. *Psychonomic Science,* 1965, **3**, 63–64.

Hull, C. L. *Principles of behavior.* New York: Appleton, 1943.

Irwin, S., & Benuazizi, A. Pentylenetrazol enhances memory function. *Science,* 1966, **153**, 1351–1358.

Kamin, L. J. The retention of an incompletely-learned avoidance response. *Journal of Comparative Physiological Psychology,* 1957, **50**, 457–460.

Kamin, L. J. The retention of an incompletely-learned avoidance response: Some further analyses. *Journal of Comparative and Physiological Psychology,* 1963, **56**, 713–718.

Lachman, R. The model in theory construction. *Psychological Review,* 1960, **67**, 113–129.

McAllister, D. E., & McAllister, W. R. Incubation of fear: An examination of the concept. *Journal Experimental Research in Personality,* 1967, **3**, 180–190.

McAllister, W. R., & McAllister, D. E. Variables influencing the conditioning and the measurement of acquired fear. In W. F. Prokasy (Ed.), *Classical conditioning.* New York: Appleton, 1965. Pp 172–191.

Swets, J. A., Tanner, W. P., & Birdsall, T. G. Decision processes in perception. *Psychological Review* 1961, **68**, 301–340.

Tarpy, R. Incubation of anxiety as measured by response supression. *Psychonomic Science,* 1966, **4**, 189–190.

Thompson, C. P., Sachson, S. M., & Higgins, R. L. Distribution of intertrial responses in shuttle-box avoidance conditioning. *Journal of Comparative Physiological Psychology,* 1969, **69**, 563–572.

Thompson, R. F. Primary stimulus generalization as a function of acquisition level in the cat. *Journal of Comparative and Physiological Psychology,* 1958, **51**, 601–606.

Webster, C. D., & Rabedeau, R. G. The effect of intersession interval in shuttlebox conditioning of the guinea-pig. *Psychonomic Science,* 1964, **1**, 73–74.

Zammit-Montebello, A., Black, M., & Suboski, M. D. Incubation of passive avoidance in rats: Shock intensity and pretraining. *Journal of Comparative and Physiological Psychology,* 1969, **69**, 574–582.

CHAPTER 5

COMPONENT DYNAMICS WITHIN COMPOUND STIMULI

Thomas W. Baker

Introduction [1]

THE PROBLEM

In a review article on compound stimuli (Baker, 1968), the varieties of compound conditioned stimuli were divided on an operational basis into three main categories: (1) those compounds involving a successive

[1] My deepest thanks and appreciation go to my research assistant, Mr. E. James Kehoe, now at the Iowa University Department of Psychology, for his untiring efforts on this research. This research was supported in part by an NSF grant to the author (GB-15061) and in part by an NSF COSIP grant to Lawrence University.

or serial ordering of the components (Seq), (2) those involving the simultaneous presentation of the components (Sim), and (3) those involving a successive but partially overlapping order of their components (OL). At the time of the writing of the review article there was little evidence to suggest that these operationally delineated types of compounds could be meaningfully grouped or understood in terms of their conformity to some single set of laws; i.e., some set of functional relationships which would describe and predict the relative efficacy of various components within a particular type of compound. The search for some viable generalizations regarding component behavior was made more difficult by the almost complete absence of studies directly comparing component behavior in more than one type of compound. Since there appears to be some evidence that the pattern of component strength in a serial compound which has been classically conditioned in an appetitive situation does relate to the latency of the CR in a single CS situation (cf. Baker, 1968), the variables governing speed of conditioning, latency of response, etc., become critical in any cross-compound–type analysis. Despite recent attempts to make cross-compound–type analyses (e.g., Borgealt, Donahoe & Weinstein, 1968; Thomas, Berman, Serednesky & Lyons, 1968), only a few studies involving direct comparisons (Baker, 1965; Baker & Kehoe, 1969; Levis, 1970, 1971; Levis, Bouska, Eron, & McIlhon, 1970) have been made.

The controversies regarding the functional similarity of components in different types of compounds have stemmed from essentially three hypotheses regarding the processes responsible for component strength; these hypotheses stress either the processes of generalization, configuration, or information. Both Borgealt *et al.* (1968) and Levis (1970, 1971; Levis *et al.*, 1970) have attempted to explain the response strength exhibited by a particular component within the framework of a generalization process. However, within this framework, Borgealt *et al.* (1968) have stressed the generalization from the training to the test situation, whereas Levis (1970; Levis *et al.*, 1970) has emphasized the degree of generalization which presumably takes place within the compound itself during training. The former has been measured by resistance to extinction of the component during test, while the latter has been measured by the latency of the response during acquisition.

It should be pointed out that these two forms of generalization are by no means incompatible with each other and in fact it is very possible that both operate, given the opportunity to do so. Specifically, with respect to an overlapping-type compound, Borgealt *et al.* (1968) argue that the first component yields greater resistance to extinction since it is the only component which appears singly in both training and test. Levis (1970, 1971; Levis *et al.,* 1970), however, emphasizes that the component closest to the US gains the maximum response strength. In an overlapping compound, the first component is more similar to the second in that it overlaps with it, and thus generalization backward from the second to the first is facilitated. Although Levis's argument predicts a shorter response latency in the overlapping compound as opposed to the sequential, one difference in prediction between the two hypotheses does seem to emerge: Under the within-compound generalization of Levis, the first component should never gain greater response strength than the second.

The difference in prediction yielded by the two types of generalization hypotheses is obscured in the conventional test for component strength. Since the usual procedure to assess component strength is to present the component alone and measure the amplitude or frequency of response to it in either a within- or between-*S*s design (cf. Baker, 1968), the test situation is a generalization test (cf. Baker, 1969; Borgealt *et al.,* 1968). The result is then most properly a function of the summation of two generalization gradients: (a) the generalization occurring within the compound during training and (b) the generalization between the training and testing situation. Until each gradient can be specified, it is impossible to predict the relative response strengths each component has acquired. Indeed, given this framework, predictions become situation specific, so much so that the reconciliation of "incompatible" results simply involves an adjustment of the hypothetical generalization gradients.

Other investigators (Razran, 1965; Thomas *et al.,* 1968) have supported the configuration hypothesis. Specifically, this hypothesis states that the effectiveness (as measured by response strength) of a particular component shifts as a function of the number of conditioning trials to the compound. Under this hypothesis, the components eventually lose their effectiveness and the compound itself remains as the only functional stimulus.

The evidence for this hypothesis is meager. Studies which have not confounded a differentiation procedure with test for component strength (i.e., those studies employing a between-*S*s design in which *S*s are tested only once) have found no evidence for the configuration hypothesis (Baker, 1969; Morrow, Seiffert, & Kramer, 1970; Thomas *et al.,* 1968, Experiment 3). Studies involving a within-*S*s design (e.g., Baker, 1969; Thomas *et al.,* 1968, Experiments 1 and 2), which employ successive training and test sessions on an individual subject, have obtained results compatible with the configuration hypothesis. However, the decrease in response to the components as a function of number of conditioning trials found in these studies can readily be attributed to the successive test/extinction trials to the components. The merits of the configuration hypothesis seem to lie in the fact that it does entertain a changing or dynamic relationship among the components as a function of training. From the evidence to be presented later it does appear that some kind of hypothesis is necessary which predicts relative changes among the components as a function of training.

The third hypothesis is the information hypothesis, which states that the first component in an overlapping-type compound is a reliable predictor of forthcoming events (UCS), whereas the second component in the compound is redundant. The information hypothesis asserts that the conditioned reinforcing strength of a compound will be directly related to its reliability. This hypothesis, although conceptually attractive, is unable to handle demonstrable changes in component strength as a function of the CS_1-CS_2 interval and also the interval between the termination of conditioning and the beginning of extinction (Baker & Schoeninger, 1969). Thomas *et al.* (1968) have argued that the high secondary reinforcing strength exhibited by the CS_1 in the Egger and Miller (1962) study was simply a result of testing component strength at a time during which the CS_1 predominated. The argument was made on the basis that the elements in an overlapping compound as used by Egger and Miller (1962) show similar functional relationships over training as do elements of a sequential compound as employed by Thomas *et al.* (1968).[2]

Empirical Investigation

This problem of similarity between the sequential- (Seq) and overlapping- (OL) type compounds was one of the main concerns of the investigations to be reported here. Specifically, a sequential compound, in which the second component immediately follows the offset of the first, was contrasted with an overlapping compound in which the offsets of the two components are simultaneous but the first component onset precedes the second component onset by a fixed number of seconds. These compound stimuli were classically paired with food for fixed numbers of trials after

[2] Thomas *et al.* (1968) employed two measures: (1) the number of responses to produce the stimulus and (2) the number of responses during the stimulus. Using pigeons as *S*s and the key peck as the response, this is an appropriate partitioning of the response class. However, with short duration stimuli in a bar-press situation, the number of responses during the stimulus presentation would not be a reliable measure. It should be noted that the conclusions arrived at from Thomas's data are inversely related to the measure employed.

which the secondary reinforcement strength of each component was assessed.

One sequential compound and two varieties of an overlapping compound were employed, using both a within-*S*s and a between-*S*s design. Two separate designs were employed in view of the considerations detailed by Grice (1966) and previous findings by Baker (1969).

The sequential compound was composed of two components, each of 1.5 sec duration. One overlapping compound consisted of a 3.0-sec CS_1 and a 2.5-sec CS_2. A second overlapping compound was also examined. It differed from the one just described only in the duration of the second component, which was 1.5 sec. This difference also changes the CS_1-CS_2 interval from 0.5 sec in the former to 1.5 sec in the latter. The overlapping compound with the 0.5-sec CS_1-CS_2 interval replicates the interval employed by Egger and Miller (1962) and will be referred to as OL 2.5. The second overlapping compound will be designated as OL 1.5 and was introduced to provide a test for both the generalization hypothesis of Borgealt *et al.* (1968) and the information hypothesis. It will be recalled that the generalization hypothesis of Borgealt *et al.* (1968) states that the first component in an overlapping compound is more effective when tested singly because it is the only component which appears alone in training and thus undergoes less of a generalization decrement in the test situation. Since the present study reported here employed test stimuli of 1.5 sec duration, the first component in the OL 1.5 compound should suffer less generalization decrement from training to testing that the CS_1 in the OL 2.5. Hence, according to the generalization hypothesis, the CS_1 in the OL 1.5 compound should exhibit greater secondary reinforcement than the CS_1 in the OL 2.5 compound. The difference in the CS_1-CS_2 intervals between the two compounds should not, however, alter predictions regarding the relative secondary reinforcement strength of the CS_1's from each compound according to the information hypothesis. The sequential compound provides information necessary to evaluate the argument by Thomas *et al.* (1968) that the components of OL compounds exhibit similar dynamic changes taking place among the components of the sequential compound as a function of the number of classic pairings.

METHOD

The *S*s consisted of 48 male albino Holtzman rats maintained at 80% of their normal body weight as determined by an *ad lib.* food and water control group. The components employed in the compound stimuli consisted of an increase in the level of white noise and the illumination of three jeweled (white, red, and green) 28-V lamps arranged in a horizontal row across the front panel over the bar. These stimuli had been functionally equated in a secondary reinforcement study run previous to the present work.

DESIGN

In the within-*S*s design there were 3 groups of 4 *S*s each. Each group received one of the three compound stimuli (OL 1.5, Seq, OL 2.5) and each *S* was tested following 50, 150, 450, and 900 pairing of the compound with food. In the between-*S*s design there were 12 groups of 4 *S*s each. Each group received either 150, 450, or 900 pairings. (The 12 *S*s from the within-*S*s design provide data at the 50-trial training level for the between-*S*s design since this is the first test for those *S*s.) Again the *S*s were divided evenly among the three compounds employed in the conditioning sessions. Complete counterbalancing was achieved both with respect to the modality of the stimulus component and its order in the compound and with respect to the order in which the components were tested for their secondary reinforcing strength.

APPARATUS

A Grason–Stadler 2-bar, operant rat test chamber was employed. The chamber was housed in a Grason-Stadler sound-insulated chest located in a sound-insulated room adjacent to the room housing the Grason–Stadler solid-state programmer. All events were automatically timed and recorded. The white noise was provided by a Grason–Stadler noise generator (model 455C), and the visual stimuli were as described previously. The positive reinforcement consisted of one 45-mg Noyes pellet dispensed simultaneously with the termination of the CS_2. The houselight was on and the left-side bar was covered at all times.

PROCEDURE

Initial training procedures were identical for all *S*s. Each *S* received magazine and bar-press training on the first day. Second-day training consisted of 5 min of a CRF schedule followed by 20 min on a Probability–30 (P–30) schedule. The P–30 schedule was maintained for 25 min each day on days 3 and 4. On day 5 the right bar was covered and compound stimulus-food pairings commenced. Twenty-five pairings were given each day on a VI–60-sec schedule. Tests for the secondary reinforcing strength of the components and compound were given on the day following completion of the prescribed number of classic pairings. On test days, the right-side bar was uncovered and the *S* was permitted to bar-press for food on a P–30 schedule for 10 min. This 10-min period constituted the warm-up period prior to test. Immediately following, the feeder was disconnected and one stimulus component of 1.5 sec duration was available on the same schedule for 5 min. During the next 5 min the other stimulus employed as a component in the compound was made available, again on the same schedule. The final 5 min consisted of a test to the compound used in the pairings. The compound retained its regular duration of 3.0 sec and was available on the same P–30 schedule. The number of bar presses occurring in these 5-min periods was taken as the measure of the secondary reinforcing strength of the particular stimuli available during that time. Subjects in the within-*S*s design would then resume the classic pairing procedure on the day following a test day.

RESULTS

Each *S*'s score was calculated as follows: The number of bar presses given in a 5-min period of test to a particular component or compound was divided by the number of responses given in the warm-up period. A constant was then added to this ratio score for each *S* prior to a $\log_{10}$ transformation. Since third test scores (i.e., responses reinforced by the compound) were highly variable, they were omitted from the following analyses. Results of the between-*S*s design will be considered first. Data from the first two tests at each level of training were entered into a $3 \times 4 \times 2 \times 2$ analysis of variance with repeated measures on the fourth factor. The levels of this analysis correspond to the three compounds, the four levels of training, the order in which the components were tested, and, finally, the components themselves. Two effects are significant: (1) the interaction of compound type with test order ($F = 5.62$, 2/24 *df*, $p < .01$) and (2) the interaction of component with test order ($F = 29.85$, 1/24 *df*, $p < .01$). Discussion of these strong test-order effects will be reserved until results from the two designs are compared.

TABLE 1

Mean Log Ratios of the Compound-by-Component Interaction

	CS_1	CS_2
Seq	1.481	1.565
OL 2.5	1.510	1.380
OL 1.5	1.475	1.468

The only other significant effect is the compound-by-component interaction ($F = 3.75$, $2/24$ *df*, $p < .05$). The means involved in this interaction are presented in Table 1. Subsequent tests indicate that the CS_2 in the sequential compound yielded more responses than the CS_1, but that just the reverse was true in the OL 2.5 compound. No significant difference was found among the components of the OL 1.5 compound.

The interesting aspect of this analysis is that level of training had no apparent effect in changing the relative strength of the component. This result is to be contrasted with that obtained from the within-*S*s design, i.e., those *S*s exposed to successive conditioning and testing. A $3 \times 2 \times 4 \times 2$ analysis with repeated measures on the third and fourth factors was performed on the log ratio data obtained from the 12 *S*s involved in this design.

The highly significant effect of training level simply reflects less responding on each successive test (extinction) ($F = 26.85$, $3/18$ *df*, $p < .01$). The test order by component interaction is also significant ($F = 33.03$, $1/6$ *df*, $p < .01$), as in the previous analysis, and will be discussed later. The other effect of interest, however, is the compound type

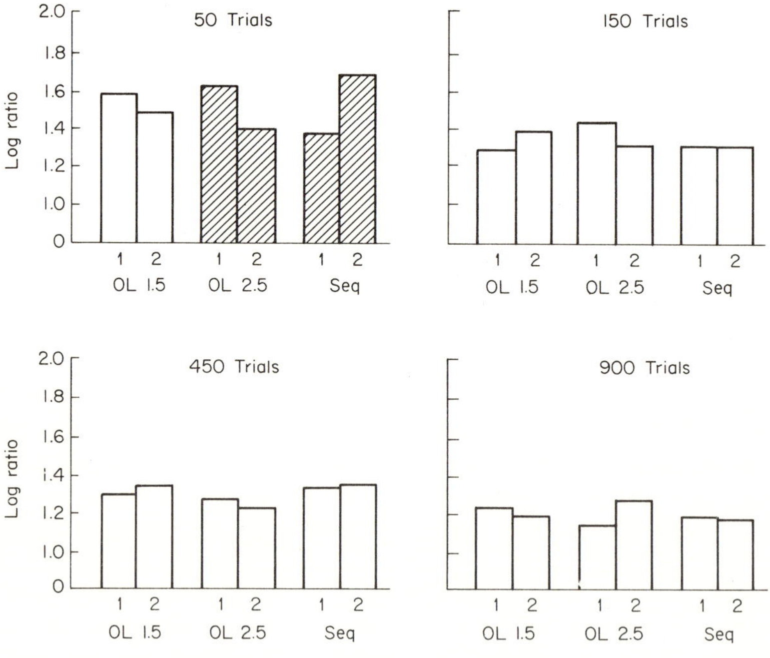

Fig. 1. Log ratio responses to the CS_1 and CS_2 in each of the three compound stimuli as a function of training in a within-*S*s design. Diagonal lines indicate the significant differences.

by training level by component interaction ($F = 3.45$, 6/18 *df*, $p <$ .05). The means of this interaction are shown graphically in Fig. 1. The hatched areas indicate those differences between components at a particular training level which are significant by subsequent test at the .05 level. The results at the 50-trial training level reflect those found for the between *S*s design across all training levels. The interaction indicates that these differences disappear after 150 trials and no significant differences appear thereafter. These data appear fairly straightforward and consistent with other investigations until one considers the highly significant effects of test order which were not expected based on results from other investigators, notably Egger and Miller (1962). However, these investigators had a 24-hr interval separating tests to each component.

Rather than attempt to look at all of the significant effects of test order and its interaction with the other variables, I thought it more profitable to attempt development of a model which might be able to predict the order effects, i.e., predict what an *S*'s score would be, depending on whether it received the CS_1 first in the test and CS_2 second, or just the reverse. If a parsimonious model could be developed to account for the order effects, then it would be possible to ask what the *S*'s response to a component would have been if it were possible to unconfound that response with the order in which the test had been given.

THE MODEL

The model is essentially simplistic. It assumes that at the time of test the compound stimulus has a secondary reinforcement strength, which shall be labeled X. Further, in a two-component compound, each component can be expressed in terms of its distance from X; thus the model conceptualizes the components as generalized stimuli from the compound.

Before proceeding further, some notation had best be introduced. As noted before, X will designate the hypothetical secondary reinforcement strength of the compound. Likewise, Y_1 and Y_2 will represent the hypothetical strengths of the two components CS_1 and CS_2, respectively. T will indicate the log response ratio given in the test situation to either components or compound. Further, T will have two subscripts to designate first the order of test and second the stimulus tested. The CS_1 will be designated with a subscript 1, the CS_2 with subscript 2, and the compound with subscript 3. Hence the designation T^{12} indicates that on the first test, the CS_2 component was available, and the designation T_{33} indicates that the compound was available on the third test.

We can now proceed with the model. The strategy of the model is to hypothesize the values which the components possess in terms of distance from the compound, then to use those values in predicting the magnitude of secondary reinforcement which will be obtained in a particular test order. This rationale produces the following equation:

$$Y_1 = X - b_1 T_{11} \tag{1}$$

In this equation b_1 is the parameter appropriate to the first test or extinction session. T_{11} is the log response ratio obtained to the CS_1 on the first test. If a test to the CS_2 immediately follows, then the appropriate equation for the second test is:

$$Y_2 = X - b_2 T_{22} \tag{2}$$

Here, b_2 is the parameter appropriate to the second test. We wish to use these values of Y_1 and Y_2 to predict the log response ratios which we would obtain in a reverse order of test, i.e., the order in which the CS_2 is tested first and the CS_1 second. To distinguish predicted from obtained log response ratios, we will add a prime to the designation for the predicted ratio. Thus the log response ratio predicted for the CS_2 in a first test would be:

$$T'_{12} = Y_2 - X/-b_1 \tag{3}$$

and the prediction for the CS_1 in a second test position:

$$T'_{21} = Y_1 - X/-b_2 \tag{4}$$

If we substitute for Y_2 and Y_1 from Eqs. (2) and (1), respectively, we have:

$$T'_{12} = X - b_2 T_{22} - X/-b_1 = b_2/b_1 T_{22} \tag{5}$$

and

$$T'_{21} = X - b_1 T_{11} - X/-b_2 = b_1/b_2 T_{11} \tag{6}$$

The model thus states that the parameters for the first and second test orders are reciprocally related. Because of this relationship, we will set $b_1/b_2 = b_c$ and, hence, $b_2/b_1 = 1/b_c$. The objective is to find that value of b_c which will minimize the sums of squares between the predicted log ratio scores and the obtained; i.e., we wish to minimize the quantity:

$$SS = (T_{21} - T'_{21})^2 + (T_{12} - T'_{12})^2 \tag{7}$$

and by substitution from Eqs. (5) and (6):

$$SS = (T_{21} - b_c T_{11})^2 + (T_{12} - 1/b_c T_{22})^2 \tag{8}$$

To minimize the *SS*, the first derivative with respect to b_c was obtained and set equal to zero. After appropriate algebraic manipulations, a fourth-degree polynomial was obtained. An IBM PO LRT subroutine[3] was then used to calculate the real roots.

[3] IBM Application Program (H20-0205-3); System/360 Scientific Subroutine Package (360-CM-03X) Version III.

The data used in Eq. (8) were the mean log ratio responses from the separate test-order groups at each level of training for each component under each compound. After the real root (i.e., that value of b_c) which minimized the sum of squares had been selected for each group, each *S*'s score, in the test order which was under prediction, was multiplied by the appropriate b_c or $1/b_c$. These scores will be referred to as the adjusted log ratios. The original order of test data for those *S*s were then used to obtain the appropriate b_c's for the opposite test order, thus giving an adjusted score for every subject. In summary then, reciprocally related test-order parameters were determined from mean log ratio scores which would minimize the sums of squares between one test order and the opposite order. This procedure was then reversed, yielding a group parameter for each component, at each test for each compound. Each *S*'s score was then multiplied by the particular b_c or $1/b_c$ for his group, yielding a new adjusted score.

It will be recalled that the objective of this model was to eliminate the order of test effects and ask what would the relative component strength

TABLE 2

Summary of the Analysis of Variance on the Adjusted Log Ratio Scores for the between-Ss Design [a]

Source	*df*	*SS*	*MS*	*F*
A	2	.07746	.0387	1.935
B	3	.12277	.0409	2.0450
C	1	.02850	.0285	1.4250
AB	6	.52832	.0881	4.4000[b]
AC	2	.01902	.0095	<1
BC	3	.10144	.0338	1.6900
ABC	6	.06964	.0116	<1
S/ABC	24	.48008	.0200	
D	1	.00006	.0001	<1
AD	2	.16151	.0807	2.75
BD	3	.39215	.1307	4.46[c]
CD	1	.30708	.3070	10.47[b]
ABD	6	.56739	.0945	3.22[c]
ACD	2	.16435	.0821	2.80
BCD	3	.04164	.0138	<1
ABCD	6	.08511	.0141	<1
SD/ABC	24	.70419	.0293	

[a] A, compound; B, training level; C, testing order; D, CS_1 versus CS_2.

[b] $p < .01$.

[c] $p < .05$.

be after adjustment for the order of test. Two measures were employed to assess the achievement of the model in this regard. One measure involved the correlation of the log ratio responses given to the CS_1 by the T_{11} groups with the adjusted log ratio response given to the CS_1 by the T_{21} groups. A similar correlation was obtained with respect to the CS_2 between the log ratio response by the T_{12} groups and the adjusted log ratio response of the T_{22} groups. These correlations averaged approximately .70. The other measure was simply to run the same analyses of variance as had been performed on the unadjusted scores on the adjusted scores and determine if the order of test effects were now absent. These analyses for both the between-*S*s design and the within-*S*s design appear in Tables 2 and 3, respectively. It is apparent from the summary tables that in both cases the only remaining significant effect that contains the order of test variable is the interaction of test order with component. The mag-

TABLE 3

Summary of the Analysis of Variance on the Adjusted Log Ratio Scores for the within-Ss Design [a]

Source	*df*	*SS*	*MS*	*F*
A	2	.14977	.0748	3.113
B	1	.00449	.0044	<1
AB	2	.10445	.0522	2.171
S/AB	6	.14434	.0240	
C	3	1.21334	.4044	23.874[b]
AC	6	.50597	.0843	4.977[b]
BC	3	.13841	.0461	2.723
ABC	6	.14664	.0244	1.442
SC/AB	18	.30501	.0169	
D	1	.00290	.0029	<1
AD	2	.39495	.1974	10.524[c]
BD	1	.11392	.1139	6.071[c]
ABD	2	.03144	.0157	<1
SD/AB	6	.11258	.0187	
CD	3	.08431	.0281	1.605
ACD	6	.59132	.0985	5.629[b]
BCD	3	.06976	.0232	1.328
ABCD	6	.23599	.0393	2.246
SCD/AB	18	.31513	.0175	

[a] A, compound; B, testing order; C, training level; D, CS_1 versus CS_2.
[b] $p < .01$.
[c] $p < .05$.

TABLE 4
Means of the Adjusted Log Ratio Scores for the Training Level × Component Interaction of the between-Ss Design

	CS_1	CS_2
50	1.59	1.65
150	1.67	1.49
450	1.52	1.69
900	1.70	1.65

nitude of this F ratio decreased considerably in the adjusted score analyses from 29.85 to 10.47 for the between-*S*s design and from 33.03 to 6.07 for the within-*S*s design. This has taken place with virtually no change in the error variances. It thus appears that this simple model which implies reciprocally related extinction parameters for first and second test has accounted for a considerable amount of the variance due to different test orders.

The scope of this chapter does not permit an intense look at the behavior of the b_c and $1/b_c$ coefficients. Such an analysis would reveal some interesting data related to the question of successive acquisition and extinction and to the problem of differential order effects across the two types of design.

For the purposes of this chapter, the most interesting aspect of the model lies in the pattern of the adjusted scores. No longer are the two de-

TABLE 5
Means for the Compound × Training Level × Component Interactions from the Analyses of Variance on the Adjusted Log Ratio Scores for Both Designs

	Within-*S*s design							
	50		150		450		900	
	CS_1	CS_2	CS_1	CS_2	CS_1	CS_2	CS_1	CS_2
OL 1.5	1.84	1.55	1.45	1.40	1.38	1.60	1.52	1.24
Seq	1.22	1.62	1.35	1.43	1.39	1.59	1.26	1.36
OL 2.5	1.73	1.79	1.44	1.21	1.48	1.29	1.21	1.35

	Between *S*s design							
	50		150		450		900	
	CS_1	CS_2	CS_1	CS_2	CS_1	CS_2	CS_1	CS_2
OL 1.5	1.84	1.55	1.68	1.53	1.49	1.70	1.80	1.56
Seq	1.22	1.62	1.70	1.56	1.50	1.68	1.75	1.61
OL 2.5	1.73	1.79	1.61	1.38	1.57	1.67	1.56	1.78

signs yielding different results. As can be seen from Tables 4 and 5, the compound × training level and compound × training level × component interactions are now significant in both designs. Figures 2 and 3 display these third-order interactions for the within-*Ss* and between-*Ss* designs, respectively. There are several points of interest in these results.

A comparison of Figs. 1 and 2 reveals the changes that have occurred in the within-*Ss* design as a result of adjusting the scores. With respect to the OL 1.5 compound, there were no significant differences among the components in the unadjusted scores (cf. Fig. 1.) However, in the adjusted scores, the CS_1 has a greater log ratio response than the CS_2 at the 50-trial level, which becomes reversed at 450 trials and then reverses again at 900 trials. The CS_2 of the sequential compound is, as before adjustment, significantly greater than the CS_1 at 50 trials but also at 450 trials after adjustment. In the OL 2.5 compound, the superiority of the CS_1 over the CS_2 does not show up significantly in the adjusted scores until the 150-trial level, whereas it appears at 50 trials in the unadjusted scores.

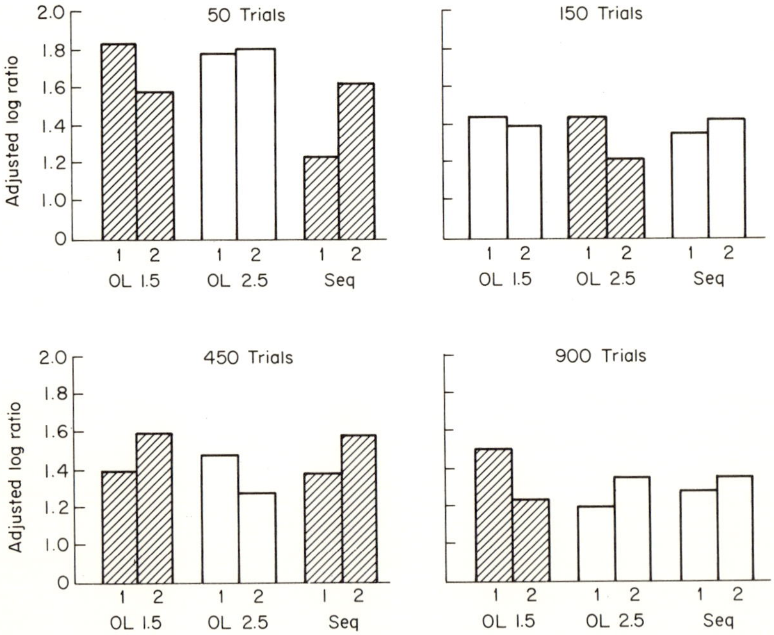

Fig. 2. Adjusted log ratio responses to the CS_1 and CS_2 in each of the three compound stimuli as a function of training in a within-*Ss* design. Diagonal lines indicate the significant differences.

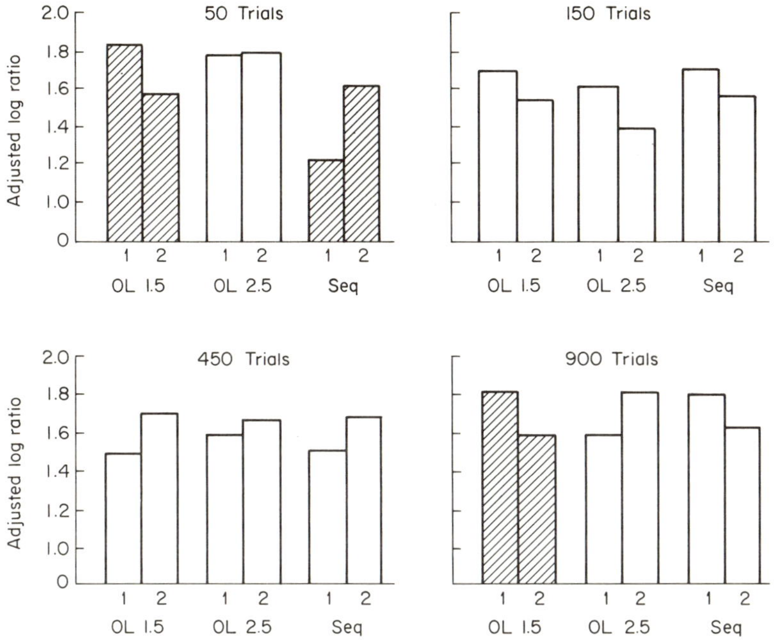

Fig. 3. Adjusted log ratio responses to the CS_1 and CS_2 in each of the three compound stimuli as a function of training in a between-*S*s design. Diagonal lines indicate the significant differences.

One might wonder at this point which set of data is reliable, if any. In the unadjusted scores, the separate designs yielded different results. In the adjusted scores, the results are now different in a within-design comparison. However, the comparison of the adjusted scores for both designs is far more promising (cf. Figs. 2 and 3). The data are identical for both designs at the 50-trial level because, it will be recalled, the same subjects are included in both designs. However, the other similarities are pronounced and merit attention. The CS_1 of the OL 1.5 compound is significantly greater than the CS_2 at the 900-trial level in both designs, and the magnitude of the mean difference is almost identical in both designs. The other significant differences in the within-*S*s design (i.e., OL 1.5: $CS_2 > CS_1$ at 450; Seq: $CS_2 > CS_1$ at 450; and OL 2.5: $CS_1 > CS_2$ at 150), are found in the between-*S*s design. Although these differences did not reach significance at the .05 level in the between-*S*s design (as a result of the larger error term employed in the subsequent tests), the magnitude and direction of the difference between the components at each of the three points mentioned previously are almost the same in both designs. The stability of the differences between the means across the two designs is very interesting. It appears that the considerations raised by Grice (1966) have not only been met but extended. After finding that separate designs yield different results, the source of these differences has apparently been isolated and extracted by the model employed. After adjustment for order of test effects, the two designs now yield highly compatible results.

INTERPRETATION OF THE ADJUSTED SCORES

The data definitely permit one observation, i.e., a nondynamic conceptualization such as the information hypothesis (Egger & Miller, 1962) is totally inadequate to handle these results. Alternative interpretations of the variety presented in the introduction appear inadequate to handle all of the data. An overview of the data will be attempted first, followed by some suggested hypotheses to help in understanding these results.

The high degree of compatibility among the data yielded by the two designs after adjusting the scores will now be utilized in an attempt to comprehend the results. It will be noted that in the between-*S*s design there exists a significant training level × component interaction (cf. Table 2). The means involved in this interaction are presented in Table 4. This interaction indicates that across the three compounds employed there is an overall tendency for the relative strengths of the two components to change back and forth. Specifically, early in training the second component dominates, then later, the first, then at 450 the shift is back to the second, and finally, at 900, the shift takes place once again and the first predominates. This overall analysis is not incompatible with the specific significant differences found in the compound × training level × component interactions for both designs (cf. Figs. 2 and 3). The only exception to this general statement is the behavior of the components in the OL 1.5 compound at the 50-trial level.

It seems to me that this generality of the pattern exemplified in the training level × component interaction of the between-*S*s design permits one to make some broad yet tentative conclusions, bearing in mind the presence of the significant three factor interactions present in both designs. There does seem to be in these results evidence to suggest that the three compounds under study share some common functional relationships. The problem is to comprehend the shifting pattern of component strength across training levels.

The following hypothesis is extended for sequential and overlapping compounds paired with appetitive reinforcement. Early in training the second component is strongest because of its proximity to the UCS. As training progresses, there is generalization back to earlier components in the sequence. This process will be more pronounced to the extent that the components overlap and also as the CS_1-CS_2 interval is shortened up to a point (cf. Levis, 1971). This increased generalization to the CS_1 along with the beginning of a generalization as a result of differences between training and test stimuli (Borgealt *et al.,* 1968) combine to yield the CS_1 more effective at the 150-trial level. With additional training, the generalization between components begins to diminish, i.e., a steepening of the gradient, thus producing a CS_1 distinct from the CS_2 but leaving the CS_2 with the majority of the conditioned reinforcement strength. This would produce the $CS_2 > CS_1$ effect at the 450-trial level. Beyond this point, it appears that a form of sequence conditioning is taking place (dynamic stereotype) such that after the first component has been differentiated from the second, the sequence itself is conditioned; i.e., the first component predominates and response to the second exceeds that to the first only when the components are presented in their appropriate order (Beritov, 1918, as cited in Razran, 1965). The presence of sequence conditioning would account for the reappearance of first-component superiority.

This general statement of the hypothesized processes involved needs only slight modification to account for the few exceptions found in the compounds under study. It may be helpful to use the sequential compound as the baseline or point of reference for the proposed processes. The changes in the components can be seen by reference either to Fig. 2 and 3 or to the table of means involved in the three factor interactions (cf. Table 5). The sequential compound illustrates the early predominance of the second component. Presumably, with respect to the analysis offered here, the OL 2.5 has moved beyond this stage at the 50-trial level and is approaching $CS_1 > CS_2$. The OL 1.5 has essentially completed the backward generalization process and thus accounts for the one exception in the data to the general view outlined previously. The proposed processes not only take place more rapidly in the OL 1.5 compound but also, apparently, more explicitly, as illustrated by the number of statistically significant shifts occurring within that compound in both designs.

The analysis is consistent with the proposal by Thomas *et al.* (1968) to view the overlapping compound on the same functional dimension as the sequential compound. However, the component shifts observed at the 450 and 900 training levels are inconsistent with the configuration hypothesis. There is no evidence in any of these results to indicate a loss of conditioned reinforcing strength in both components after extended training. The hypothesis of sequence conditioning (presumably that which takes place in the final stage) is quite different from that of configuration. The latter implies a loss of individual component identity, whereas the former necessitates component differentiation.

If the analysis presented here is correct, it would predict that in all two-component compounds which have been paired with an appetitive reinforcer the component strength should reveal a 2121 order as a function of training. The reasons for the predominance of a component at any one stage, however, appear dependent on changing gradients of generalization both within the compound itself and with respect to the test situation and finally to the inception of sequence conditioning following complete differentiation of the components.

Conclusions

After assessment of the secondary reinforcing strength in three separate compound stimuli as a function of the number of classic pairings certain findings emerged. The pattern of component strength was found to be a function of the particular design employed, i.e., either within *S*s or between *S*s. A model was developed based on a hypothesis concerning these differences. After adjustment of each score in terms of the model, the separate designs were then found to yield consistent results. The pattern of component strength was interpreted to be similar for all these types of compounds; further, the results dictated the need for a dynamic model which could account for the changes in relative strength as a function of the number of pairings. An outline of such a model was introduced which essentially incorporates three processes: (1) generalization between the components within the compound; (2) generalization between the training and test situations; and (3) the final appearance of sequence conditioning which necessitates component differentiation as opposed to a process of configuration.

REFERENCES

Baker, T. W. Strength of components of a compound CS as determined by their temporal relation. Paper presented at the meeting of the Psychonomic Society, Chicago, October 1965.

Baker, T. W. Properties of compound conditioned stimuli and their components. *Psychological Bulletin,* 1968, **70,** 611–625.

Baker, T. W. Component strength in a compound CS as a function of number of acquisition trials. *Journal of Experimental Psychology,* 1969, **79,** 347–352.

Baker, T. W., & Kehoe, E. J. Component strength in two types of compound stimuli. Paper presented at the meeting of the Psychonomic Society, St. Louis, November 1969.

Baker, T. W., & Schoeninger, D. W. Resistance to extinction of components in a compound stimulus as a function of the CS_1–CS_2 interval and practice conditions. *Journal of Experimental Psychology,* 1969, **80**, 304–310.

Borgealt, A., Donahoe, J. W., & Weinstein, A. Conditioned suppression and the information hypothesis: Effects of extended training on bar pressing and cardiac responses. Paper presented at the meeting of the Midwestern Psychological Assiociation, Chicago, May, 1968.

Egger, M. D., & Miller, N. E. Secondary reinforcement in rats as a function of information value and reliability of the stimulus. *Journal of Experimental Psychology* 1962, **64**, 97–104.

Grice, G. R. Dependence of empirical laws upon the source of experimental variation. *Psychological Bulletin* 1966, **66**, 488–498.

Levis, D. J. Serial CS presentation and shuttle box avoidance conditioning: A further look at the tendency to delay responding. *Psychonomic Science* 1970, **20**, 145–147.

Levis, D. J. Effects of serial CS presentation on a finger withdrawal avoidance response to shock. *Journal of Experimental Psychology* 1971, **87**, 71–77.

Levis, D. J., Bouska, S., Eron, J., & McIlhon, M. Serial CS presentation and one-way avoidance conditioning: A noticeable lack of the delay in responding. *Psychonomic Science* 1970, **20**, 147–149.

Morrow, M. C., Seiffert, P. D., & Kramer, L. L. W. GSR conditioning and pseudoconditioning with prolonged practice. *Psychological Reports* 1970, **27**, 39–44.

Razran, G. Empirical codifications and specific theoretical implications of compound-stimulus conditioning: Perception. In W. F. Prokasy (Ed.), *Classical conditioning.* New York, Appleton, 1965. Pp 226–248.

Thomas, D. R., Berman, D. L., Serednesky, G. E., & Lyons, J. E. Information value and stimulus configuring as factors in conditioned reinforcement. *Journal of Experimental Psychology* 1968, **76**, 181–189.

CHAPTER 6

SENSORY PRECONDITIONING[1]

Richard F. Thompson

Sensory preconditioning (SPC) has intrigued students of learning since its discovery by Brogden in 1939. However, it has not received extensive theoretical or experimental analysis, perhaps in part because it could not conveniently be fitted into theories of learning prevalent at the time. In this chapter it will be argued that SPC may reflect a fundamental and widespread form of learning in higher animals.

[1] This work was supported in part by Research Scientist Award MH 06650, research Grant MH 19314 from the National Institute of Mental Health, and research Grant NS 07661 from the National Institutes of Health.

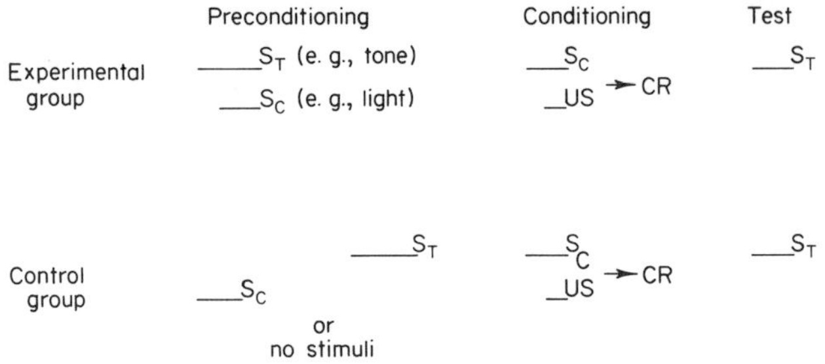

Fig. 1. Operational definition of sensory preconditioning (SPC). Experimental *S*s are given paired presentations of S_T and S_C in the preconditioning phase, then some response (CR) is conditioned to S_C in the conditioning phase, and the strength of that response to S_T is measured (typically by extinction and/or retraining) in the test phase. Control *S*s are typically given unpaired presentations of S_C and S_T, or no stimuli, in preconditioning and then treated identically to experimentals. Response of the experimental *S*s relative to response of the control *S*s during the test phase defines SPC.

The basic operational definition of SPC is shown in Fig. 1. The SPC condition involves initial unreinforced paired presentations of two stimuli which will become the conditioning (S_C) and test (S_T) stimuli. These are typically a light and a tone. Some form of response is then conditioned to S_C and strength of the response is subsequently tested to S_T. Subjects commonly give some conditioned responses to S_T. A similar procedure was used in earlier Russian studies of conditioning (Prokofiev & Zeliony, 1926). However, this situation per se cannot be distinguished from transfer. As Brogden first emphasized, it is necessary to compare responses to S_T for the preconditioning subjects against responses to S_T of control subjects not given paired S_T-S_C preconditioning. A significantly greater test response level to S_T by the control subjects constitutes the operational definition of SPC. The control group provides a baseline measure of degree of cross-modal generalization in subjects not given paired preconditioning trials. In his original experiment, Brogden (1939) did not present any stimuli to the control group prior to conditioning. Reid (1952) challenged SPC in a negative report where pigeons given unpaired S_T and S_C during preconditioning did not differ from animals given paired preconditioning. However, the subsequent literature is in agreement that, at least with mammals, both control procedures (i.e., no stimuli or unpaired stimuli) yield the same absence of cross-modal generalization (Brogden, 1947; Chernikoff & Brogden, 1949), particularly if the animals are trained to a relatively high criterion during the conditioning phase (Thompson, 1959). Hence either procedure is satisfactory.

Sensory preconditioning was for a time a key issue in the hotly debated controversy over reinforcement theory. Since no reinforcement was given during the preconditioning phase, SPC appeared to be an example of unreinforced learning. Reinforcement theorists countered with the argument that the so-called neutral stimuli (S_T and S_C) did in fact have reinforcing properties. In ordinary learning, the US or reinforcing stimulus can be shown to be reinforcing by independent measures. Operationally, a stimulus is reinforcing if the probability of some response is increased with repeated presentations of the stimulus, the most widely used examples being food approach and shock avoidance. In actual fact, the conditioning and test stimuli typically used in SPC are not reinforcing; they cannot be shown to have reinforcing properties independent of the SPC paradigm. Consequently, a strict reinforcement argument is either wrong or circular when applied directly to SPC. This issue will be explored further after an examination of the SPC literature.

Characteristics of Sensory Preconditioning

Sensory preconditioning has been characterized by several authors as a weak and unstable phenomenon that does not seem to "fit" the facts of learning. The parametric characteristics of SPC simply do not make sense in terms of the well-known characteristics of ordinary reinforced learning. In this section the features of SPC will be reviewed. As it turns out, SPC is a surprisingly consistent phenomenon, exhibiting very similar properties over a wide range of organisms, responses, conditioning or training procedures, and stimuli. The only problem is that these properties are not those of reinforced learning.

ORGANISMS, CONDITIONING PROCEDURES, AND RESPONSES

Sensory preconditioning has been obtained in the rat, cat, dog, monkey, normal human, and retarded human. There have been only two published studies reporting no SPC. Brogden (1942) failed to obtain it for human GSR. However, several subsequent studies have obtained clear and significant SPC using this response system (Bitterman, Reed, & Kubala, 1953; Coppock, 1958; Lovibond, 1959; Uno, 1966; Wickens & Cross, 1963), so Brogden's negative finding was likely due to particular conditions used. The other negative report used the pigeon (Reid, 1952). A phylogenetic generalization is tempting, but the evidence is meager. Seidel (1959) asserts, without documentation, that lower organisms do not show SPC.

Conditioning procedures have included instrumental shock avoidance in runway, hurdle box, wheel, leg flexion, finger withdrawal, and finger flexion; instrumental reward bar press; classical GSR (human), salivation (dog and human), milk licking, and, most recently, due to the imaginative study by Prewitt (1967), classical CER lick suppression. The latter technique appears to yield very reliable SPC (Parkinson, 1968; Prewitt, 1967; Tait, Marquis, Williams, Weinstein, & Suboski, 1969). Stimuli used in SPC have typically been sound and light, the sound most commonly as the S_T and the light as S_C. In one study acid was employed as S_C (Enzie, 1969). Intramodal stimuli have also been used successfully —e.g., colors in the monkey (W. L. Brown, Urmer, & Carr, 1958) and human (Uno, 1966), tones in the cat (Kendall & Thompson, 1960), and lights differing in location in humans (Bitterman *et al.*, 1953).

Unfortunately, the majority of SPC experiments have not been concerned with parametric investigation of stimulus and training variables but rather have attempted critical tests of "S-S" vs. "S-R" theories of learning. Since these global theoretical positions contain a convenient number of ambiguities, and SPC is a rather variable phenomenon, such has not been possible.

EFFECTS OF STIMULUS AND TRAINING VARIABLES

Number of SPC Trials

Brogden and Gregg (1951) were the first to vary number of SPC trials, using 2, 10, and 20 trials in a human auditory acuity procedure. Significant overall SPC was obtained, but the differing number of SPC trials had no significant effect. However, 2 and 10 trials both gave numerically larger SPC effects than 20 trials. Brogden and associates (Hoffeld, Kendall, Thompson, & Brogden, 1960) completed an extensive study of number of SPC trials using shock avoidance conditioning of cats in the wheel. The number of SPC trials used was 0, 1, 2, 4, 8, 10, 20, 40, 80, 200, 400, and 800; separate groups of 6 animals were trained under each condition. As indicated in Fig. 2, the rather unexpected result was obtained that 4 trials yielded maximum SPC. Furthermore, several animals in the 1- 2-, and 800-trial groups only gave no evidence of SPC. Recently, Prewitt (1967) compared 1, 4, 16, and 64 trials of SPC training using CER lick suppression in the rat. She found that 16 trials gave numerically maximum SPC. More specifically, 16 trials gave more than 4 and 1, 4 gave more than 1, and 64 were somewhat less effective than 16, not differing significantly from either 4 or 16 (see Fig. 2).

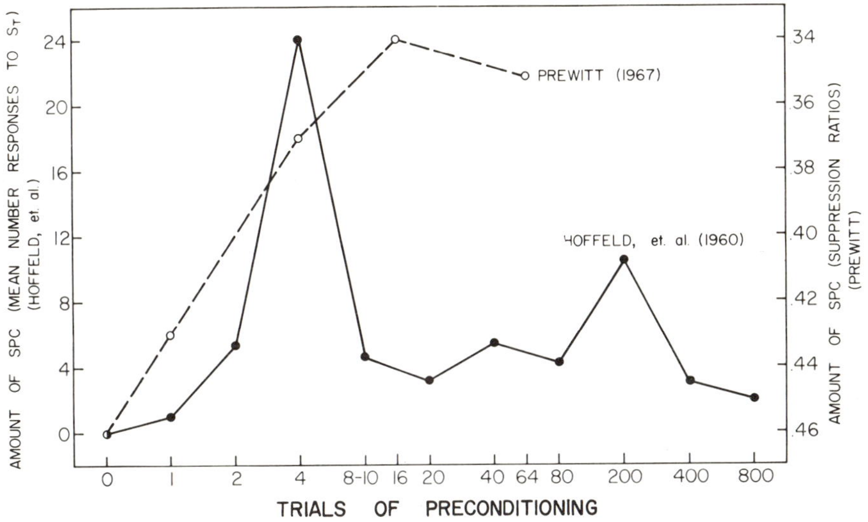

Fig. 2. The effect of number of preconditioning trials on the strength of SPC determined in two separate studies using quite different conditioning procedures. Both agree in finding maximum SPC with relatively few preconditioning trials.

Time Relations

There have been several studies of the time relations between S_T and S_C during the preconditioning phase, particularly in relation to forward vs. backward preconditioning. Silver and Meyer (1954) were the first to compare forward, simultaneous, and backward preconditioning. The stimuli were light and buzzer, *S*s were rats, the conditioned response was running to avoid shock, and the SPC test was reacquisition (i.e., transfer) to the S_T. All three preconditioning conditions yielded clearly superior relearning compared to control conditions. There was a substantial amount of backward and simultaneous preconditioning. In addition, the forward preconditioning group was significantly superior to the backward and simultaneous groups. As in ordinary reinforced conditioning, forward preconditioning is better than simultaneous or backward preconditioning. However, in marked contrast to conditioning is the fact that a substantial amount of simultaneous and backward preconditioning did occur. C. P. Brown and King (1969) noted that Silver and Meyer gave massed trials, resulting in an interval of 3.7 sec between S_T on a given backward trial and S_C on the next trial, which could be brief enough for forward preconditioning. Brown and King compared forward and backward SPC using light and sound with classically conditioned human salivary response to citric acid and found significant forward but not backward SPC. However, the conditioned response itself appeared somewhat weak and variable in their study. Coppock, in his elegant study of SPC using human GSR, obtained forward but not backward SPC (1958). Tait and associates (1969) used Prewitt's CER lick suppression technique to compare forward and backward SPC with light and tone in rat. They report significant forward SPC but no backward SPC. Unfortunately, they did not run a control group for SPC so it is not actually possible to determine whether they obtained no backward SPC or less backward than forward SPC.

The most extensive parametric studies of stimuli time relations during preconditioning have been completed by Brogden and associates. Hoffeld, Thompson, and Brogden (1958) compared SPC in groups given simultaneous 2-sec tone (S_T) and light (S_C) and tone precedences of .5, 1, 2, and 4 sec, tone and light terminating simultaneously, against a control group not given preconditioning. All groups showed preconditioning relative to controls, but the only group showing relatively more preconditioning was that given the *longest* S_T, a 6-sec tone with the light (S_C) occurring during the last 2 sec (see Fig. 3).

This unexpected finding was replicated in a more extensive study by Wynne and Brogden (1962). They used somewhat different conditions

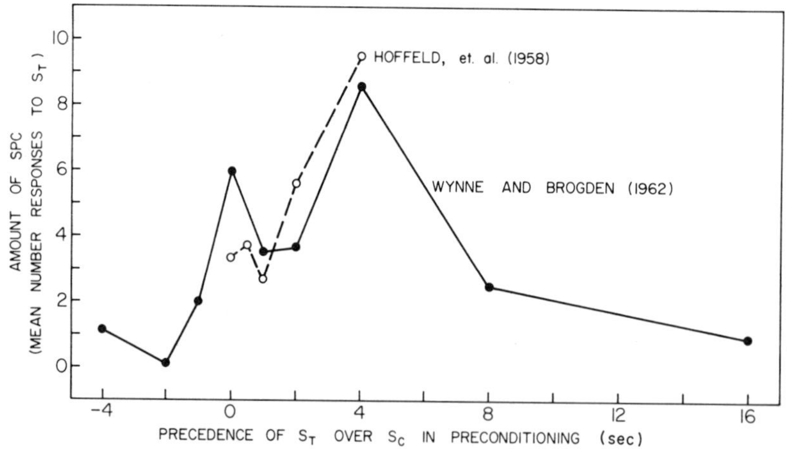

Fig. 3. Effects of preconditioning stimuli time relations on strength of SPC. Two separate studies agree in finding maximum SPC with a 4-sec precedence of S_T (tone) over S_C (light).

in that the tone S_T lasted only 2 sec, and they employed S_T precedence intervals of −4, −2, −1, 0, 1, 2, 4, 8, and 16 sec. The negative values are thus backward preconditioning, e.g., −4 means that the light (S_C) was on 2 sec, followed by 2 sec of no stimuli, followed by 2 sec of tone. Condition zero represents simultaneous S_T-S_C and, at the opposite extreme, 16 means that tone was on for 2 sec followed by 14 sec of no stimuli followed by 2 sec of light. A control group given no preconditioning was also run. The only significant difference among the experimental groups was the significantly greater SPC for the group given 4 sec of tone precedence, as in the previous study (see Fig. 3). When groups were compared against a pooled control (from this and the previous experiment), −4-, −2-, and 16-sec conditions did not differ statistically and were numerically approximately the same; 0-, 1-, 2-, and 4-sec conditions differed significantly, and −1 and 8 conditions were numerically greater but did not reach statistical significance. In short, 4 sec of precedence again gave most SPC, 0–8 sec gave less, and 16 sec and backward conditions gave none. An interesting point emphasized by Wynne and Brogden is that the 4-sec tone precedence here and in the previous study gave identical amounts of SPC even though a trace procedure was used here and a delay precedence used previously.

The remaining study of time relations, by Wickens and Cross (1963), used human GSR to shock with light and tone preconditioning stimuli and precedence times for tone of 0, 100, 400, and 600 msec. Both stimuli terminated together. The measure of SPC was GSR magnitude during extinction testing to tone following light conditioning. Results of this study are somewhat complex. Groups did not differ on the first extinction trial, but on succeeding trials the 0-, 100-, and 400-msec conditions tended to give more SPC than the 600-msec condition. This is actually consistent with the studies of Hoffeld *et al.* (1958) and Wynne and Brogden (1962) in that both show some degree of bimodality (see Fig. 3), the lesser peak occurring in the 0- to 500-msec range. However, the longer precedence times relatively much more effective in Brogden's studies were not explored here.

Stimulus Intensity

In only one study has the intensity of the UCS been varied in the conditioning phase. Doubros (1965) used two levels of shock intensity in a finger flexion paradigm with human mentally retarded *S*s and tone and light as the preconditioning stimuli. Significant SPC was obtained, but the different levels of UCS intensity had no effect.

Thornton (1956) tested effects of high and low intensity levels of both the preconditioning stimuli (loud tone-bright light vs. weak tone-dim light) in a hurdle-jump shock avoidance response in rats. Interestingly, when these groups were compared against corresponding controls, the high intensity preconditioning group showed no SPC but the low intensity preconditioning group did. Wokoun (1959) varied intensity of the preconditioning stimuli in a fairly complex experiment using a shock avoidance response in rats. Some details are not clear (the report is only available as a thesis abstract), but it appears that three levels of light intensity and a constant intensity buzzer were used for the preconditioning stimuli. However, the different values of light were apparently used as S_T in 3 groups and S_C in 3 groups. Results are of considerable interest. For S_T, stimulus intensity was *inversely* related to amount of SPC. For S_C, stimulus intensity tended to be an inverted U, the intermediate intensity giving the numerically largest SPC.

Motivational Variables

Bahrick (1952; 1953) demonstrated in two separate experiments that SPC is greater in animals (rats in running shock avoidance) given preconditioning under conditions of food and water deprivation than under conditions of satiation. Seidel (1958) used a similar training situation but gave all animals preconditioning under food deprivation and then trained and tested one group with food deprivation, one group with water deprivation, and one satiated group. A control group given no preconditioning was run with food deprivation. All three experimental groups showed SPC, the satiated and hungry groups showing more than the thirsty group.

In a recent study Adamec and Melzack (1970) noted that transfer of drive state may have been a problem in the Bahrick and Seidel studies and used food deprivation in an appetitive SPC situation where cats were given paired click-train (S_T) and light (S_C), then trained to lick milk when light was given and tested by retraining to click-train. Separate SPC groups were given preconditioning under 48-hr food and water deprivation and satiated conditions and corresponding control groups given random unpaired click-train and light under these conditions. All animals were then trained to light and tested to tone on 48 hr of deprivation. The study demonstrated significant overall SPC and significantly greater SPC for the group given preconditioning under deprivation.

The effects of training and stimulus variables on SPC can be summarized as follows: A relatively few trials (4 to 16) of preconditioning yield maximum SPC. A large number of trials may yield no SPC. This differs markedly from ordinary reinforced conditioning. Forward preconditioning with an S_T precedence of about 4 sec yields maximum SPC. Several studies have reported SPC with simultaneous S_T-S_C and one (Silver & Meyer, 1954) obtained SPC with backward preconditioning. The fact that forward SPC is much more effective than backward SPC is consistent, but the occurrence of maximum SPC with 4-sec precedence, the occurrence of significant simultaneous SPC, and the occasional finding of backward SPC are not. The intensity variable has not been explored extensively; what data exist suggest that intensity of UCS does not have a strong effect, and intensity of S_T and S_C may have an inverted U or no clear relationship to strength of SPC. These tentative facts are also at variance with reinforced conditioning. Motivational studies agree in finding that SPC tends to be stronger when preconditioning is given under conditions of food and water deprivation; however, deprivation during subsequent conditioning yields inconsistent results. The effect of deprivation on SPC is in the same direction as in ordinary reinforced learning but is less powerful.

Orienting and SPC—A Type-I Analysis

Sensory preconditioning can be treated at two levels of discourse, as with other behavioral constructs (see J. S. Brown, 1965). At the type-I level, the phenomenon is defined operationally in terms of procedures and resultant behavior and the parametric characteristics of stimulus and training variables are determined. The type-I analysis deals with performance. At the type-II level a theoretical construct may be inferred to account for the existence and characteristics of SPC. In this section SPC will be examined in relation to other forms of behavior at the level of performance.

Perhaps because reinforcement theory dominated psychology for so long, some very obvious facts of animal behavior have been underemphasized. When a stimulus occurs in the presence of a higher organism, several types of behavior may result. The animal may do nothing, he may approach or avoid the stimulus, or he may make some other type of response. Approach or avoidance, and an increasing probability of such with repetition, define stimuli that are reinforcing. The vast majority of stimuli encountered in an organism's real world are not reinforcing. When higher animals, ranging, certainly, from rat to man, are given a stimulus not previously present, they characteristically respond with some form of orienting or exploratory behavior. The importance and ubiquity of this type of response has been emphasized by many students of behavior (e.g., Berlyne, 1960; Hinde, 1966; Sokolov, 1963; Thompson & Spencer, 1966; Welker, 1961). If the stimulus is repeated, and has no clear appetitive or aversive consequences, behavioral orienting decreases or *habituates.* Repetition of the stimulus leads to decreased response probability; therefore, the stimulus is by definition not reinforcing.

There is no satisfactory terminology for stimuli that thus influence the organism but are not reinforcing. In physiological terms they are adequate—they excite receptors and cause activity in sensory pathways of the brain. In behavioral terms they can all serve as conditioned stimuli—the organism can be trained to respond to their occurrence by coupling with reinforcing stimuli. "Neutral" is a poor word; the organism does in fact respond with some form of orienting behavior to initial presentations of most stimuli—such stimuli are not really neutral. We introduce the term effective here for purposes of discussion, and distinguish two categories: *effective-reinforcing* stimuli, which yield behavioral responses and upon repetition result in increased probability of response, and *effective* stimuli, which, at least upon initial presentation, lead to some form of response but upon repetition result in decreased probability of response.

This distinction is not meant necessarily to imply a fundamental theoretical dichotomy here, merely an operational difference. Stimuli obviously could be placed on continua from ineffective to strongly reinforcing. A very loud tone is negatively reinforcing. As it becomes weaker, it loses reinforcement value and becomes an effective stimulus. As it becomes even weaker, it may become less effective. However, "effectiveness," like "reinforcement," is a behavioral term. It is defined here in relation to orienting, or, more generally, elicited, behavior, and need have no obvious relationship to physical stimulus scales. Stimuli that serve as releasers for fixed action patterns are, in our terms, very effective, but are often not physically strong. The effectiveness of a stimulus depends as much or more on organismic variables than on physical stimulus variables and is in fact defined by its effectiveness in eliciting behavior.

As noted previously, the behavioral characteristics of SPC differ substantially from those of ordinary reinforced learning. This general point has been made by several students of SPC (Hoffeld *et al.,* 1958; 1960; Kendall & Thompson, 1960; Prewitt, 1967; Seidel, 1958). In fact, as Thompson and Kramer (1965) perhaps first pointed out, the parametric characteristics of SPC strikingly resemble those of behavioral orienting. These correspondences are summarized briefly here.

NUMBER OF TRIALS

When an effective stimulus is presented for the first time, some form of orienting or other elicited behavior occurs. For a wide range of condi-

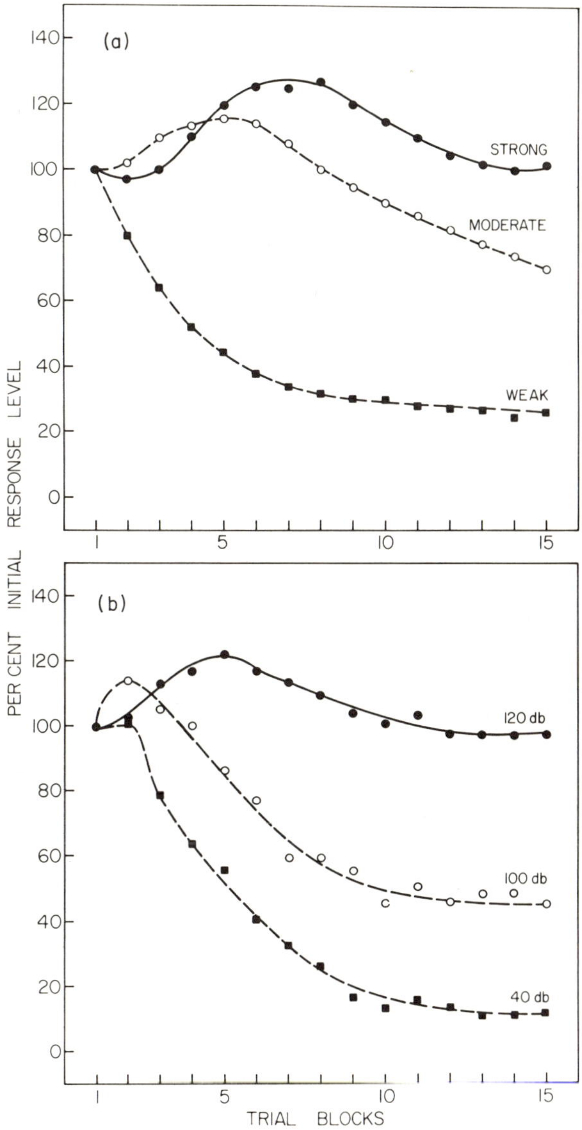

Fig. 4. Amplitude of response to repeated "effective" stimulus as a function of stimulus intensity for two quite different response systems, (a) hindlimb flexor reflex of acute spinal cat to skin shock (Groves & Thompson, 1970) and (b) intact human skin potential base level to sound (Raskin *et al.*, 1969).

tions with relatively more effective stimuli, subsequent presentations do not lead to immediate decrement but rather to a transient increase in orienting, followed by eventual habituation, as recently emphasized by Groves and Thompson (1970). Two quite diverse illustrations of this are shown in Fig. 4, the spinal flexion reflex of acute spinal cat (from Groves & Thompson, 1970) and the palmar skin potential of intact human (from Raskin, Kotses, & Bever, 1969). Note that with intermediate stimuli there is an initial period of a few trials where the response is maximal. If the stimulus is strong, the period of "sensitization" (i.e., increased response) is prolonged and peaks later. For weak stimuli, there is no apparent effect—however, these data are averaged over trial blocks. Even with very weak stimuli, orienting behavior is quite commonly greater to the second than the first stimulus presentation. Compare this figure with the analogous data for sensory preconditioning shown in Fig. 2. The correspondence is interesting.

TIME

The author is not familiar with any systematic parametric studies of effect of stimulus duration on degree of behavioral orienting. However, where comparions have been made, longer stimuli produce better orienting than brief stimuli. Thompson and Welker (1963) found significantly greater head orienting by cats to a 2-sec auditory stimulus than a .1-sec stimulus. R. C. Davis, Buchwald, and Frankmann (1955) report that some components of orienting behavior have latencies from 4 to 20 sec. This latter point may appear to conflict with the fact that Wynne and Brogden (1962) found poor SPC with precedence times of 8 and 16 sec during preconditioning. However, they used a trace procedure. Even these long times may be effective with a delay paradigm. Alternatively, cat behavioral orienting may be less at 8 and 16 than 2 sec. The data do not exist. In any event, both SPC and orienting are better with stimuli of considerably longer duration than the .5 sec maximally effective CS-US interval in conditioning.

STIMULUS INTENSITY

Here again, there is a correspondence in the effects of stimulus intensity on SPC and orienting behavior. Although data are meager, it appears that there is not a positive relationship between intensity of S_T (and S_C) and amount of SPC. Instead it tends to be inverse or an inverted U (Wokoun, 1959). Data are more extensive here for orienting. Razran

(1961) notes that the "orienting response" is weaker for very strong stimuli than for moderate levels. In a wide variety of situations, elicited behavior and performance have an inverted-U relationship to stimulus intensity, as noted by many authorities in relation to arousal and activation (Duffy, 1962; Hebb, 1955; D. B. Lindsley, 1951, 1960; Malmo, 1959; etc.). In contrast, ordinary reinforced conditioning has a positive (although not strong) relationship to SC intensity.

DEPRIVATION

Little systematic data exist. As noted previously, studies of SPC in general find more SPC if preconditioning is done under conditions of food and water deprivation. A methodological issue of considerable magnitude, namely, the problem of transfer, has not been adequately controlled (see J. S. Brown, 1961). There are no SPC studies where deprivation has been varied in an orthogonal design to permit independent evaluation of its effects on each of the three phases of the SPC paradigm, e.g., deprived vs. satiated in preconditioning, conditioning, and testing. There is also sparse systematic evidence relating orienting behavior to deprivation, although the general inverted-U relationship between stimulus intensity and orienting is believed to hold for conditions of deprivation as well (see, e.g., Berlyne, 1960). In the only direct study of this issue in relation to SPC, Adamec and Melzack (1970) recorded orienting behavior in their animals and found that the deprived cats made more behavioral orienting responses during preconditioning than did satiated animals. Deprivation would seem to be a dimension on which SPC and ordinary reinforced conditioning are consistent—both are better with deprivation. The possible inverted-U relation for orienting does suggest a differential prediction—it should be possible to increase deprivation to a point where SPC deteriorates but reinforced learning does not.

OTHER PROPERTIES AND PREDICTIONS

Sensory preconditioning has been characterized by several writers as weak and unstable. Actually, as we have seen here, it has quite reliable relations (or lack of relations) to variables of stimulus and training. However, in any given experiment it is a highly variable phenomenon between *S*s in the same condition. In this way too it resembles orienting. Extreme interanimal variability under constant external conditions is characteristic of both orienting and SPC and in distinct contrast to the much lower within-group variability in ordinary reinforced learning. In terms of measured behavioral strength, orienting and SPC are indeed much weaker than reinforced conditioning. Furthermore, both habituate with increased training.

The suggestion explored in this section that SPC and orienting resemble one another is a strictly empirical hypothesis. It is not asserted that SPC *is* orienting, merely that there is a correspondence. Several types of predictions follow even from this limited "theory." Definitions of orienting is a problem we prefer to ignore here. They range from behavioral head pointing to Sokolov's complex syndrome defining the "orienting reaction" in humans (see discussion in Thompson & Bettinger, 1970). However, it is possible to establish operational definitions of behavioral orienting for particular organisms and stimuli (see, e.g., Adamec & Melzack, 1970; Thompson & Shaw, 1965). Given some measure of orienting, our view predicts a significant positive correlation between the degree or amount of orienting shown by animals to the stimuli during preconditioning and the strength of subsequently tested SPC. This is actually a fairly strong prediction. It suggests that in spite of the very large interanimal variability in SPC, individual animal performance on the SPC test can be predicted by an independent measure taken during preconditioning. The experiment has not yet been done.

The study by Adamec and Melzack (1970) is the only direct investigation of orienting and SPC. They demonstrated a group effect consistent with the prediction but did not do individual analyses. Two other studies bear on this issue. Parks (1968) has also given a clear statement of the possible relation between SPC and orienting. He reasoned that unpaired presentations of S_T and S_C prior to preconditioning would result in habituation of elicited orienting behavior and hence poorer SPC relative to animals not given this initial experience. His experiment, using rats in a shock avoidance situation, verified this prediction. Tait and associates (1969), in a different context, gave preconditioning followed by extinction training to S_T and then conditioned and tested rats in the CER lick suppression paradigm. The experiment is complicated because varying numbers of stimuli were also given prior to preconditioning so that the total number of stimuli prior to conditioning was constant for all groups, and backward groups were run as controls. None the less, amount of SPC was inversely related to number of preconditioning extinction trials, a finding which they interpret in terms of classical conditioning but which is in fact at least equally consistent with the orienting-response hypothesis.

In general, conditions that increase orienting to the preconditioning stimuli should yield better SPC. In the important study by Wickens and Briggs (1951), *S*s required to make the same verbal response to both preconditioning stimuli during preconditioning showed more SPC, regardless of whether stimuli were paired or unpaired, than *S*s responding to only one of the stimuli in unpaired pretraining. Although the authors interpret their findings in terms of response-mediated stimulus generalization, the results are also very consistent with the orienting hypothesis. It is likely that *S*s required to respond verbally to both stimuli will show considerably greater orienting to the stimuli by other measures as well than *S*s not required to respond.

A number of other predictions can be suggested, based on properties of orienting behavior. Thus, as indicated previously, high deprivation should lead to poor SPC. The relations between stimulus intensity, number of trials, and degree of responsiveness indicated in Fig. 4 for responses elicited by effective stimuli lead to interesting possibilities. Sensory preconditioning should increase with number of preconditioning trials for intense stimuli, should decrease with number of training trials for weak stimuli, and should be maximal with a few preconditioning trials for intermediate stimuli. This is, of course, completely at variance with the properties of reinforced learning. The third part of the prediction is consistent with the studies of Brogden and associates (Hoffeld *et al.*, 1958, 1960; Wynne & Brogden, 1962) and Prewitt (1967). No data exist to evaluate the remainder of this prediction.

Behavioral Theories of SPC

The most significant theoretical statement made about SPC is contained in Brogden's (1939, pp. 330, 331) original discussion of the phenomenon:

> That the flexion-response is elicited by the stimulus not associated with shock must be due to an association formed when the bell and the light were presented contiguously, prior to the conditioning of flexion to one of them. . . . Some "bond" must have been formed between the bell and the light, and some "trace" of this bond retained.
>
> Since sensory preconditioning is a phenomenon of phasic activity, it is of importance as a form of behavior-modification. It is a basic principle of psychology that organisms are capable of making responses in the light of past experience. Much of this modification in behavior takes place under circumstances which fit the principles of conditioning. It is likely that in the commonplace environment of any organism, the conditions of the experiment on dogs herein reported will be fulfilled in nature. The experience of two contiguous sensory stimuli completely divorced from any phasic activity is frequent to any organism. If one of these stimuli becomes the signal for the response of a given reaction-pattern, the other will then elicit a similar response.

This straightforward view that contiguous experience of two sensory stimuli results in a lasting modification of the organism became complicated as subsequent authors attempted to fit the phenomenon into "S-R," "R-R," and "S-S" theories of learning. By sufficiently scholastic argumentation SPC can be interpreted in each of these theoretical contexts. However, the arguments as originally given are unconvincing and require ad hoc assumptions about inferred responses, particularly for R-R and S-R approaches. In brief, S-R theory (see Coppock, 1958; Osgood, 1953; Seidel, 1959) assumes that both S_T and S_C evoke unobserved responses, S_T becomes connected to the response to S_C through unknown need reduction, and, hence, following reinforced conditioning of S_C to a CR, S_T comes to elicit the CR. The fatal weakness here is the assumption that there is reinforcement to establish the connection between S_T and the response to S_C. The hypothetical unobserved mediating responses could relate to orienting behavior. Guthrie's response contiguity ("R-R") approach could also handle SPC, as noted by Brogden (1947), simply by assuming that unobserved responses elicited by S_T and S_C occur contiguously, the necessary and sufficient condition for learning according to Guthrie. This is a more parsimonious view than S-R theory in that no reinforcement is necessary, but again it requires unobserved mediating responses, which, of course, could be some form of orienting. Finally, Birch and Bitterman (1949) interpret SPC as S-S contiguity learning—all that is necessary is "a process of afferent modification . . . when two afferent centers are continuously active, a functional relation is established between them such that the subsequent innovation of one will arouse the other" (pp. 302, 358). This is the simplest of the three views, does not require unknown reinforcement or mediating responses, and most closely parallels Brogden's original suggestion. However, it is a general theory of learning based on purely hypothetical brain events.

These three views, which characterize classic learning theory approaches to SPC, face the same difficult problem. Each interprets SPC as one particular example of the general phenomenon of conditioning. Therefore, according to all these views, SPC must follow the same laws as does ordinary reinforced conditioning. As we have seen, this is simply not true. Performance in SPC and reinforced learning differ fundamentally in term of effects of number of training trials and stimulus time relations, appear to differ in terms of stimulus intensity effects, and may differ in degree if not in kind for motivational variables.

A quite different interpretation of SPC has been in terms of "attention." This apparently was first suggested by Seidel: "Thus, it is proposed that the important stimuli for the organism in the preconditioning situation are constituted by the stimulus complex to which it attends" (1959, p. 72). Attention was invoked in terms of orienting behavior as an explanation of SPC by Thompson and Kramer (1965) and by Adamec and Melzack (1970). The basic idea is simply that an organism will develop SPC to the extent that he attends to the stimuli during preconditioning. As Thompson and Kramer (1965) noted, attention can be defined operationally in terms of orienting responses. The correspondence between SPC and orienting behavior listed here appeared to provide strong evidence for this view. Adamec and Melzack (1970) reasoned further that arousal and attention should be increased under conditions of deprivation, and, hence, orienting behavior and SPC should both increase, as indeed they did.

Unfortunately, there is a fundamental difficulty with the attention hypothesis. As Brogden noted (1965, personal communication), "attention" adds nothing to our understanding of SPC or, for that matter, any other behavioral phenomena. The present author was not always convinced of this view. A recent and comprehensive edited volume on attention (Mostofsky, 1970) illustrates the point. A careful reading of the contributions, written by many of the leading authorities in the field of attention (The present author, while not claiming this distinction, even contributed a chapter) reveals *not a single useful or meaningful definition of attention.* There are, to be sure, a number of straightforward operational definitions in terms of orienting responses, observing responses, differential responding, selective listening, etc. At this level "attention" merely provides a shorthand descriptor for measured performance. The basic problem is that attention is almost invariably also invoked as an explanation—a type-II hypothetical construct to *explain* differential responding or selective listening. However, it is an empty construct with properties so implicit that they are known only to the particular author and only in an uncommunicable form. To assert that an animal makes a differential response to one of two stimuli because he selectively attends to that stimulus represents no significant advance over the assertion that God or secondary reinforcement makes it happen. The explanation of SPC in terms of a behavioral construct of attention has no merit.

It has been emphasized throughout this discussion that the properties of SPC and orienting behavior are closely parallel. There is also an obvious difference. Orienting is a response or pattern of responses to a stimulus or stimulus complex. Sensory preconditioning is fundamentally an associative process. It is not merely response to a stimulus but rather subsequent response to S_T after pairing with S_C and training to S_C. In order to explain SPC in terms of orienting, it is necessary to make some kind of assumption regarding the nature of the association formed between S_T and S_C. We adopt Brogden's original suggestion simply that there is some bond formed as a result of pairing and some trace of this bond retained. Another way of stating it is that contiguous experiences are to some degree retained. It is a small step from this to a general notion of plasticity. As Hebb (1949) emphasized, higher organisms tend to retain experiences; it is a general property of a more developed nervous system. At least partial retention of contiguous experiences is a common fact in ordinary life and in the verbal learning laboratory for humans. Sensory preconditioning would then reflect the fundamental process of plasticity; reinforced learning might be a special case. As Brogden and his associates suggested: "Perhaps the only difference between standard conditioning and sensory preconditioning is in terms of performance and that the primary role of reinforcement is in terms of performance" (Hoffeld, *et al.*, 1960, p. 203).

This is probably an overstatement, particularly in reference to well-learned and/or strongly reinforced behavior. However, it may well be true for the intial phases of conditioning. Assuming that SPC reflects a basic plasticity of the higher nervous system, we are still left with the question of why SPC and orienting are such closely parallel phenomena. Actually, it appears that conditions yielding maximum SPC are those giving an increased orienting response, i.e., sensitization. Sensitization per se is a very basic form of plasticity, as is the subsequent habituation with continued repetition in the absence of reinforcement. For a wide variety of responses and conditions there is a transitory increase in evoked behavioral response to the first few presentations of an effective stimulus. These data have been interpreted in terms of a "dual-process" theory of response to repeated stimulation, where the outcome is assumed to be the net result of two *inferred* processes, habituation and sensitization, which are always induced by repetition, or even first occurrence, of an effective stimulus (for an extended discussion, see Groves & Thompson, 1970; Thompson, Groves, Teyler, & Roemer, 1972). We argue further here that sensitization is the necessary condition for the development of SPC and, more generally, for the initial phase of learning. Sensitization is then the fundamental inferred process underlying the initial development of behavioral plasticity. This was, of course, the assumption implicit in my earlier analysis of SPC performance where predictions were made about SPC on the basis of conditions that maximize sensitization of orienting behavior.

It is not suggested that SPC is merely behavioral sensitization. Rather, the initial development of an association between two contiguous stimuli is facilitated, or even made possible, by the existence of a hypothetical state of sensitization. In fact, sensitization does develop in the initial trials of ordinary reinforced conditioning in many learning situations (Harris, 1941; Kimble, 1961). Furthermore, backward conditioning, which probably reflects sensitization, occurs largely on initial training trials (Champion, 1962; Jones, 1961; Spooner & Kellogg, 1947).

It could be argued that the impressive correspondences noted here between orienting and SPC provide strong evidence for response mediation theories (either "S-R" or "R-R") of SPC. This, of course, does not follow. Correlation does not imply causation. We adopt the equally possible interpretation of this correlation in terms of a common underlying factor, hypothetical sensitization, which leads to stronger orienting behavior and greater associative plasticity. Sensory preconditioning is interpreted as a reflection of this fundamental plasticity relatively uncontaminated by the powerful effects of reinforcement on performance. The assumption that *behavioral* responses must occur to mediate learning, as in S-R and R-R theories, is an obsolete inheritance from early behaviorism. The evidence from many sources is now overwhelming that behavioral responses are not necessary for learning (see, e.g., Miller, 1969). Consequently, it is an unnecessary complication to postulate that behavioral orienting serves as a mediator for SPC. Our view, that both orienting and SPC reflect an underlying hypothetical neural process of sensitization or plasticity, is more parsimonious and has the further advantage of being testable. Something, obviously, must mediate behavior. Even hard-core behaviorists are coming to recognize that this "something" is the central nervous system.

Possible Neural Substrates of SPC

Since no direct evidence exists regarding neural mechanisms of SPC, this section will, unfortunately, be brief. Some information is available regarding neural correlates of orienting. In general, behavior orienting, arousal, or sensitization is accompanied by the low voltage, fast cortical EEG arousal pattern, reticular activation, changes in amplitudes of some brain-evoked potentials, and certain autonomic responses (for reviews, see Groves & Thompson, 1970; Lacey, 1967; D. B. Lindsely, 1960; Malmo, 1959; Sokolov, 1963). Further, there appears to be a positive relationship between amount of ongoing neuronal activity in nonspecific polysensory regions of the cerebral cortex and degree of behavioral orienting (Thompson & Bettinger, 1970; Thompson & Shaw, 1965). Consequently, these neural indexes ought to correlate with SPC as well. It was in this sense that the term attention was used by Thompson and Kramer

(1965) and Adamec and Melzack (1971)—as a descriptor for the constellation of neural and physiological events that appear to accompany orienting and, hence, by inference, SPC as well. The usefulness of attention in this context is no greater than in behavioral terms—it is a description of measurable events. Physiological psychologists are prone to use "attention" in this sense.

There are several reports of sensory-sensory "conditioning" of some individual neurons in visual cortex (D. F. Lindsley, Chow, & Gollender, 1967; Morrell, 1967) and motor cortex (O'Brien & Fox, 1969). Only a relatively small proportion, about 10%, of units in visual cortex seem to show the effect. These studies were, of course, not done in the context of SPC, but results are at least suggestive. Polysensory "association" cortex might seem a more logical substrate for sensory preconditioning. First and most obvious, it is polysensory, being influenced by all modalities of stimuli (see review by Thompson, Robertson, & Mayers, 1972). Second, activity in these regions is related to degree of behavioral orienting (Thompson & Shaw, 1965). Third, ablation of polysensory cortex prevents subsequent development of SPC (Thompson & Kramer, 1965). However, Scharlock, de Nosaquo, and Stewart (1963) reported that lesions of auditory cortex presented the development of SPC, so the lesion effect cannot be considered unique to association cortex. Finally, according to Seidel (1959), lower organisms do not exhibit SPC; they, of course, do not have association cortex. If polysensory association cortex plays a critical role in SPC, it should be possible to demonstrate substantial direct sensory-sensory conditioning in these regions, and activity there during preconditioning should correlate with subsequent strength of SPC. If activity in polysensory association cortex is indeed related to the development of SPC, it would provide a neural substrate for Brogden's hypothetical "bond" and Birch and Bitterman's "S-S" theories of SPC. A major problem for them was postulation of unknown associations between afferent systems of different modalities. More generally, association cortex may provide an essential substrate for the development or at least facilitation of associative plasticity in higher organisms. Empirical tests of this hypothesis remain to be done.

A peripheral sensory stimulus activates primary sensory pathways projecting to lateral thalamic nuclei and sensory specific regions of the cerebral cortex. It also activates nonspecific systems—reticular formation and medial thalamus—which have powerful functional projections to polysensory association regions of the cortex. Wester (1971) has recently shown that direct electrical stimulation of the thalamus can evoke clear behavioral orienting in cats. Repeated electrical stimulation of the lateral thalamus leads only to rapid habituation of orienting. However, behavioral orienting to repeated stimulation of medial thalamus does not habituate and often shows marked increases. In terms of the present argument, medial thalamic stimulation increases hypothetical sensitization. Consequently, medial thalamic stimulation should increase both behavioral orienting and SPC to subsequently presented peripheral stimuli. These predictions have not yet been tested. The behavioral sensitization produced by medial thalamic stimulation is particularly relevant to our argument. Wester (personal communication) has shown in other work that this effective brain stimulus does not have behavioral reinforcing properties; in present terms it is a very effective stimulus but not an effective-reinforcing stimulus.

Conclusions

Sensory preconditioning has been obtained in a number of mammals, ranging from rat to man, with a variety of conditioning procedures, classical and instrumental, appetitive and aversive, and a wide range of stimuli, both cross-modal and intramodal. Virtually all published studies of SPC are positive demonstrations of the phenomenon. The few parametric studies of effects of stimulus and training variables on SPC agree in finding maximum SPC with a relatively few trials of preconditioning and a relatively long precedence interval of the test stimulus during paired preconditioning trials. Preconditioning stimulus intensity has an uncertain, possibly inverted-U, relation to amount of SPC. Preconditioning under conditions of food and water deprivation is more effective than under satiation, but effects of deprivation during conditioning are less certain.

As emphasized through the discussion, most of these parametric behavioral properties of SPC are fundamentally different from those of ordinary reinforced learning. They are, in fact, closely parallel to the effects of stimulus and training variables on behavioral orienting responses. This correspondence forms the basis of the empirical theory developed here that SPC and orienting are fundamentally similar phenomena. A number of testable behavioral predictions are derived from this view. In more general theoretical terms, it is assumed, following Brogden's original suggestion, that SPC reflects a basic associative plasticity of the higher vertebrate brain. Possible neural substrates of SPC are considered, and it is proposed that some form of increased sensitization or plasticity in polysensory association systems and cerebral cortex provides the neural basis for SPC, as well as increased orienting and related elementary aspects of behavioral plasticity. Sensory preconditioning is an example of the fundamental process of learning that probably occurs almost continuously in the ordinary natural environment of higher animals, including man.

REFERENCES

Adamec, R., & Melzack, R. The role of motivation and orientation in sensory preconditioning. *Canadian Journal of Psychology,* 1970, **24**, 230–239.

Bahrick, H. P. Latent learning as a function of the strength of unrewarded need states. *Journal of Comparative and Physiological Psychology,* 1952, **45**, 192–197.

Bahrick, H. P. Sensory preconditioning under two degrees of deprivation. *Journal of Comparative and Physiological Psychology,* 1953, **46**, 39–42.

Berlyne, D. E. *Conflict, arousal, and curiosity.* New York: McGraw-Hill, 1960.

Birch, H. G., & Bitterman, M. E. Reinforcement and learning: The process of sensory integration. *Psychological Review,* 1949, **56**, 292–308.

Birkimer, J. C. Sensory preconditioning and higher order conditioning with discriminative stimuli in instrumental reward learning. *Dissertation Abstracts,* 1967, **27**, (9-B), 3302–3303.

Bitterman, M. E., Reed, P. C., & Kubala, A. L. The strength of sensory preconditioning. *Journal of Experimental Psychology,* 1953, **46**, 178–182.

Brogden, W. J. Sensory pre-conditioning. *Journal of Experimental Psychology,* 1939, **25**, 323–332.

Brogden, W. J. Tests of sensory preconditioning with human subjects. *Journal of Experimental Psychology,* 1942, **31**, 505–517.

Brogden, W. J. Sensory preconditioning of human subjects. *Journal of Experimental Psychology,* 1947, **37**, 527–539.

Brogden, W. J. Sensory conditioning measured by the facilitation of auditory acuity. *Journal of Experimental Psychology,* 1950, **40**, 512–519.

Brogden, W. J., & Gregg, L. W. Studies of sensory conditioning measured by the facilitation of auditory acuity. *Journal of Experimental Psychology,* 1951, **42**, 384–389.

Brown, C. P., & King, M. G. Backward sensory preconditioning: The ineffectiveness of the procedure under optimal conditions. *Australian Journal of Psychology,* 1969, **21**, 55–58.

Brown, J. S. *The motivation of behavior.* New York: McGraw-Hill, 1961.

Brown, J. S. Generalization and discrimination. In D. I. Mostofsky (Ed.), *Stimulus generalization.* Stanford, Calif.: Stanford University Press, 1965. Pp. 7–23.

Brown, W. L., Urmer, A. H., & Carr, R. M. The facilitative effect of sensory preconditioning on instrumental learning in the rhesus monkey. *Journal of Comparative and Physiological Psychology,* 1958, **51**, 461–463.

Champion, R. A. Stimulus-response contiguity in classical avoidance conditioning. *Journal of Experimental Psychology,* 1962, **64**, 35–39.

Chernikoff, R., & Brogden, W. J. The effect of instructions upon sensory pre-conditioning of human subjects. *Journal of Experimental Psychology,* 1949, **39**, 200–207.

Coppock, W. J. Pre-extinction in sensory preconditioning. *Journal of Experimental Psychology,* 1958, **55**, 213–219.

Davis, J. L., & Thompson, R. F. Sensory preconditioning of cats in a shuttle box avoidance situation. *Psychonomic Science,* 1968, **13**, 37–38; *Psychonomic Science,* 1969, **15**, 142. (Erratum)

Davis, R. C., Buchwald, A. M., & Frankmann, R. W. Autonomic and muscular responses and their relation to simple stimuli. *Psychological Monographs,* 1955, **69** (20, Whole No. 405) .

Doubros, S. G. Sensory preconditioning with the mentally retarded. *American Journal of Mental Deficiency,* 1965, **70**, 282–286.

Duffy, E. *Activation and behavior.* New York: Wiley, 1962.

Enzie, R. F. Direct measurement of the mediating response in sensory preconditioning. *Dissertation Abstracts,* 1969, **29**, (10-B), 3937.

Groves, P. M., & Thompson, R. F. Habituation: A dual-process theory. *Psychological Review,* 1970, **77**, 419–450.

Harris, J. D. Forward conditioning, backward conditioning, pseudo-conditioning, and adaptation to the conditioned stimulus. *Journal of Experimental Psychology,* 1941, **28**, 491–502.

Hebb, D. O. *The organization of behavior.* New York: Wiley, 1949.

Hebb, D. O. Drives and the c.n.s. (conceptual nervous system) . *Psychological Review,* 1955, **62**, 243–254.

Hinde, R. A. *Animal behavior: A synthesis of ethology and comparative psychology.* New York: McGraw-Hill, 1966.

Hoffeld, D. R., Kendall, S. B., Thompson, R. F., & Brogden, W. J. Effect of amount of preconditioning training upon the magnitude of sensory preconditioning. *Journal of Experimental Psychology,* 1960, **59**, 198–204.

Hoffeld, D. R., Thompson, R. F., & Brogden, W. J. Effect of stimuli time relations during preconditioning training upon the magnitude of sensory preconditioning. *Journal of Experimental Psychology,* 1958, **56**, 437–442.

Holmes, P. A. The effect of stimulus intensity and unconditioned responsivity on sensory preconditioning using the CER. *Dissertation Abstracts,* 1968, **29**, (6-B), 2220.

Jones, J. E. The CS-UCS interval in conditioning short and long latency responses. *Journal of Experimental Psychology,* 1961, **62**, 612–617.

Karn, H. W. Sensory pre-conditioning and incidental learning in human subjects. *Journal of Experimental Psychology,* 1947, **37**, 540–544.

Kendall, S. B., & Thompson, R. F. Effect of stimulus similarity on sensory preconditioning within a single stimulus dimension. *Journal of Comparative and Physiological Psychology,* 1960, **53**, 439–442.

Kimble, G. A. *Hilgard and Marquis' conditioning and learning.* New York: Appleton, 1961.

Lacey, J. I. Somatic response patterning and stress: Some revisions of activation theory. In M. Appley & R. Trumbull (Eds.) , *Psychological stress.* New York: Appleton, 1967. Pp. 14–37.

Lindsley, D. B. Emotion. In S. S. Stevens (Ed.) , *Handbook of experimental psychology.* New York: Wiley, 1951. Pp. 473–516.

Lindsley, D. B. Attention, consciousness, sleep, and wakefulness. In American Physiological Society, J. Field, (Eds.), *Handbook of physiology.* Section 1, *Neurophysiology.* Vol. III. Baltimore, Md.: Williams & Wilkins, 1960. Pp. 1553–1593.

Lindsley, D. F., Chow, K. L., & Gollender, M. Dichoptic interactions of lateral geniculate neurons of cats to contralateral and ipsilateral eye stimulation. *Journal of Neurophysiology,* 1967, **30**, 628–644.

Lovibond, S. H. Sensory preconditioning: Central linkage or response mediation. *Journal of Experimental Psychology,* 1959, **58**, 469–475.

Malmo, R. B. Activation: A neuropsychological dimension. *Psychological Review,* 1959, **66**, 367–386.

Miller, N. E. Learning of visceral and glandular responses. *Science,* 1969, **163**, 434–445.

Morrell, F. Electrical signs of sensory coding. In G. C. Quarton, T. Melnechuk, & F. O. Schmitt (Eds.), *The neurosciences: A study program.* New York: Rockefeller University Press, 1967. Pp. 452–469.

Mostofsky, D. I. (Ed.) *Attention: Contemporary theory and analysis.* New York: Appleton, 1970.

O'Brien, J. H., & Fox, S. S. Single-cell activity in cat motor cortex. II. Functional characteristics of the cell related to conditioning changes. *Journal of Neurophysiology,* 1969, **32**, 285–296.

Osgood, C. E. *Method and theory in experimental psychology.* London and New York: Oxford University Press, 1953.

Parkinson, S. R. Sensory preconditioning of a conditioned emotional response. *Psychonomic Science,* 1968, **11**, 119.

Parks, E. R. The orientation reaction as a mediator in sensory preconditioning. *Dissertation Abstracts,* 1964, **24**, (8), 3438.

Parks, E. R. The orientation reaction as a mediator of sensory preconditioning. *Psychonomic Science,* 1968, **11**, 11–12.

Prewitt, E. P. Number of preconditioning trials in sensory preconditioning using CER training. *Journal of Compartive and Physiological Psychology,* 1967, **64**, 360–362.

Prokofiev, G., & Zeliony, G. Des modes d'associations cérébrales chez l'homme et chex les animaux. *Journal de Psychologie Normale et Pathologique,* 1926, **23**, 1020–1028.

Raskin, D. C., Kotses, H., & Bever, J. Autonomic indicators of orienting and defensive reflexes. *Journal of Experimental Psychology,* 1969, **80**, 423–433.

Razran, G. The observable unconscious and the inferable conscious in current Soviet psychophysiology: Interoceptive conditioning, semantic conditioning, and the orienting reflex. *Psychological Review,* 1961, **68**, 81–147.

Reid, R. L. A test of sensory pre-conditioning in pigeons. *Quarterly Journal of Experimental Psychology,* 1952, **4**, 49–56.

Scharlock, D. P., de Nosaquo, S., & Stewart, D. L. Sensory preconditioning in cats following bilateral ablation of temporal cortex. *Perceptual and Motor Skills,* 1963, **17**, 847–850.

Seidel, R. J. An investigation of mediation in preconditioning. *Journal of Experimental Psychology,* 1958, **56**, 220–225.

Seidel, R. J. A review of sensory preconditioning. *Psychological Bulletin,* 1959, **56**, 58–73.

Shaw, J. A., & Thompson, R. F. Inverse relation between evoked cortical association responses and behavioral orienting to repeated auditory stimuli. *Psychonomic Science,* 1964, **1**, 399–400.

Silver, C. A., & Meyer, D. A. Temporal factors in sensory preconditioning. *Journal of Comparative and Physiological Psychology,* 1954, **47**, 57–59.

Sokolov, Y. N. *Perception and the conditioned reflex.* Oxford: Pergamon Press, 1963.

Spooner, A., & Kellogg, W. N. The backward conditioning curve. *American Journal of Psychology,* 1947, **60**, 321–334.

Tait, R. W., Marquis, H. A., Williams, R., Weinstein, L., & Suboski, M. D. Extinction of sensory preconditioning using CER training. *Journal of Comparative and Physiological Psychology,* 1969, **69,** 170–172.

Thompson, R. F. Effect of acquisition level upon the magnitude of stimulus generalization across sensory modality. *Journal of Comparative and Physiological Psychology,* 1959, **52,** 183–185.

Thompson, R. F., & Bettinger, L. A. Neural substrates of attention. In D. I. Mostofsky (Ed.), *Attention: Contemporary theory and analysis.* New York: Appleton, 1970. Pp. 367–401.

Thompson, R. F., Groves, P. M., Teyler, T. J., & Roemer, R. A. A dual-process theory of habituation: Theory and behavior. In H. V. S. Peeke & M. J. Herz (Eds.), *Habituation: Behavioral studies and physiological substrates.* Vol. 1. New York: Academic Press, 1972, in press.

Thompson, R. F., & Kramer, R. F. Role of association cortex in sensory preconditioning. *Journal of Comparative and Physiological Psychology,* 1965, **60,** 189–191.

Thompson, R. F., Robertson, R. T., & Mayers, K. S. Cortical association response areas of the cat. In G. M. French (Ed.), *Behavior and cortical function.* Glenview, Ill.: Scott, Foresman, 1972, in press. (a)

Thompson, R. F., & Shaw, J. A. Behavioral correlates of evoked activity recorded from association areas of the cerebral cortex. *Journal of Comparative and Physiological Psychology,* 1965, **60,** 329–339.

Thompson, R. F., & Spencer, W. A. Habituation: A model phenomenon for the study of neuronal substrates of behavior. *Psychological Review,* 1966, **173,** 16–43.

Thompson, R. F., & Welker, W. I. Role of auditory cortex in reflex head orientation by cats to auditory stimuli. *Journal of Comparative and Physiological Psychology,* 1963, **56,** 996–1002.

Thornton, G. L. The effect of stimulus intensities upon sensory preconditioning. *Proceedings of the Iowa Academy of Science,* 1956, **63,** 620–626.

Uno, T. Sensory preconditioning and classical conditioning of autonomic responses. *Proceedings of the 74th Annual Convention of the American Psychological Association,* 1966, **1,** 55–56.

Welker, W. I. An analysis of exploratory and play behavior in animals. In D. W. Fiske & S. R. Maddi (Eds.), *Functions of varied experience.* Homewood, Ill.: Dorsey Press, 1961. Pp. 175–226.

Wester, K. Habituation to electrical stimulation of the thalamus in unanesthetized cats. *Electroencephalography and Clinical Neurophysiology,* 1971, **30,** 52–61.

Wickens, D. D., & Briggs, G. E. Mediated stimulus generalization as a factor in sensory pre-conditioning. *Journal of Experimental Psychology,* 1951, **42,** 197–200.

Wickens, D. D., & Cross, H. A. Resistance to extinction as a function of temporal relations during sensory preconditioning. *Journal of Experimental Psychology,* 1963, **65,** 206–211.

Wokoun, F. W., Jr. The effect of stimulus intensity in sensory preconditioning. *Dissertation Abstracts,* 1959, **20,** 1881.

Wynne, J. D., & Brogden, W. J. Supplementary report: Effect upon sensory preconditioning of backward, forward, and trace preconditioning training. *Journal of Experimental Psychology,* 1962, **64,** 422–423.

CHAPTER 7

INTRATASK INTERFERENCE AS A SOURCE OF FACILITATION IN TRANSFER AND RETENTION[1]

William F. Battig

The concept of interference has long played a central role in experimental analyses of human verbal and motor acquisition, transfer, and retention. Until very recently, interference from prior or interpolated learn-

[1] In a contribution of this nature, it would be exceedingly remiss not to follow W. J. Brogden's policy of giving at least full acknowledgment to student contributions. The research reported herein was heavily dependent on the work of several of the

ing was being widely accepted as the major if not the only cause of retention loss or forgetting (e.g., Keppel, 1968). The "proactive" and "retroactive" sources thereof have been interchangeably referred to as either interference or inhibition. The virtual synonymity of "interference" with "negative transfer" indicates the negative connotations of the former term to be equally basic to analyses of transfer phenomena (Battig, 1966a).

Despite its importance in contributing negatively to transfer and retention, however, the concept of interference has played at best a secondary role in research on the initial acquisition phase of learning. This has been true even though the typical experimental task employed in human-learning research is characterized by a great deal of interference, both within and external to the task to be learned. Yet in 1960, when Sam Brown and I originally became interested in the role of interference produced by the remainder of the list in the paired-associate (PA) learning of individual pairs (Brown, 1964), we found essentially no previous literature relevant thereto except for Gibson's (1940) formulation based on the closely related concept of stimulus generalization. Brown's work effectively demonstrated that interference produced by other unlearned pairs represented a significant source of retardation in PA learning. Thus the negative effects of interference in producing forgetting and negative transfer also appeared to extend to the retardation of original acquisition. Consequently, we began to give serious attention to the role played by intratask interference in the acquisition of PA and other types of verbal-learning tasks, finding this to be very useful in helping to account for some of the surprising results emerging from some of our experiments concerned with quite different problems (Battig, 1966a).

In retrospect, it is difficult to specify exactly when and why we began to conceive of intratask interference as anything other than a major source of retardation in human learning. Clearly, it required a combination of results from several different experiments showing more positive

author's students. Sam C. Brown, Russell B. Johnson, and Mary E. Schild were largely responsible for the work leading to the initial formulation of the topic of this chapter. Shu-jen Huang and John K. Berry, along with undergraduate assistants too numerous to name individually, were extensively involved primarily in the several unsuccessful attempts to provide a direct and convincing demonstration of the phenomenon. Finally, James W. Pellegrino deserves most of the credit for the eventual success in the latter venture, and for our decision to write on this topic for the present volume. Grateful acknowledgment is also made to the United States Public Health Service for research grants (M-05769, HD-00929, HD-01062, and HD-03058) supporting most of this work, and to a grant from the National Science Foundation (GB-25433) which facilitated the writing of this chapter.

transfer and/or better retention produced by high intratask interference during acquisition before we began to take seriously the possibility that such an inverse relationship might be of some general importance. Our first recorded statement to this effect apparently was made at a symposium at the April 1963 meetings of the Southeastern Psychological Association, where a description of Mary Schild's 1963 master's thesis (Schild & Battig, 1966), was concluded as follows:

> There may well be an important general principle at work here, with considerable practical as well as theoretical significance, that the simplest and most efficient methods with respect to initial learning may be inferior in the long run to more complex methods or types of learning, the implications of which are certainly deserving of experimental attention.

Despite the considerable "intratask interference" associated with giving this symposium paper, however, we had no recollection whatever of the just-quoted statement less than two years later, when our first formal statement of this principle was delivered in a paper prepared for the Tulane conference on "Acquisition of Skill" in March 1965. In this paper, subsequently appearing as a chapter in Bilodeau's book by this title (Battig, 1966a), the initial formulation of the principle that *intertask facilitation is produced by intratask interference* was attributed to Russell Johnson's (1964) Ph.D. dissertation. Although Johnson was still collecting his data at the time of the symposium, it was primarily his results that led us to take the principle seriously enough to begin to design experiments explicitly intended to test it and try to establish its generality and boundary conditions.

Whatever its origin, the subsequent development of the principle and of research bearing upon it can most clearly be described in terms of four distinct phases, each of which will constitute a separate section of this report. First, there was the substantial amount of research in our laboratory in the early 1960s, all of it concerned primarily with other problems, that provided the indirect evidence leading us to take the principle seriously. Second, there were several largely abortive attempts to demonstrate the principle directly, which taught us primarily about the serious interference with its direct and uncontaminated experimental investigation produced by a host of methodological problems. Third (and to a large extent concurrent with the second phase), several lines of support for the principle and its generality began to emerge from other laboratories, again concerned primarily with other types of problems. Finally, as we were about to conclude that the best way to study this phenomenon was indirectly rather than directly, we managed to identify and free our research of the major difficulties responsible for the inconclusiveness of our efforts in the second phase. Thus in the fourth and final section I will report some recent experiments providing the conclusive demonstration of the intratask interference as a source of facilitation in transfer and/or retention that had so long eluded us.

Initial Indirect Evidence

Most of this research has been described in detail elsewhere so that only a brief review is called for here. In the Schild–Battig (1966) Experiment I (Schild's master's thesis), 8 groups representing all possible combinations of recall or anticipation methods, uni- or bidirectional PA learning, and uni- or bidirectional pronunciation were employed. A correlation of .40 across groups indicated subsequent written recall to be best for conditions producing greater original learning difficulty (anticipation, bidirectional learning, and/or pronunciation). Johnson's (1964) even more complicated experiment (see also Battig, 1966a) included 12 basic groups representing different combinations of (a) high or low similarity of 9 nonsense-shape stimuli, (b) 3 dissimilar or 9 similar responses, and (c) congruence or incongruence of stimulus with response classes, in a paired-associate stimulus-predifferentiation task. Mean subsequent recognition accuracy for the stimulus shapes was only 31.9% with minimal intratask interference in the stimulus-predifferentiation task increasing to values of 34.1, 36.3, 36.9, and 42.2% with progressive increases in intratask interference produced by high shape similarity, 9 similar responses, and/or increased incongruence of shape and response classes. Battig, Brown, and Schild (1964) found that items from the middle of an initial serial list actually produced better performance (49.0%) when included in a second transfer list than was found for otherwise comparable items taken from the beginning positions of the initial list (32.4%). Finally, Battig, Merikle, and Schild (1965) showed that while free-recall learning of three-letter anagrams is slower if *S*s are required to recall these in the letter order presented than if they can be recalled as the word solution, the former condition showed greater positive transfer (27.8%) to a subsequent PA list than did the latter (15.0%).

These experiments cover a variety of learning phenomena and tasks, including, respectively, (1) bidirectional associations in PA acquisition and retention, (2) stimulus-predifferentiation training in subsequent perceptual recognition, (3) serial acquisition and transfer as a function of serial positions of items repeated in the two lists, and (4) free-recall learning of anagram materials and the effects thereof upon subsequent

PA transfer. Moreover, they offer little indication that the principle is either limited in its application or especially difficult to investigate directly. Some further supportive evidence emerged from the work of Battig *et al.* (1965), who obtained nearly as much positive transfer to PA performance from a high-interference recognition task (22.5%) as from the high-interference free-recall task (requiring reproduction of the exact anagram letter order). This latter finding was of particular interest because it supported some earlier unpublished research (Spera, 1963; Thompson, 1964) suggesting maximal transfer to PA learning from an individual-item pretraining procedure requiring multiple-choice recognition of the item to be learned from a large set of highly similar alternatives. Because of the relevance of this multiple-choice recognition (MCR) technique also to what at that time was our primary goal of isolating and determining the relative importance of the several component processes involved in PA learning (Battig, 1968), it was adopted in our first experiments designed directly to evaluate increased intratask interference as a source of subsequent intertask facilitation, as described in the following section.

Failures of Efforts to Obtain Direct Evidence

MULTIPLE-CHOICE–RECOGNITION PRETRAINING

In retrospect, it is clear that two unfortunate major decisions were made at the outset of the second phase of this research, wherein we attempted to obtain direct empirical support for the principle rather than relying on indirect evidence. First, the use of number and similarity of incorrect alternatives in a multiple-choice recognition (MCR) pretraining task turned out to produce more methodological problems than it resolved. Moreover, the nature of these problems was largely responsible for misguiding us into substituting a subsequent intratask-interference producing variable (double-function lists) that produced even more serious complications. Our second questionable decision was to concentrate upon transfer rather than retention measures as our index of facilitation produced by increasing intratask interference. While the first decision was somewhat arbitrary and based on a lack of relevant information, the second was based on what still seems a persuasive logical analysis indicating that transfer should be less contaminated than retention measures. This follows because any intratask interference present during acquisition might likewise be present while retention is being measured, thus representing a negative factor on performance that could well obscure any facilitation. By contrast, transfer tasks (we thought) could be designed so that intratask interference would be operative only within the original acquisition task but not on the transfer task. Thus our first direct experiments, as described in detail elsewhere (Battig, 1966b; Battig & Berry, 1966), both used MCR tasks as the source of intratask interference, and evaluated primarily subsequent transfer to a PA list including pairs of items from the MCR task. Since the outcome of these experiments largely determined our subsequent research strategy, they are summarized briefly here.

Our first direct attempt (Battig & Berry, 1966) was designed principally to demonstrate directly and conclusively that subsequent PA learning would show greater facilitation when the individual PA items had previously been learned in an MCR task including several highly similar incorrect alternatives. Thus the key manipulation was number of alternatives (two or eight) in the pretraining task, and whether correct and incorrect alternatives (all CVC trigrams) were similar or dissimilar to one another.[2] Completely contrary to our expectations, subsequent PA performance was not significantly affected by either number or similarity of pretraining alternatives. In fact, the pretraining task involving the most intratask interference (eight highly similar alternatives) actually produced numerically *less* PA transfer to pairs of pretrained items than did the lowest intratask interference conditions (two dissimilar alternatives in a typical verbal-discrimination pretraining task).

Fortunately, this experiment also included some additional variable manipulations and performance measures which help to account for the surprising results. In particular, a subsequent recognition retention test given 24 hr later clearly demonstrated that during pretraining there had been substantial learning of incorrect as well as correct alternatives. Thus our high intratask-interference pretraining conditions had produced pri-

[2] This experiment had also included systematic variations in type of PA procedure, including not only the usual procedure whereby the entire list is presented once on each trial (noncorrection procedure) but also a correction procedure (Battig, 1955) wherein pairs are temporarily dropped from the list after each correct recall so that each trial consists of one correct recall of each pair. While this variable produced some interesting effects, these bore little if any relevance to the elucidation of the effects of pretraining intratask interference on PA performance. Since the correction procedure serves to reduce overall amount of intratask interference and to put this primarily under the control of the subject rather than the experimenter, it was abandoned in our subsequent research. It is worth noting, however, that correction as compared with noncorrection PA procedures may well provide a useful vehicle for systematically varying amount and type of intratask interference. Thus, since we soon will have access to computerized automation of various types of correction procedures, this variable may play a focal role in our future research on this problem.

marily intertask interference with PA performance from incorrect pretraining alternatives similar to correct PA items. Further support for this interpretation derived from our systematic variation also of length of the PA list (8 or 12 pairs), and number of these pairs constituted from pretrained items (0, 4, or 8 pairs). The consequent inclusion of both unmixed and mixed PA lists, with varying proportions of pretrained and nonpretrained pairs within the latter, further demonstrated that an "isolation" effect served to facilitate PA performance on whichever type of pair was in the minority within a mixed PA list (see also Battig, 1966c). When these latter confoundings were taken into account, it became possible to reinterpret the pattern of transfer results as showing that increased intratask interference during pretraining had represented a source of facilitation in subsequent PA performance on pretrained items. Further supportive evidence derived from the findings that 24-hr PA retention was actually somewhat better for 12- than 8-pair lists. The aforementioned confounding effects, however, clearly had been more powerful than the effects that the experiment had been designed to test. Thus we had clearly failed in our purpose of providing a direct demonstration that intratask interference produces intertask facilitation.

The Battig–Berry results contrasted sharply with our previous experiments showing marked PA facilitation on pairs of items pretrained on an MCR task where the correct alternative(s) had to be selected from among several highly similar incorrect alternatives (Battig *et al.*, 1965; Spera, 1963; Thompson, 1964). The consistency of the lack of PA facilitation over the several variable conditions of this experiment further questioned seriously the generality, and perhaps even the validity, of the previous findings. Consequently, our next experiment (Battig, 1966b) represented a replication of the high-intratask-interference MCR conditions employed by Battig and Berry (1966), along with those used by Thompson (1964) showing large amounts of PA facilitation. Also included in this experiment were some additional conditions designed to shed further light on the reasons for the discrepant results. The most plausible reason appeared to be differences in learning material. Battig and Berry (1966) had used CVC trigams, whereas Thompson's (1964) materials were CVCCVC disyllables (e.g., ZAKVEB). Thus, in addition to replicating both types of materials, Battig (1966b) included combinations of the two types, e.g., CVCs being used in MCR pretraining with CVCCVCs on the PA task and vice versa. For conditions employing CVCCVCs on the MCR task, another variable was whether the two CVCs constituting these items were paired in the same way or differently in the PA list. Either all PA pairings were identical to MCR pairings, all were changed from the MCR to PA task, or half stayed the same and half were changed.

The results replicated the Battig–Berry finding of no PA facilitation when CVCs were used both on the MCR and PA tasks. However, when CVCCVCs were used on either the MCR or PA tasks, or on both tasks, marked PA facilitation was obtained for pairs of items appearing on the MCR task. Thus the Battig–Berry failure to obtain facilitation clearly reflected their use of CVC items, which produced counteracting interference due to MCR learning of incorrect alternatives similar to the CVCs used on the PA task. Minimization of the latter contamination through the use of CVCCVC materials apparently permitted the intertask facilitation produced by MCR pretraining to show up clearly in PA performance.

However, another important finding in this experiment kept us from making the mistake of accepting MCR pretraining with CVCCVC materials as a satisfactory technique for further research on this problem. When CVCCVCs were used on both tasks, PA facilitation was no less when the pairings of their constituent CVCs were changed from the MCR to the PA task than when these pairings were identical for both tasks. This indicated that the high difficulty of the CVCCVC items had also contributed substantially to the observed facilitation, perhaps more so than the greater intratask interference produced during the MCR task with such materials. More specifically, it appeared that a list of 12 pairs of CVCCVC items was virtually impossible to learn, and that *S*s typically approached it by selecting and trying to learn only those pairs including CVCs from the MCR task, while ignoring the remaining pairs. Thus the experiment not only clarified the discrepant previous results but offered a compelling argument against the use of more complex as well as simpler types of items in future research. Consequently, the MCR pretraining procedure was abandoned, making it necessary to try another, hopefully more suitable technique for varying intratask interference as our next step in investigating the problem.

DOUBLE-FUNCTION LISTS AND EXPERIMENT GIANT

Since the major problem with the MCR procedure appeared to be the carryover of the irrelevant learning involved therein to interfere with subsequent transfer and/or retention performance, the principal criterion for selecting its successor was that this source of contamination be eliminated. Double-function lists appeared especially promising for this purpose inasmuch as such lists possess the unique feature of producing substantially more intratask interference with only half as many constituent items as compared with the typical single-function list. More specifically, the increased intratask interference within double-function PA lists results from the use of each item twice, as a stimulus term for one pair and as a response term for an entirely different pair.

Hindsight indicates that our goal of demonstrating directly that intratask interference leads to intertask facilitation would have been much better served if we had begun with a simple experiment wherein pairs of items learned under double- as compared with single-function conditions were compared as to subsequent transfer to single-function second lists. This alone appeared sufficient to eliminate both the carryover of irrelevant learning under high intratask-interference conditions to contaminate transfer performance and the excessive difficulty of the transfer list so that apparent facilitation could be attributed to *S*s selection of particular pairs to learn.

Such transfer conditions did in fact represent an integral part of our next experiment, but far from all of it. Instead, they became only a small part of Experiment Giant, including seven major independent variables, 320 different experimental conditions, and 1920 subjects. For several years we had been claiming that complex psychological phenomena could best be studied with complex multifactor experiments (Battig, 1962), a position solidified by our previous two MCR experiments (Battig, 1966b; Battig & Berry, 1966). What otherwise might have been completely uninterpretable results in these experiments made sense largely because other nonfocal variables and experimental conditions were included therein. Moreover, had Battig and Berry systematically varied type of learning materials, the Battig (1966b) follow-up would have been unnecessary.

Thus our commitment to increasingly complex multifactor designs as the road to resolution of our (and psychology's) research problems had developed to the point where our contribution to the 1966 Kentucky conference included the following: "The most efficient possible experimental approach (although an impractical one without the cooperation of a large number of PA researchers) would probably represent a single mammoth investigation involving the simultaneous manipulation of all PA task and procedural variables known or suspected to have any effect whatever within any kind of PA learning task" (Battig, 1968, p. 167).[3]

Thus Experiment Giant grew out of our increasing commitment to large-scale multifactorial experiments combined with our desire not to

[3] The generally skeptical reaction of other researchers to this suggestion is typified by Tulving and Madigan's (1970 Annual Review, p. 449) facetious characterization of it as the ICBM (Intercontinental Battig Method).

overly commit ourselves to only one of the many possible sources of variation in intratask interference, as we had in the MCR research described previously. Consequently, Experiment Giant included double- vs. single-function lists along with the following other means of varying intratask interference: (1) intralist formal similarity (high vs. low), (2) constituent items which were alike (homogeneous) or widely different (heterogeneous) in meaningfulness, (3) constant or varied serial orders of presentation, and (4) fast (3-sec) or slow (5-sec) presentation rates. In addition, transfer from both single-function and double-function verbal-discrimination pretraining to PA performance was also evaluated and compared.

Although data collection for Experiment Giant began early in 1966, it was not completed until shortly before we moved from Maryland to Colorado in June 1967. A foulup within the National Institute of Child Health and Human Development prevented immediate transfer to Colorado of the grant supporting this research, thus depriving us of the services of Shu-jen Huang (the graduate assistant who had so effectively handled the complex data-collection process) until June 1968. Therefore, it was over two-and-one-half years after the experiment was begun before it became apparent that the double-function manipulations of intratask interference had been even less successful in directly demonstrating intertask facilitation than had our previous attempts using MCR pretraining. The results indicated instead that the chained structure (e.g., A-B, B-C, C-D, D-A) of our double-function lists had represented a very important cue used by *S*s in learning these lists. Thus, since this chained structure was necessarily eliminated within single-function second lists, such conditions actually showed less second-list facilitation than any other combination of single- or double-functon first and second lists. Unfortunately, this contamination proved to be especially operative under the high intratask-interference conditions of the other variables. To make matters worse, there was no evidence whatever for PA facilitation produced by double-function verbal-discrimination pretraining, even when the latter pairings were identical to those used in the PA transfer task. Consequently, Experiment Giant proved to be almost totally useless as a test of intratask interference as a source of intertask facilitation. Its many substantial empirical and theoretical contributions proved highly relevant to a wide variety of other current issues in PA-learning research, however, as demonstrated in the long-delayed completed written report of Experiment Giant (Battig & Huang, 1971).

More influential for our subsequent research were some further problems complicating data tabulation and analysis for Experiment Giant. Dr. Huang's replacement during 1967–1968 contributed primarily an amazing variety of erroneous data tabulations, the last of which were not discovered and corrected until almost two years thereafter. The most critical of these tabulation errors misled us for some months into believing that the data had actually shown maximal facilitation under conditions with double-function first lists followed by single-function second lists. Before this error was discovered, we had already begun another experiment using double-function lists as the intratask-interference–producing variable, as described later in this section.

CONTINGENT-TRIAD–DISCRIMINATION PRETRAINING

So as not to be completely dependent upon Experiment Giant, during 1967–1968 we also tried another technique for producing high intratask interference during a pretraining task. Like double-function lists, this technique too eliminated a major difficulty with our original MCR procedure by producing substantial increases in intratask interference with a small number of different items. The technique was an elaboration of one introduced as a pretraining familiarization procedure in one of our serial-learning experiments (Battig & Young, 1969), and can best be described as involving contingent-triad discrimination (CTD). In this CTD task, eighteen partially overlapping different combinations of three from a total set of six CVC syllables were presented on each CTD trial. Each of the six CVCs appeared in nine of the eighteen triads, each time with a different combination of two other CVCs; e.g.

DAF TOC
TOC VEB, KIV VUT

The *Ss'* task was to select the arbitrarily designated "correct" CVC within each triad. Each of the six CVCs was correct for three of the nine triads in which it appeared, and was presented in a different one of the three triangular spatial positions each time it was correct. Thus a correct response required that *S* pay equal attention to all three CVCs within each triad, with each CVC also being "associated" equally often with each of the five other CVCs.

In the first experiment, 5 successive CTD trials were given, involving forty-five separate presentations of each CVC. That this CTD task in fact involved extremely high intratask interference was indicated by only slightly above-chance performance with no improvement whatever over the 5 trials. Intertask facilitation was evaluated in terms of subsequent PA performance on 3 pairs constituted from the 6 CTD items. These were included in a mixed PA list containing also "new" pairs of CVCs not seen previously along with pairs pretrained by an "associative rating" (AR) procedure shown previously to produce substantial facilitation of subsequent PA performance (Burke & Battig, 1968). The PA pairs representing each of the three types (CTD, AR, and New pairs) were, of course, counterbalanced across *S*s.

The results of this first CTD experiment are best described as suggestive but inconclusive enough to lead to two further experiments. Mean total errors for CTD pairs (8.93) were only insignificantly less than for AR (9.67) or New pairs (9.93). This nonsignificance proved attributable to the extremely deviant performance of 2 of the 30 *S*s, each of whom made over three times as many errors on AR or CTD pairs as on the other two types. Exclusion of these 2 deviant *S*s produced a marginally significant superiority of CTD over New pairs (although AR pairs still did not differ significantly from either). Moreover, a subsequent PA written-recall test showed a marginally significant superiority in number of individual CVCs recalled correctly for CTD (4.39) over AR (4.10) and New pairs (3.81).

Thus the experiment was replicated, differing only in its use of fewer (3) CTD trials and a different experimenter. These results showed PA errors to be insignificantly greater on CTD (8.20) than either AR (7.40) or New pairs (7.70), with virtually identical post-PA recall for all three types. Clearly, the suggestion from the first experiment of greater PA facilitation for high-intratask-interference CTD items had been illusory. Apparently, the CTD-task requirements had been too discrepant from PA tasks for there to be any substantial transfer between them.

Rather than giving up on the CTD procedure at this point, however, the latter interpretation led us to try once again, this time substituting for the PA-transfer task a free-recall task that presumably differed less from the CTD task requirements. Instead of a PA list, CTD and AR pretraining were followed instead by an 18-item free-recall list including 6 CDT and 6 AR items along with 6 New items. Like its PA predecessor, however, these results showed virtually identical numbers of free-recall errors for CTD (13.60) and New items (13.70), with a nonsignificant superiority to both shown for AR items (11.90). Fortunately (unlike its two predecessors), an additional free-recall variable manipulation bearing no relevance to the present problem provided sufficiently valuable information concerning the PRNI (priority of recall of newly learned items) effect in free recall to merit publication (Battig & Slaybaugh, 1969).

TRANSFER OF RULE LEARNING

The completion of this last experiment in the summer of 1968 came at the time that the analysis of Experiment Giant had reached the point where its failure to directly test and demonstrate intratask interference as a source of intertask facilitation also first became evident. Thus a radically different approach to the problem appeared to be called for. Although it was far from clear just what kind of approach this should be, we decided to focus more directly upon what *S*s might be doing under conditions of intratask interference that could lead to subsequent intertask facilitation. We had previously argued that this was the role played by complex "coding" or "grouping" processes in PA learning (Battig, 1966d). Moreover, it appeared to have been the operation of such processes (e.g., the use of structural relationships within double-function lists, selection of CVCCVC pairs containing pretrained MCR items to concentrate on learning) that was most clearly indicated to occur during learning under high intratask interference in our previous experiments. Consequently, we decided to try to observe and measure directly such processes under conditions of varying intratask interference, and to ascertain whether their use was demonstrably greater when intratask interference was high.

Our approach to this problem by building in a subtle but consistent "rule" relating the two members within each PA pair reflected primarily the joint influence of Lyle Bourne (our colleague at Colorado) and Willard Runquist (who had spent part of the summer of 1968 working with us on Experiment Giant). Both had experienced considerable success in the analysis of the very different research areas of conceptual behavior (e.g., Bourne, 1970) and stimulus simularity in PA learning (Runquist & Joinson, 1968), on the basis of relational "rules" used and/or learned by *S*s. Their work suggested to us that with high intratask interference, it might be *S*s' increased efforts to find and apply such rules to one or more items that produced any subsequent intertask facilitation. Consequently, in our next experiment we attempted to demonstrate this, using partially double-function lists (which we thought would be free of the structural complications that had contaminated Experiment Giant) as our source of intratask interference.

In this experiment, 4 different groups of 12 *S*s each learned a different PA list to a criterion of 40 total correct responses summed over all trials. The 8-pair list for the critical High-R group included 4 CVCs used twice as stimulus and response terms for different pairs, with a consistent rule whereby the first and third response-term letters alphabetically followed the corresponding letters of the paired stimulus term (e.g., SOC-TID, RAB-SOC). This alphabetical following rule also applied to the Low-R group, but their list was entirely single-function (e.g., SIF-TOG, RAB-SOC). By re-pairing the CVCs used in the High-R and Low-R lists, this alphabetical rule was eliminated for otherwise comparable High-NR (e.g., CEL-TID, KOW-CEL) and Low-NR groups (e.g., SIF-MEW, KOW-CEL).

All groups subsequently learned the same 8-pair PA transfer list, as did a fifth "control" group with no prior PA learning. To measure learning and usage of the alphabetical-following rule, two transfer pairs (RAB-SOC and MUR-NOS) were taken from both the High-R and Low-R lists, whereas two others (FAK-GUL and VAR-WIS) followed this rule but were new pairs for all *S*s. The other 4 transfer pairs did not follow this rule, two having appeared in both High-NR and Low-NR lists (KOW-CEL and BIK-LEX) with the other two being new pairs (DUB-PIX and HEW-TUC).

Contrary to expectation, the High-R group performed no better on either Old-R or New-R transfer pairs than did the Low-R group. Post hoc examination of the data and structure of the partially double-function lists suggested this to reflect our unintended provision within both High lists of another rule more potent than the alphabetical-following rule. Since 4 CVCs were used twice, these High lists could readily be subdivided into four sets of 2 pairs containing a common item, which would provide a highly effective means of coping with the double-function–produced interference. Such a strategy, however, could only interfere with transfer performance since the transfer list was strictly single function, including at most 1 pair from each of the four first-list groupings.

Before discarding the rule-learning approach, we decided to try again with a new technique for varying intratask interference in terms of the sequence in which the materials were presented. Our High-Interference condition involved a sequence wherein each PA pair was both preceded and followed immediately by two stimulus terms different from the one for that pair, with 8 alternating other pairs and stimuli always intervening between each pair presentation and its stimulus term alone for response-term recall. The Low-Interference condition followed the typical PA recall procedure used in all previous experiments. The Low-R and Low-NR lists from the previous experiment were each used for half of the *S*s with the High- and Low-Interference sequences. The procedure otherwise was closely comparable to the previous experiment, with the same transfer list used for all 4 groups (as well as the fifth "control" group).

The results, however, actually showed insignificantly worse transfer performance on both Old-R and New-R pairs for the High-R than the Low-R group. Since overall transfer performance was actually worse for both High-Interference groups, it appeared that the shift to the transfer list (presented by the low-interference recall method for all groups) had interfered generally with their transfer performance, thereby probably eliminating any carryover of the alphabetical-following rule to the transfer list. Clearly, the rule-learning approach involved methodological complications of its own and was not the end of our search for a satisfactory means of demonstrating intratask interference as a source of intertask facilitation.

Support from Other Laboratories

Four years of repeated failures to demonstrate directly intratask interference as a significant source of intertask facilitation normally would have caused us to question at least the generality of this relationship, if not its basic validity. That this did not happen can be attributed largely to results obtained in several other laboratories showing what we interpreted as clear-cut evidence for intratask interference as producing facilitated retention or transfer (although such an interpretation typically was not considered by the researchers themselves).

Such evidence was not unknown to us prior to this time (e.g., Postman, 1963, p. 41; Underwood & Erlebacher, 1965), but most immediately influential was the first of a series by Nancy Anderson (our colleague at Maryland) done in England in 1965. Anderson found better delayed serial recall of lists of consonants of high (68%) than low acoustic similarity (41%), even though the latter had shown better immediate recall. Unfortunately, our planned subsequent collaboration on this research was precluded by our move to Colorado. Thus by the time these results were published, Anderson (1969) became persuaded that they were relevant only to the demonstration of a basic distinction between short- and long-term retention and made no mention of their consistency with our work. Baddeley (1966) presented similar results and conclusions based on retention of acoustically similar words rather than letters. Using more elaborate between- and within-list acoustic-similarity variations in stimulus and response words of PA lists, Dallett (1966, Experiment II) also reported better subsequent retention for high (42.9%)

than low similarity (16.7%). More recently, similar findings have been reported for both formal and associative similarity within PA lists. Joinson and Runquist (1968) obtained better retention for high (66.0%) than low formal similarity (45.0%) within subsets of two stimulus terms, although only with moderate acquisition levels. Underwood and Ekstrand (1968, Experiment I) showed superior retention for lists wherein two associatively related words occurred in different pairs (72.8%) than for low-similarity lists (53.0%), a result consistent with the work of Johnson (1964) and subsequently confirmed by Postman (1971). Only Dallett and Runquist, however, even mentioned interpretations compatible with ours.

Several other investigators reported more convincing replications and/or extensions of some of our work described in the two preceding sections. Especially noteworthy here was Young and Thomson's (1967) demonstration of superior retention following acquisition of double- (87.5%) than single-function PA lists (77.2%), exactly the results that our intertask transfer comparisons had consistently failed to show. Ceraso's (1967) finding of better retention for longer (52.2%) than shorter PA lists (37.5%) was consistent with the results of Battig and Berry (1966), whereas Zechmeister, Biers, and Underwood's (1969) experiments extended the Schild–Battig (1966) finding of better retention for bidirectional (74.5%) than unidirectional PA lists (48.0%). Although we had discussed our work at length with both Young and Underwood but not with Ceraso, only the latter even suggested an interpretation similar to ours.

Also deserving of mention here is Zavortink and Keppel's (1968) demonstration of superior retention of serial lists presented with different starting and ending points on each trial (83.3%) as compared with the usual serial-learning procedure (68.5%). So is the frequently reported finding that early PA acquisition is better if a given pair is repeated in immediate succession than if several other items intervene between successive repetitions, but subsequent retention is superior for the latter over the former conditions (e.g., Bregman, 1967; Greeno, 1964; Peterson, Hillner, & Saltzman, 1962).

Our laboratory too contributed to this wealth of evidence from experiments concerned with other problems through Shu-jen Huang's 1968 Ph.D. dissertation on the role of numerical cues in serial learning (Huang & Battig, 1969). She found that under conditions where serial learning was significantly retarded by the added numerical cues, subsequent serial recall and designation of serial positions was actually superior to easier serial-learning conditions.

The experiments reviewed here showed superior retention in PA tasks following increased intratask interference produced by (1) acoustic, formal, and associative intralist similarity, (2) double-function lists, and (3) longer lists, (4) bidirectional learning, and (5) spaced repetition conditions. In serial learning, superior retention or transfer resulted from intratask interference produced by (1) varied starting points and (2) incompatible numerical cues. Thus, despite our consistent failures to demonstrate the phenomenon directly, we remained convinced that we were dealing with a real phenomenon of considerable generality and importance. Mainly because other researchers not only failed to share our conviction but typically refused even to consider it as an interpretation of their results, we still felt impelled to provide a direct and unimpeachable demonstration of intratask interference as a source of facilitated transfer and/or retention. How we finally accomplished this will be described in the following section.

Direct Evidence from Our Laboratory

It was not until the spring of 1969 that we finally pinpointed the probable variable distinguishing successful indirect demonstrations from unsuccessful attempts at direct demonstrations as reflecting the concern of the former with direct retention rather than transfer measures. Thus our next effort involved intratask interference produced by sequential manipulations representing a less extreme modification of the technique employed in the last of our "rule-learning" experiments, but without any "rules" and with a series of retention measures rather than a subsequent transfer task.

The sequential variations were closely comparable to those employed previously by Jones and Bourne (1964, Experiment IV). Using 8-pair PA lists, they had found PA performance to be significantly retarded if 4 of the stimulus terms were presented alone in succession followed in the same order by these same 4 pairs, as compared either with standard PA anticipation and recall procedures or the modification just discussed with blocks of 2 instead of 4 stimuli and pairs. By using 12- instead of 8-pair lists, we added another modified condition involving blocks of 6 items. Thus the experiment included five different sequences, indicated symbolically as follows:

Grp 12 S1-S2-S3-S4-S5-S6-S7-S8-S9-S10-S11-S12-P1-P2-P3-P4-P5-P6-P7-P8-P9-P10-P11-P12
Grp 6 S1-S2-S3-S4-S5-S6-P1-P2-P3-P4-P5-P6-S7-S8-S9-S10-S11-S12-P7-P8-P9-P10-P11-P12

Grp 4 S1-S2-S3-S4-P1-P2-P3-P4-S5-S6-S7-S8-P5-P6-P7-P8-S9-S10-S11-S12-P9-P10-P11-P12
Grp 2 S1-S2-P1-P2-S3-S4-P3-P4-S5-S6-P5-P6-S7-S8-P7-P8-S9-S10-P9-P10-S11-S12-P11-P12
Grp 1 S1-P1-S2-P2-S3-P3-S4-P4-S5-P5-S6-P6-S7-P7-S8-P8-S9-P9-S10-P10-S11-P11-S12-P12

Groups 1 and 12 represent the standard PA anticipation and recall procedures, whereas the numerical designations for the other 3 groups indicate the size of the blocks (S standing for stimulus terms alone and P for stimulus–response pairs) in which the two types of items (all high-meaningful nonword CVCs) were presented. There were 20 *S*s in each of the 5 groups, all learning the same list to the same criterion of 60 total correct responses summed over all trials. Immediately after the criterion trial, each *S* was given the same series of three retention tests. The first of these was a 12×2 matrix with the two columns labeled "left-hand members" and "right-hand members," with *S*s instructed to write down as many pairs and individual CVCs as they could remember. Next came a recognition test, consisting of the 24 CVCs from the list along with 70 other CVCs similar to them presented in alphabetical order, with *S*s instructed to designate those CVCs that had just been learned. Finally, an associative-matching test was given. The 12 stimulus and 12 response CVCs were provided in separate columns in alphabetical order, and *S* was asked to write on a blank line next to each stimulus CVC the response CVC paired with it.

The 5 groups differed significantly in mean total errors to criterion, with group 12 showing the best performance (90.5 errors), followed in order by groups 6 (102.2), 4 (111.0), 1 (123.0), and 2 (139.5). Number of correctly recalled responses proved to be the only retention measure showing significant group differences, with groups 1 (7.85) and 2 (7.25) showing the best retention and group 12 the worst (5.80), whereas groups 6 (6.75) and 4 (6.35) were intermediate between them. Even though rather small in magnitude and limited to just one of the three retention measures, retention clearly increased, although acquisition difficulty also had increased systematically with decreasing block size. Thus we finally had succeeded in demonstrating unequivocally better retention with increasing intratask interference in an experiment in which this was what we were trying to do.

An even more important contribution of this experiment may have been its introduction of the issue of intratask interference as facilitating retention to James Pellegrino, one of the three experimenters running the *S*s therein. Following its conclusion, Pellegrino decided to investigate the phenomenon with a classic retroactive-interference paradigm, wherein controlled variations could be introduced in interference within the interpolated as well as the original learning task (Pellegrino, 1972). His source of intratask interference was high formal similarity (letter overlap) among CVC-word responses. Eight experimental groups of 12 *S*s each represented all possible combinations of high and low intralist response similarity (1) within the first PA list and (2) in the second PA list, along with (3) A-B, A-D and A-B, C-D relationships between the first and second lists, e.g., whether or not the stimulus terms in addition to the response terms were different for the two lists. To avoid confounding of stimulus with response similarity conditions, the stimuli within all lists were of a medium level of intralist similarity intermediate between the high and low response intralist-similarity conditions. Interlist stimulus and response similarity was both low and approximately equal whenever different items were used for the two lists. The first lists for all groups were learned via the standard PA recall procedure to the same criterion of 1 perfect trial, followed immediately by the second lists to a criterion of 60 total correct responses. Second-list learning was followed immediately by a series of four successive retention tests, including the three that had been used in the previous experiment along with the "modified modified free recall" (MMFR) test typically used as the basic measure of retroactive interference (Keppel, 1968).

More specifically, all *S*s were first asked to write down as many of the pairs or individual CVCs from both lists as they could recall (uncued free recall). Next, the MMFR test provided each of the stimulus words from both lists, and *S*s were asked to write down in a blank space adjacent to each stimulus word the response word paired with it. This was followed by a recognition test, wherein *S*s were asked to identify the response words for both lists from an alphabetical list of 135 similar CVC words. Finally, the associative-matching test presented all stimulus and response words from both lists, and *S*s were asked to pair these together correctly.

Two additional control groups of 12 *S*s each were also run, learning only the high- or low-similarity first lists. Instead of the second list, these *S*s worked for an equivalent amount of time on an irrelevant (pyramid puzzle) task, followed by the same series of four retention tests for the first list only. Except for the elimination of second-list learning, the control groups were otherwise identical to the high- and low-similarity first-list experimental conditions. Within and across conditions, first and second lists were completely counterbalanced so that for all groups with the same similarity conditions for a given list, exactly the same lists were used equally often.

First-list high- and low-similarity acquisition differences were surpris-

TABLE 1

Mean Percent Retention on MMFR Task

List-1 similarity	A-B, A-D Paradigm, list-2 similarity			A-B, C-D Paradigm, list-2 similarity			Control
	High	Low	Total	High	Low	Total	
High	78.42	87.50	82.95	95.17	94.42	94.79	96.50
Low	63.17	72.92	68.04	84.67	91.67	88.17	96.50
Total	70.79	80.21	75.50	89.92	93.04	91.48	

ingly small and reached significance only for later trials as indexed by percent of occasions after the first correct response on which errors were made (percent after errors). This meant that any retention differences could not be attributed to greater practice for high- than low-similarity first lists because these did not differ significantly in number of acquisition trials. Differences favoring low- over high-similarity second-list acquisition were somewhat larger in magnitude, reaching significance for all performance measures, but again were greater on later than on initial second-list trials. First-list similarity had little if any effect on second-list performance, thus confirming our previous impression that intertask transfer is relatively insensitive to effects produced by intratask interference during initial acquisition.

Pellegrino's retention results, however, provided far and away the most impressive evidence yet obtained for facilitation produced by intratask interference during initial acquisition. As shown in Table 1, with the MMFR measure there was markedly superior retention for high- over low-similarity first lists following either A-D or C-D second lists. As shown in the last column, however, retention was identical and very high for both high- and low-similarity control groups. Likewise, second-list high- and low-similarity MMFR differences were very small. Thus controlled interpolated learning appears to be the key to getting sizable facilitation of retention following original acquisition under high intratask interference, and the very small effects indicated for response learning only in our previous experiment can be attributed to the lack of any interpolated learning therein.[4]

[4] A recently published experiment by Wright and Gescheider (1970) confirms this interpretation. They used sequential variations very similar to ours, but with alternation of pairs with other stimulus terms as in our earlier rule-learning experiment. All their *S*s learned two successive nonoverlapping PA lists (similar to Pellegrino's A-B, C-D conditions), with retention for both lists measured only after second-list learning. Under these conditions, all three retention measures (backward stimulus recall, stimulus recognition, and associative matching) showed a marked superiority for high-intratask-interference conditions.

The last row of Table 1 shows that intratask interference within the interpolated A-D or C-D list also significantly affected first-list retention, although negatively rather than positively. Thus not only did high intratask interference in the first list lead to better retention but high intratask interference in the second list significantly reduced first-list retention. Consequently, there was nearly three times as much forgetting of the low-similarity first list when the second-list was of high intralist similarity than was observed for the high-similarity first list with a low-similarity second list.

The poorer first-list retention following high- than low-similarity second lists was found only for the MMFR measure shown in Table 1. Both the uncued-free-recall and recognition retention measures, however, also showed superior retention for high-similarity first lists. Because the magnitude of this effect differed systematically across these tests, comparisons between them also give some information as to just what component PA processes contributed to the retention differences (Battig, 1968). Four types of PA processes can be distinguished on the basis of their differential involvement in the four types of retention tests. These are stimulus learning (S), response learning (R), response differentiation (D), and stimulus–response associative learning (A). All four processes are involved in the first (uncued free-recall) retention test. Because the stimuli were provided to *S* for the second MMFR test, this excludes stimulus (S) learning and involves only the other three processes. The third recognition test required *S* to identify only responses that are provided for him. Thus response differentiation (D) is required but not stimulus or response learning nor associative learning. Finally, the last associative-matching test provides *S* with both stimulus and response terms, thus eliminating stimulus learning, response learning, and response differentiation processes, and leaving only the stimulus–response associative (A) process.

The results in Table 2 indicate that high response similarity in the first

TABLE 2
Mean Percent Retention on Each Task

Measure	Processes [a]	High	Low	Difference
Uncued free recall	S, R, D, A	73.73	49.77	23.96
MMFR	R, D, A	88.88	78.10	10.77
Recognition	D	86.96	81.38	5.58
Associative matching	A	95.81	95.10	0.71

[a] S, stimulus learning; R, response learning; D, response differentiation; A, stimulus–response associative learning.

list had produced not only better response learning and differentiation but also greater stimulus learning. The latter is indicated by the fact that the uncued free-recall difference favoring high over low similarity was over twice as large as was the difference on the MMFR test, which differed from uncued free recall only in that stimulus factors were not involved. That uncued recall of stimulus terms was markedly superior for high- over low-similarity first lists further supports this conclusion. Thus, even though the stimuli were identical for high- and low-similarity lists, high response similarity clearly produced greater stimulus learning.

Less direct and conclusive is the evidence in Table 2 indicating that both response learning and response differentiation were greater for high- than low-similarity responses but that stimulus–response associations were not. The significantly superior response recognition for high- over low-similarity first lists shows this most directly with regard to response differentiation. And since these differences for associative matching were very small and nonsignificant, this indicates either that the associative stage was not affected or that this test was insensitive to such effects. That the latter cannot be ruled out is suggested by the extremely high associative-matching performance by the low-similarity groups such that there is little if any "room" for the high-similarity groups to perform any better. In any event, the doubling of the high-low differences for MMFR as compared with recognition measures clearly reflects stronger response learning within high-similarity lists.

Since the four tests were always given in the same order, the actual figures in Table 2 may be influenced by *S*s' performance on preceding tests, as well as by the processes involved therein. The sequence of tests, however, provided that each successive test presented most if not all of the relevant information available from *S*s' performance on the previous test(s), so this contamination probably is not serious. Even if it were, there appears no reason to expect such effects to be different for high- and low-similarity lists, so it is unlikely that the high-low differences of primary concern here would be seriously contaminated thereby.

Pellegrino's experiment also contributed many other interesting results (e.g., that uncued free recall is significantly better for the A-B, A-D than the A-B, C-D paradigm, contrary to the MMFR results in Table 1), which are described in detail elsewhere (Pellegrino, 1972). For present purposes, what is most important about his results is their convincing demonstration that facilitation produced by intratask interference during initial acquisition is most strongly shown in measures of first-list retention rather than intertask transfer, when controlled interpolated learning occurs during the retention interval. That facilitated retention of high-similarity first lists was found equally for A-B, A-D and A-B, C-D paradigms (see Table 1) further tells us that the interpolated learning need not be related to the list to be tested for retention. This is important because further research on this question could become unduly complicated if the two tasks had to be interrelated in ways that might cause interpolated learning to carry over to influence the retention of the initial task, as we found in our early experiments to be true of the MCR procedure (Battig & Berry, 1966).

Pellegrino's results should not, however, be taken to indicate that transfer performance cannot be facilitated significantly following acquisition under high intratask interference. Such facilitated transfer has been shown especially with high intralist stimulus similarity (e.g., Ellis, 1970). A particularly impressive demonstration thereof comes from Judith Pagel's Ph.D. dissertation research at Colorado (Pagel, 1971), on which data collection was completed during the writing of the present report. This experiment involved variations in intralist similarity (high or low) of CVC stimuli very much like those of Pellegrino (1972) for response similarity, except that both lists were always at the same similarity level. Pagel's transfer paradigms, however, both involved identical responses (digits 1–7) for both lists, one (the A-B, A-Br paradigm) involving also the same stimuli but different pairings and the other (A-B, C-B paradigm) involving different stimuli for the two lists.

Despite her usage of high-meaningful digit responses maximally conducive to negative transfer, Pagel's results actually showed significantly fewer trials to criterion on her second (transfer) list than her first list under high-similarity conditions, even for her A-Br paradigm. Under this paradigm, mean percentage transfer with high-similarity stimuli was +10.3%, as contrasted with −10.3% with low-similarity stimuli. This difference between high- and low-similarity obtained for both high- and low-meaningful stimuli (another variable in this experiment). Thus learning of CVC stimuli under high-similarity conditions had clearly facilitated transfer performance when these same CVCs were paired differently with the same digit responses, even though these are the conditions usually leading to maximum negative transfer (Battig, 1966a).

Although not directly designed to test this principle, one other just-completed experiment deserves mention here because it indicates the facilitative effects of intratask interference on subsequent retention to operate under conditions more characteristic of verbal learning tasks outside the experimental laboratory. This experiment was actually carried out as an undergraduate classroom exercise designed to provide basic data relevant to acquisition, retention, and transfer phases of verbal learning. The learning materials were a set of forty words developed by Patricia Lauer for her master's thesis (Lauer, 1971). These included five members of each of eight conceptual categories and also five words beginning with each of eight different first letters, thus permitting either conceptual or alphabetical bases for organization. After writing down the first forty words they could think of (to provide a baseline against which to evaluate subsequent learning), each *S* was given a list of these forty words and instructed to arrange them into nonoverlapping groups in any way (s) they could, being provided with two columns labeled "first groupings" and "second groupings" in which to write their groupings of the words. Three different groups of *S*s had the forty words either (1) blocked by category, so that all five members of each category appeared together, (2) blocked by first letter, so that all five words with the same first letter appeared together, or (3) presented randomly, so that words from each category and with each first letter were maximally spread throughout the list. Immediately after the grouping task, all *S*s were asked to write down as many of the forty words as they could. A week later, all *S*s were again asked for written recall of these words, followed immediately by a recognition test including the original forty words along with twenty incorrect words from the same eight categories and with the same eight first letters.

These results, along with Lauer's (1971), showed categorical organization to be far more prevalent with this list than alphabetical organization. Not only did most *S*s group words categorically far more easily than alphabetically, but categorical clustering during recall was over five times as great as alphabetical clustering. All present retention measures, however, showed significantly poorer performance by the group for which the words had been blocked by category than for the other two (alphabetical and random) groups. Mean percent immediate recall was 54.4% for the categorical group as compared with 68.5 and 71.3% for the random and alphabetical groups. Differences of similar magnitude were shown for the other retention measures, which additionally showed significantly greater recall and recognition of incorrect words for the categorical groups. That this inferior retention by the categorical groups could be attributed solely to the blocking of the words by category (with consequent lesser interference within the grouping task) was indicated by the virtually identical performance of this to the other two groups in a subsequent free-recall task given under identical conditions to all *S*s. Lauer (1971) obtained further evidence that the additional interference produced by ordering the words alphabetically substantially facilitates subsequent retention or transfer, finding more transfer on a subsequent list of new items if alphabetical rather than categorical cues had been presented during a final written-recall trial on the previous list.

Conclusions and Implications

On the basis of the evidence described in the preceding sections, it appears that the facilitation of retention produced by interference within the acquisition task is of sufficient magnitude and generality to be of considerable theoretical as well as practical significance. Even our several failures to obtain supporting evidence for this phenomenon typically showed no significant difference, rather than the retardation of transfer and/or retention performance produced by intratask interference during acquisition that would have been expected from previous analyses (e.g., Gibson, 1940). Moreover, our unsuccessful experiments all involved identifiable special features or confoundings inherent in the particular experimental manipulations and/or types of transfer tasks employed such that any additional learning produced by intratask interference failed to carry over sufficiently to be demonstrated in subsequent performance measures. Especially Pellegrino's (1972) results suggest that the range of processes involved in the facilitation produced by intratask interference is quite general rather than limited to any single type of process. Our present impression (admittedly based on insufficient data) is that the *S* is likely to invoke any additional learning processes that he can to overcome intratask interference during acquisition, and that subsequent facilitation results to the extent that this additional learning makes the material more resistant also to whatever factors would cause it subsequently to be forgotten. This suggests that individual *S*s may differ substantially and often idiosyncratically as to how they try to overcome intratask interference so that our present research is focused primarily on the development of methods for identifying and assessing the magnitude of differences both between and within individuals as to the learning process (es) employed under conditions of high intratask interference during acquisition.

An important qualification is that our research to date has dealt exclusively with sources of interference intrinsic to the learning task, materials, and procedure. There is no evidence, so far as we know, to suggest that sources of extrinsic interference irrelevant to the learning task itself also operate to facilitate subsequent retention and/or transfer, although that possibility certainly seems deserving of empirical investigation.

The present phenomenon and our interpretation of it appear generally incompatible with most prevailing theoretical formulations applied to complex human learning, as indicated by the alternative and conceptually very different interpretations favored by other investigators obtaining evidence consistent with ours (as described in the third section of the present chapter). Thus it would carry us too far afield to try herein to bridge the tremendous theoretical and conceptual gap that appears to preclude a meaningful discussion of the general theoretical implications of intratask interference as a source of subsequent facilitation. Instead, we will confine ourselves to a single example described previously (Battig, 1968) wherein we argued that the evidence responsible for rejection of the Underwood–Postman (1960) extraexperimental interference theory of retention actually is not inconsistent with the theory, and appears so only because they have ignored the facilitative effects of intratask interference. Their conditions of increased extraexperimental interference involved also concomitant increases in intratask interference so that the predicted decrease in retention produced by the former is counteracted by the facilitation of retention we have shown to be produced by the latter. Consistent with this latter interpretation is the fact that the best evidence for the Underwood–Postman theory has come from experiments where intratask interference has been eliminated by the use of single items (Turnage, 1967) or substantially reduced by using a dropout procedure (Amster, Keppel, & Meyer, 1970).

As for practical significance, it is difficult to conceive of anything more contrary to the basic assumptions underlying currently emphasized learning and educational procedures than the present evidence indicating that making the learning task more difficult may facilitate rather than retard subsequent usage of this learning. We have had even less success in convincing educational than psychological researchers of the importance of their taking this inverse relationship seriously. This is perhaps to be expected at a time when not only our educational system but our general culture as well has become increasingly predicated on the philosophy that necessary but allegedly unpleasant activities involved in learning and education should be minimized, making learning as simple and painless as possible. Thus empirically unsupported proposals such as the programmed-learning emphases upon learning through reward for correct responses, with incorrect ones eliminated by careful "programming" of the learning materials, clearly become much easier for educators to accept than anything (such as the present proposal) arguing for the importance of interference and additional learning to overcome it as the key features of an effective learning system. Unfortunately, this is true even though there is probably more empirical evidence contrary to than supporting reward for correct responses as necessary as for effective learning, and certainly no evidence anywhere nearly as wide-ranging and convincing as that offered in the present report.

In any event we find it hard to take very seriously the common criticism of basic research as being too far removed from real-life problems to contribute effectively to the solution thereof. Here is clearly a case where something of immense practical importance had developed directly from a totally basically oriented research program, and where we have become quite concerned with seeing its practical significance for education recognized and properly taken into account in the development of educational technology. In this instance, the communicative problem cannot be attributed to our inability or lack of concern for making our findings available for application to real-life problems; rather, it is because our recommendations are too discrepant from currently prevailing views concerning optimal learning conditions for their implications to receive proper serious consideration. This appears true even though the common-sense idea that one has to work hard in order to learn or accomplish anything is certainly far from new, and the present proposal that intratask interference during learning leads to facilitated transfer and/or retention really represents little if anything beyond a specialized way of formulating this basic idea.

REFERENCES

Amster, H., Keppel, G., & Meyer, A. Learning and retention of letter pairs as a function of association strength. *American Journal of Psychology,* 1970, **83**, 22–39.

Anderson, N. S. The influence of acoustic similarity on serial recall of letter sequences. *Quarterly Journal of Experimental Psychology,* 1969, **21**, 248–255.

Baddeley, A. D. The influence of acoustic and semantic similarity on long-term memory for word sequences. *Quarterly Journal of Experimental Psychology,* 1966, **18**, 302–309.

Battig, W. F. Parsimony in psychology. *Psychological Reports,* 1962, **11**, 555–572.

Battig, W. F. Procedural problems in paired-associate learning research. *Psychonomic Monograph Supplements,* 1965, **1**, No. 1.

Battig, W. F. Facilitation and interference. In E. A. Bilodeau (Ed.), *Acquisition of skill.* New York: Academic Press, 1966. Pp. 215–244. (a)

Battig, W. F. Transfer from multiple-choice recognition to paired associate performance as a function of item length. *Canadian Journal of Psychology,* 1966, **20**, 252–261. (b)

Battig, W. F. A shift from "negative" to "positive" transfer under the A-C paradigm with increased number of C-D control pairs in a mixed list. *Psychonomic Science,* 1966, **4**, 421–422. (c)

Battig, W. F. Evidence for coding processes in 'rote' paired-associate learning. *Journal of Verbal Learning and Verbal Behavior,* 1966, **5**, 177–181. (d)

Battig, W. F. Paired-associate learning. In T. R. Dixon and D. L. Horton (Eds.), *Verbal behavior and general behavior theory.* Englewood Cliffs, N.J.: Prentice-Hall, 1968. Pp. 149–171.

Battig, W. F., & Berry, J. K. Effects of number and similarity of pretraining alternatives on paired associate performance on pretrained and new items under correction and noncorrection procedures. *Journal of Experimental Psychology,* 1966, **72**, 722–730.

Battig, W. F., Brown, S. C., & Schild, M. E. Serial-position and sequential associations in serial learning. *Journal of Experimental Psychology,* 1964, **67**, 449–457.

Battig, W. F., & Huang, S. J. Experiment giant: Effect of five sources of variation in intratask interference on paired-associate learning and transfer. *Psychonomic Monograph Supplements,* 1971, 4, No. 9.

Battig, W. F., Merikle, P. M., & Schild, M. E. Anagram free-recall and recognition learning, and paired-associate transfer. *Journal of Verbal Learning and Verbal Behavior,* 1965, **4**, 44–52.

Battig, W. F., & Slaybaugh, G. D. Evidence that priority of free recall of newly-learned items is not a recency artefact. *Journal of Verbal Learning and Verbal Behavior,* 1969, **8**, 556–558.

Battig, W. F., & Young, R. K. Simultaneous serial-recall learning of two serial orders of the same list. *Journal of Verbal Learning and Verbal Behavior,* 1969, **8**, 393–402.

Bourne, L. E., Jr. Knowing and using concepts. *Psychological Review,* 1970, **77**, 546–556.

Bregman, A. S. Distribution of practice and between trials interference. *Canadian Journal of Psychology,* 1967, **21**, 1–14.

Brown, S. C. Interpair interference as a function of level of practice in paired-associate learning. *Journal of Experimental Psychology,* 1964, **67**, 316–323.

Burke, F. J., & Battig, W. F. Facilitation of paired-associate learning by prior associative ratings. *Journal of Verbal Learning and Verbal Behavior,* 1968, **7**, 695–699.

Ceraso, J. The recall of long and short stimulus lists. *American Journal of Psychology,* 1967, **80**, 221–228.

Dallett, K. M. Effects of within-list and between-list acoustic similarity on the learning and retention of paired associates. *Journal of Experimental Psychology,* 1966, **72**, 667–677.

Ellis, H. C. Transfer of stimulus differentiation and stimulus encoding alternatives. Paper read at Psychonomic Society, San Antonio, November, 1970.

Gibson, E. J. A systematic application of the concepts of generalization and differentiation to verbal learning. *Psychological Review,* 1940, **47**, 196–229.

Greeno, J. G. Paired-associate learning with massed and distributed repetitions of items. *Journal of Experimental Psychology,* 1964, **67**, 286–295.

Huang, S. J., & Battig, W. F. The role of numerical cues in serial learning. Program on Verbal Learning Report No. 3, Institute for the Study of Intellectual Behavior, University of Colorado, 1969.

Johnson, R. B. Recognition of nonsense shapes as a function of degree of congruence among components of pretraining task. Unpublished doctoral dissertation, University of Virginia, 1964.

Joinson, P. A., & Runquist, W. N. Effect of intralist stimulus similarity and degree of learning on forgetting. *Journal of Verbal Learning and Verbal Behavior,* 1968, **7**, 554–559.

Jones, R. E., & Bourne, L. E., Jr. Delay of informative feedback in verbal learning. *Canadian Journal of Psychology,* 1964, **18**, 266–280.

Keppel, G. Retroactive and proactive inhibition. In T. R. Dixon and D. L. Horton (Eds.), *Verbal behavior and general behavior theory.* Englewood Cliffs, N. J.: Prentice-Hall, 1968. Pp. 172–213.

Lauer, P. A. The use of storage and retrieval cues in free recall of organized words. Unpublished master's thesis, University of Colorado, 1971.

Pagel, J. C. A two stage markov model of transfer in the A-B, A-Br paradigm varying intralist stimulus similarity and stimulus meaningfulness. Unpublished doctoral dissertation, University of Colorado, 1971.

Pellegrino, J. W. Effects of intralist response formal similarity upon paired-associate transfer and retroactive inhibition. *Journal of Experimental Psychology,* 1972, **92,** in press.

Peterson, L. R., Hillner, K., & Saltzman, D. Supplementary report: Time between pairings and short-term retention. *Journal of Experimental Psychology,* 1962, **64,** 550–551.

Postman, L. Does interference theory predict too much forgetting? *Journal of Verbal Learning and Verbal Behavior,* 1963, **2,** 40–48.

Postman, L. Organization and interference. *Psychological Review,* 1971, **78,** 290–302.

Runquist, W. N., & Joinson, P. A. Rated similarity of low association value CVC trigrams. *Journal of Verbal Learning and Verbal Behavior,* 1968, **7,** 317–320.

Schild, M. E., & Battig, W. F. Directionality in paired-associate learning. *Journal of Verbal Learning and Verbal Behavior,* 1966, **5,** 42–49.

Spera, A. J. The effects of multiple-choice familiarization and sequential grouping on paired-associate learning. *Virginia Journal of Science,* 1963, **14,** 274–275.

Thompson, A. S. The role of stimulus and response familiarization in paired-associate learning. *Virginia Journal of Science,* 1964, **15,** 368.

Tulving, E., & Madigan, S. A. Memory and verbal learning. *Annual Review of Psychology,* 1970, **21,** 437–484.

Turnage, T. W. Unit-sequence interference in short-term memory. *Journal of Verbal Learning and Verbal Behavior,* 1967, **6,** 61–65.

Underwood, B. J., & Ekstrand, B. R. Linguistic associations and retention. *Journal of Verbal Learning and Verbal Behavior,* 1968, **7,** 162–171.

Underwood, B. J., & Erlebacher, A. H. Studies of coding in verbal learning. *Psychological Monographs,* 1965, **79** (13, Whole No. 606).

Underwood, B. J., & Postman, L. Extraexperimental sources of interference in forgetting. *Psychological Review,* 1960, **67,** 73–95.

Wright, J. H., & Gescheider, G. A. Role of immediate and delayed knowledge of results in paired-associate learning under the anticipation procedure. *Journal of Psychology,* 1970, **74,** 249–257.

Young, R. K., & Thomson, W. J. Retention of single- and double-function lists. *Journal of Verbal Learning and Verbal Behavior,* 1967, **6,** 910–915.

Zavortink, B., & Keppel, G. Retroactive inhibition of interitem associations for serial lists with constant or varied starting position. *Journal of Verbal Learning and Verbal Behavior,* 1968, **7,** 771–775.

Zechmeister, E. B., Biers, D. W., & Underwood, B. J. Bidirectional unlearning. *Journal of Verbal Learning and Verbal Behavior,* 1969, **8,** 54–58.

CHAPTER 8

ON THE PROBLEM OF WHAT IS LEARNED DURING LEARNING[1]

James F. Voss

One of the most puzzling and yet most important problems in the general area of human learning is the question of what is learned in a particular situation other than the specific contents or materials of the task. In

[1] This work was supported by the National Institute of Child Health and Human Development (Grant HD00957-07) and by Special Fellowship MH-47183 of the National Institute of Mental Health. In addition, I wish to acknowledge the support of the University of Pittsburgh and the University of California at Irvine. I also wish to thank Drs. William Battig, Judith Petrich, Charles Thompson, and Richard Thompson for their comments made on an earlier draft of the manuscript.

addition to the importance of this problem as it relates to our understanding of learning processes, this issue is of basic significance because the primary effect of cumulative experience, that which we call learning, seems to be that we acquire means or ways of responding to our environment even though the specifics of what we have learned, i.e., the contents, apparently have disappeared or have become inaccessible.

There have been a number of attempts to study what we are calling the non-content aspects of learning. Historically, the act–content distinction was related to the issue, and in more recent time, the concepts of learning sets (Harlow, 1949), response sets (Paul & Paul, 1968), and the so-called learning-to-learn effect may be regarded as an aspect of the same problem. In addition, the attempts in recent years to study rule learning (e.g., Haygood & Bourne, 1965) and strategy development (e.g., Bruner, Goodnow, & Austin, 1956) under particular task conditions also may be viewed as efforts to determine what factors other than content are acquired under specific task conditions.

The present chapter, addressed to the issue of the non-content aspects of learning, approaches the problem in a manner which may be described as pseudo-biological. According to the theoretical concepts presented, the non-content factors of learning are assumed to be responses and response systems which function in relation to task situations. It is the objective of this chapter to suggest how such systems develop, to consider what may be the properties of such systems, and to show how such systems may be related to certain research findings.

Theoretical Framework

As mentioned previously, the learning experiment typically consists of presentation of a set of materials under particular task conditions. In the usual situation, instructions are given to the subject, materials are presented, and the subject's performance is measured in terms of his acquisition of the material. There typically is no measurement of the influence of task factors, however, probably because methods of measurement have not been devised. In other words, we do not have a measure of the "effect of instructions" except in the most gross sense of the subject's ability to repeat or follow the instructions. We usually do not measure the subject's understanding of the nature of the task or his perceived role in the task, we usually do not measure the cognitive operations that may be aroused in relation to the task, and we usually do not have an idea of the orientation differences that may occur in reference to one task that may not be elicited in reference to another task.

The fact that our measurement of performance are primarily measures of content asquisition should not deter us from at least speculating about the nature of the non-content processes that may be involved in the learning situation, and this chapter constitutes such a speculation. The general model or theoretical framework that is presented is viewed as one approach to the issue, an approach which in the long run hopefully will be fruitful.

We begin the development of our model by assuming that, in a given task situation, the components of the task evoke task responses (T_R), with the entire set of responses related to a particular task situation called a task system (T_S).[2] These T_R and T_S, at our current state of knowledge, must be regarded as hypothetical constructs. We further assume that over the course of learning, T_S development essentially has the characteristics of a motor skill. Thus, with these assumptions, our first step is to consider what the nature of task systems may entail and to study the properties of responses and response systems that may be related to T_S development.

Properties of Response Systems

STAGES OF SKILL ACQUISITION

In one approach to the study of performance change over the course of acquiring motor skills, Fleischman and his colleagues (e.g., Fleischman, 1957, 1962, 1967) analyzed intratask components of various tasks and determined how factor loadings changed with stage of practice.

Of interest are the following findings: (1) There is no single general motor ability. (2) The components of a task change as a function of learning; e.g., reaction time, rate of movement, and perceptual components increased, whereas verbal and spatial components tended to decrease (Fleischman & Hempel, 1955). (3) It was found that a factor unique to the particular task increases in importance as training proceeds.

Another classification of motor acquisition was developed by Fitts (1962, 1964; Fitts & Posner, 1967). The first stage is termed the cognitive stage. The important features of this stage include the understanding of the task requirements, familiarization with the component parts of the

[2] Responses in this case do not refer to associates of the material or verbal responses in the typical sense of the word. Instead, response and response system are terms used as constructs to describe the organism's reaction to the task conditions, regardless of the specific task contents.

skill, etc. Performance at this level thus tends to be related more to mental ability than the later stages, and thus the stage is termed cognitive. The second stage originally was called fixation, but the term was changed to association (Fitts & Posner, 1967, pp. 12ff). The individual in this stage is essentially perfecting his skill; performance has few errors and the latency of responses is being reduced. Fitts pointed out, incidentally, that most motor-learning studies have gotten into, but not beyond, this second stage. The third stage is termed automation. This stage is characterized by a high degree of overlearning, and the individual is able to perform "automatically." In addition, individuals are able to perform the task under conditions of distraction (cf. Bahrick, Noble, & Fitts, 1954), a point made previously by James (1950).

In reference to this third stage of learning, Fitts indicated that perhaps not only the plateau of motor learning is a phantom event (Keller, 1958) but the asymptote also may be ephemeral. Data cited by Fitts suggest that in many instances high skill performance continues to improve and a relatively permanent asymptote does not occur (cf. Crossman, 1959).

Consideration of motor skill development, if applied to T_R and T_S development, leads to a number of interesting implications. Three of these are as follows: (1) T_S development is characterized by intellectual processes or understanding early in learning, but as the system develops, other aspects of the task increase in importance. This notion suggests that the role of instructions, either as stated by the experimenter or as self-stated by the subject, probably decreases in importance to a considerable extent as practice on the task proceeds and performance improves. Carried one step farther, this position suggests that a highly developed T_S is less under verbal control than a T_S that is in the earlier stages of development. (2) It would be expected that upon the occurrence of a particular task situation, a well-developed T_S is set in operation much more quickly than a less well-developed T_S. (3) There is the possibility that T_S development has no asymptote, i.e., as practice continues, the T_S continues to increase in its refinement. (4) A highly developed T_S may occur without interfering with other, simultaneously occurring, task responses. This conclusion suggests that different T_S's do not interfere with each other.

KNOWLEDGE OF RESULTS

The concepts of knowledge of results (KR) and feedback cannot be easily separated; both involve the aftereffects of a response and information that is fed back via a sense modality. A difference in the usage of the terms, however, is that KR generally has been employed in a more empirical way, referring to operational manipulations that are external to the organism, whereas feedback has been used as a term (a) describing the reception of information following a response, (b) as a descriptive principle indicating the operation of a self-regulating mechanism, and (c) as a principle of self-regulation which acts as a basis of theory building. I will employ the two terms in a somewhat arbitrary manner, using knowledge of results to refer to investigations which are designed to study how manipulating the postresponse information influences performance and using feedback in a more general way to discuss theoretical notions related to the response aftereffects (see I. McD. Bilodeau, 1966, for a discussion of terminology in this area).

Delay of KR

Lorge and Thorndike (1935) found that delay of KR did not significantly influence performance. Their situation involved a single discrete response and a response-KR interval which was filled with no particular activity. Subsequent work under these conditions generally has supported this finding (I. McD. Bilodeau, 1966). When the delay interval was filled with activity, Lorge and Thorndike (1935) also reported no effect of delay. Subsequently, I. McD. Bilodeau (1956), using a stick positioning response, found that performance decreased as the number of intervening responses between the response and KR increased, although even with 5 intervening responses the subjects were able to improve their performance. Lavery and Suddon (1962) further found that by increasing the number of training trials, performance under the condition of 5 intervening responses became equivalent to that of the condition in which there were no intervening responses.

Frequency of KR

Using a stick positioning task, E. A. Bilodeau and Bilodeau (1958) provided KR after every trial, every third trial, or every fourth trial. By presenting 10, 30, or 40 trials for the three respective conditions, they were able to assess the effects of the absolute KR frequency as well as the relative effects of proportion of KR. They found that absolute KR frequency is the critical frequency variable.

Amount of KR

Some motor tasks have component processes such that KR may be provided about one or two aspects of the task but not about the other components. The question of the effect of amount of KR, as defined by the number of task components for which KR is given, was studied by

Gould (1965). His results indicated that performance tended to improve with number of components for which KR was provided, and that the visual information was more important than information pertaining to the hand and arm position.

Augmented KR

Augmented KR refers to the presentation of some event which provides no additional information per se but is presented as a secondary or extra source of KR. The results indicate that augmented KR can have a facilitating, a deteriorating, or no effect upon performance (Adams, 1966; I. McD. Bilodeau, 1966). Because the augmented feedback seems to be a temporary effect, i.e., performance tends to increase with such feedback and decrease immediately without it, the hypothesis has been advanced that such knowledge influences performance, not learning, and is motivational in nature (Fitts, 1962; Smode, 1958). However, the finding (Lincoln, 1954) that augmented feedback during training can have a deleterious effect upon subsequent transfer performance suggests that these may be more lasting effects.

Theoretical Basis of KR

Taken as a whole, the influence of KR upon performance has had relatively little theoretical analysis. J. S. Brown (1949) described the possible roles of KR as reward, information, and motivation. Payne and Hauty (1955) described two properties of KR, the directive, an informational property, and the incentive, a motivational property. The information property of KR is obvious, i.e., the subject is told or observes his results and modifies his subsequent performance. The theoretical problem is how the information is utilized by the subject in modifying his next response.

Studies of the hypothesized motivational property of KR have been summarized by Locke, Cartledge, and Koeppel (1968). Locke *et al.* argue that KR has a goal-setting property which enables the subject to set a goal or standard level of performance for himself and work toward it. KR thus provides a motivational influence with respect to the individual's attempts to obtain the goal.

The role of KR in motor learning suggests some interesting possibilities for T_S development. Specifically, it is likely that the learning of the materials provides for the development of the T_S. In other words, as practice proceeds, the acquisition of the material attests to the effectiveness of the T_S that is developing. Thus reinforcement in the present context consists primarily of acquiring the task materials, thus indicating that the T_S is effective.

This conjecture may be tested by comparing KR with no KR or misinforming KR and determining how T_S development occurs under these conditions. Using a learning-to-learn procedure to study T_S development, the present notions lead to the hypothesis that learning to learn will not occur when there is no knowledge of results, even though amount of practice is held constant.

FEEDBACK

The discussion of feedback centers about three issues: proprioception and serial chaining as explanations of motor behavior; the limited role of feedback, as shown by deafferentation studies; and the issue of feedback and internal control.

Feedback, Proprioception, and Serial Chaining

One issue which received extensive attention during the early decades of this century was the problem of determining what sense or senses are involved in maze acquisition (see Munn, 1950, for a summary of the literature, and Adams, 1961, for an abbreviated account) and, in particular, determining whether the proprioceptive sense is necessary and/or sufficient for maze learning to occur. In the most extensive study, Honzik (1936) found that proprioception was not sufficient for acquisition to occur. Similar results were found by others, and only Hunter (1940) offered evidence that kinesthesis can produce learning, and this was in a single alternation, as opposed to a more complex, maze. Munn concluded his survey by stating, "There is no evidence that more typical maze patterns are learned either on the basis of kinesthetic processes alone or on the basis of symbolic processes alone" (p. 201).

Another approach to the issue of proprioception was that of elimination of a trained response via the use of lesions. After training rats to learn a maze, interruption of proprioceptive function was affected either by a cerebral (Lashley & Ball, 1929) or cerebellar lesion (Lashley & McCarthy, 1926). It was found that although the ability to traverse the maze was severely impaired, the animals nevertheless retained the maze habit. Thus maintenance of proprioceptive feedback at the level of the brain was not necessary to prevent forgetting of the maze habit.

At the theoretical level, the concept of serial chaining is essentially that a response produces stimuli and these stimuli elicit subsequent responses. Thus, in the execution of a motor skill, this position views the performance of the skill as a highly integrated chained reaction. This view, however, has received extensive criticism.

Woodworth (1899) pointed out that movements often are not controlled by sensory stimulation that occurs during their execution, and, in 1951, Lashley pointed out that a chaining view could not explain the rapidity with which a complex pattern of movements occurs in tasks such as piano playing. The proprioceptive feedback, Lashley maintained, is too slow to explain such movement patterns (cf. Higgins & Angel, 1970). More recently, the serial chaining view has been criticized on the basis of behavioral evidence (cf. Greenwald, 1970). In summary, we thus find that proprioceptive stimulation seems to be of limited importance for acquisition of skills such as maze learning and is not necessary for the retention of such skills, and that the theoretical position which advocates serial chaining as the basic mechanism of performance is open to question and probably not tenable.

Deafferentation

Another physiological approach to the problem of feedback has been via the use of the deafferentation technique. Deafferentation involves the elimination of the proprioceptive feedback by cutting the nerves that carry the proprioceptive feedback to the brain. The initial study of Mott and Sherrington (1895) indicated that eliminating the use of such afferent neurons in a monkey produced a loss of use of the limb. More recent work, however, has indicated that deafferentation does not lead to a loss in performance.

Gorska and Jankowska (1967) found that dogs would perform instrumentally conditioned responses following deafferentation. With respect to the characteristics of the specific response, they reported,

> The instrumental reactions of the deafferented limb, although in principle unaffected, were performed in a somewhat changed manner. They were rather awkward and ataxic and sometimes seemed to be executed by the animals with a greater "effort" than normally. These features were constant and during the period of post-operative observation no changes in the skill of the performed movements were noticed. (p. 162)

Another series of studies on deafferentation has been conducted by Taub and associates, using monkeys as subjects (Taub & Berman, 1968). As mentioned previously, Mott and Sherrington (1895) reported that deafferentation of a limb prohibited purposive action, a finding supported by Lassak (1953) and Twitchell (1954). This result was supported by Taub and associates for monkeys in a free situation, i.e., when the monkey was allowed to use the limb without any particular prior training. However, Taub and his associates, after conditioning an animal prior to the operation, found that there was an initial deficit in CR retention following deafferentation, but recovery occurred. The investigators also were able to show that animals naive to the CR preoperatively could acquire the CR postoperatively. Thus a new response was acquired by use of the deafferented limb. Finally, it also was demonstrated that after complete deafferentation of the spinal cord animals had no permanent change in conditioned response or free behavior. (It should be pointed out that studies such as these were conducted in which the animal was unable to see his limb.)

The studies on deafferentation have considerable significance, for they strongly suggest that proprioceptive feedback is not necessary for either the acquisition or the retention of a learned response. The importance of these findings with respect to T_S development thus lies in the implication that T_S probably do not develop via proprioceptive feedback. In other words, even though KR is taken to be of importance, the significance of KR is related primarily to the overall act and not to proprioceptive feedback occurring in relation to the specific T_R and T_S.

Feedback and Internal Control

The question that may be raised regarding the role of feedback is: If it is not really necessary for acquisition or retention, what role does it serve? Evarts (1971), discussing this problem in a physiological context, pointed out that the answer to this question is conditional, depending upon modality and other factors. Evarts (1971) also indicated that although feedback may not be important for the acquisition and retention of particular responses, as shown in the deafferentation work, feedback does provide a type of internal control which monitors efferent discharge. In addition, Oscarsson (1970), in discussing the role of ascending sensory pathways, suggested that the function of the ascending sensory pathways is not only to supply information regarding peripheral events but to provide information pertaining to how motor commands are being carried out as well. In other words, there are internal feedback loops which provide the brain with knowledge of what is happening to motor commands that are given. One role of feedback thus is to permit a type of internal control regarding the execution of movements.

In relation to this type of thinking, a two-phase process in motor control has received considerable support from physiological research (cf. Evarts, 1971). Sperry (1950) developed the concept of "corollary discharge," which essentially states that in addition to the neural discharges which are involved in the control of movement, there are correlated discharges to the sensorium which are important to perception and postural effects. Similarly, Teuber (1967) has asserted that a voluntary movement always involves one discharge to the effector and another discharge to the appropriate sensory systems, the function of the latter apparently being to provide the respective sensory apparatus with information regarding the anticipated change.

We find, therefore, that current theorizing suggests that upon the occurrence of neural discharge which will evoke a particular effector action, there is a discharge to the sensorium which essentially tells the sensorium what to expect. Furthermore, as the movement command is being executed, there is apparently feedback which provides the brain with information regarding the state of execution of the movement. This information, it would be expected, may be used to compare the state of the movement with the command. Theoretical statements have, of course, been developed in relation to these notions. Sokolov (1969), e.g., speaks of comparator neurons carrying out such matching, Anokhin (1968) speaks of an "acceptor-of-action" which compares the feedback information with the initial discharge, and Konorski (1967), in a similar way, considers the mechanism of feedback to high-ordered "gnostic" units.

The significance of these notions for the issues of this chapter are threefold: (1) The execution of a movement may be viewed as being initiated by a command. This command evidently may be a program which produces a sequence of activity resulting in a final action. (2) It would be expected that T_S also would develop in this way, i.e., the occurrence of a T_S or task system, as it develops, would come under the control of a command. (3) When a T_S is in operation, it would be expected that there is internal feedback which monitors the execution of the T_S. Finally, it may be mentioned that there also would be a "point of no return" such that there is a time at which the execution of the action must occur (Bartlett, 1958; Keele & Posner, 1968). These consideratons lead to the more general topic of motor programs, which we now shall consider.

Motor Programs

In recent years the concept of motor programs has been employed with increasing frequency (cf. Keele, 1968). The term motor program is not easy to define, but in general, the expression is used to refer to a controlling mechanism which, when activated, sets off a sequence of movements or responses without the necessity of any further stimulation. The general concept of a motor program, it should be noted, has been employed not only in relation to movement execution but to contour perception (Festinger, Ono, Burnham, & Bamber, 1967), speech perception (Liberman, 1970; Liberman, Cooper, Shankweiler, & Studdert-Kennedy, 1967), and the development of language (Lenneberg, 1967) as well. In the perceptual contexts, the concept refers to ways in which efferent activity is thought to be an integral aspect of a particular type of perception.

Despite the relatively wide range of usage of the concept of motor programs, little is known regarding how such programs develop. Keele (1968), in considering this problem, provided evidence indicating that movement control may shift from visual-kinesthetic feedback to some form of internal control and that such a change occurs with practice, but the parameters and mechanisms involved are unspecified.

Keele listed three things that are accomplished by bringing a motor behavior under the control of a motor program. First, the attention requirements of the task are reduced, a point discussed previously in this chapter in relation to skill acquisition. Second, successive stimuli may be anticipated more readily, an assertion that emerges primarily from consideration of tracking tasks. Third, movements become much quicker.

Within the present framework, the development of a T_S is viewed as essentially that of a development of a motor program. Thus, under specified task conditions, the activation of a program provides for the rapid processing of information. The motor program or T_S, therefore, may be viewed as a set of responses that occur under particular task conditions, and these responses provide the operations to be conducted on the input.

MOTOR PROGRAM DEVELOPMENT

A series of studies by Held and his associates, which can only be described as ingenious, may be taken as quite germane to the issue of motor program development. The general paradigm used in a number of the experiments was to present stimulus material under conditions of visual distortion (via the use of prisms) and to analyze the factors involved in correcting for the distortion, a technique which had its inception with von Helmholtz (1867, pp. 601–602). When an individual looks at an object through a prism, the diffraction of light produces a distortion such that the object is perceived to be in a different place than where it is located. Thus, if one reaches for the object, he misses it. However, von Helmholtz demonstrated that by repeatedly reaching for the object, the individual in some way compensates for the error and is able to grasp the object without error.

In a later study involving visual distortion, Stratton reported his view of the world through lenses which inverted the visual image (Stratton, 1897). He observed that initially everything was viewed as inverted, but over a period of eight days, he found he could adjust to the change. Readjustment was necessary to perceive as he did preexperimentally, but this was accomplished in a matter of hours.

One of the more interesting observations of Stratton was his reporting of a "swinging of the scene." When he moved his head, Stratton reported that the movement did not seem to be localized in the observer but was localized in both the observer and the surrounding area, i.e., with head movement, the objects appeared to move past faster than his body movement, although in the same direction. This phenomenon suggested that visual perception in this context consists of more than a simple inverted visual field; instead, the role of movement in perception was implied.

Studying the problem of movement in the correction of visual distortion, Held and Hein (1958) investigated the role of active movement in adapting to visual distortion. The experiment consisted of three stages. In the first the subject, wearing prismatic lenses which distorted the visual field, viewed the target indirectly via a mirror. He was instructed to mark the target with a stylus and did so with his arm out of view. The results indicated that the visual distortion attributable to the lenses occurred. In the second stage, the subject viewed his hand through a lens, and one of three conditions was imposed: the hand was not moved, moved actively, or moved passively. Active movement refers to the subject swinging his hand through a prescribed arc; passive movement involved the experimenter moving the hand of the subject through the same arc. The difference of movement thus was whether the subject moved his own hand or whether he relaxed his hand and let the experimenter move it. Under the no-movement condition, the subject looked at his hand for a time corresponding to the action or passive movement time. Following this procedure, the first stage was repeated.

The data indicated that only under the active movement condition did the subject adapt to the visual distortion. Similar findings were reported by Held and Bossom (1961). In yet another study, involving use of kittens, Held and Hein (1963) showed that active movement is important to the development of visual perception. In this experiment two kittens received equivalent visual stimulation, but one kitten was allowed to walk whereas the second was moved about in a wagonlike vehicle. The latter kitten was shown to suffer perceptually compared to the former.

The results of these experiments as well as others by Held *et al.* have been interpreted in terms of a type of feedback model (Held, 1961,

1965, 1968; Held & Freedman, 1963) which has its origins in a paper by von Holst (1954). In considering the issue of feedback von Holst distinguished two types, exafferent and reafferent. The former consists of feedback from the external environment; the latter consists of feedback from the action of the individual. From this general position, Held *et al.* argued that when a signal is given to make a response, not only does the signal elicit the response but the signal also produces an internal memory storage. Upon occurrence of the particular response, there is afferent feedback and the memory storage is compared to the feedback. As Held (1968) points out, this model suggests that any distortion of the feedback destroys the 1:1 relationship between the feedback and the storage, and the perception becomes uncorrelated. Active movement in the "rearrangement" experiment thus is one way in which the feedback from output signals becomes correlated with the memory storage, and it is necessary via active movement to develop the proper storage-feedback relation.

With respect to T_S development, the results of the Held *et al.* investigations strongly suggest that a T_S develops via a process of active learning. This assertion leads to a number of predictions; e.g., learning-to-learn effects should only occur when subjects actively learn the task materials. If they are shown the materials under equivalent conditions but are instructed to not learn, and make no effort to, learning-to-learn should not occur. Also, it is of interest to note that the present notions provide an alternative interpretation with respect to the results of Mandler's sorting studies (e.g., Mandler, 1967; Mandler & Pearlstone, 1966). Mandler had one subject sort unrelated words into categories and a yoked subject was shown the particular word sort. Subjects treated in the former way acquired and retained the particular sort better than those sorting under the second set of conditions. Mandler interpreted the results in terms of the importance of subjects sorting according to their own scheme of organization. The Held studies suggest that the operation of "active" vs. "passive" sorting may be an important confounding factor.

In addition to emphasizing the importance of "active" learning to T_S development, the Held *et al.* findings, taken in conjunction with other notions regarding feedback, suggest that the following factors may be involved in T_S development. First, acquisition of the materials of a particular task probably serves as a stabilizing influence on the development of T_S. However, that motor programs are modifiable has been demonstrated (e.g., Pew, 1966), and it is quite likely that such programs undergo some type of change, depending upon the outcome of the program action. Second, when the motor program is operating, there is a monitoring process which keeps the brain informed regarding the execution of the program.

Third, once a program is developed, its repeated usage provides for its increasingly rapid execution. Fourth, it would be expected that under the subsequent occurrence of identical or highly similar task conditions, the motor program would be activated that was developed or employed under the respective previous conditions. Before considering how these notions regarding task systems may be related specifically to the non-content aspects of learning, it is necessary to examine one more phenomenon of response process, namely, habituation.

HABITUATION

The concept of habituation refers to a decrease in response strength as a function of stimulus repetition. Although this phenomenon has been viewed as similar to extinction, at least at the gross level (e.g., Kling & Stevenson, 1970), the interest of this chapter in habituation is in relation to learning.

R. F. Thompson and Spencer (1966), in their review of habituation, listed nine parameters that are important to the habituation process. These parameters were later reviewed by Hinde (1970). The statements of primary interest to the present formulation are 1, 2, 3, 4, and 7:

1. Given that a particular stimulus elicits a response, repeated applications of the stimulus result in decreased response (habituation). The decrease is usually a negative exponential function of the number of stimulus presentations.
2. If the stimulus is withheld, the response tends to recover over time (spontaneous recovery).
3. If repeated series of habituation training and spontaneous recovery are given, habituation becomes successively more rapid (this might be called potentiation of habituation).
4. Other things being equal, the more rapid the frequency of stimulation, the more rapid and/or more pronounced is habituation.
7. Habituation of response to a given stimulus exhibits stimulus generalization to other stimuli.

The relation of the phenomenon of habituation to the present notions is the following principle: Given that task responses (T_R) and task systems (T_S) are acquired during the course of learning a set of materials under specific task conditions, it would be expected that upon repeated occurrences of the T_S, habituation of the T_S should occur. This effect should be especially prevalent under massed presentations of the material (principle 4).

The phenomenon of habituation also raises the question of the possible effects of sensitization (Groves & Thompson, 1970), i.e., an increase in the strength of a response as a function of repeated stimulation. Sensitization, it is pointed out by Groves and Thompson, tends to occur under conditions of more intense or stronger stimulation.

Within the present context, it may be somewhat tenuously hypothesized that rather than varying with stimulus intensity in the sense of energy level, the T_S strength would vary with the discriminatibility of the stimulus material. In other words, in a learning-to-learn paradigm, it would be expected that changing to new materials would produce sensitization, with a reduction in the relative contribution of habituation to the strength of T_S occurrence.

We find, therefore, that the following factors are hypothesized to occur with respect to T_S development. First, T_S development is assumed to facilitate acquisition because the response system, becoming more refined with practice, functions in an increasingly efficient manner. Thus acquisition of new materials should be facilitated as a function of T_S development. However, repeated occurrences of a T_S, especially under massed conditions, weaken the strength of occurrence of the T_S. Thus it would be predicted that learning should be poorer during habituation of the T_S. A problem, therefore, is how the present formulation handles this paradox of both faster and slower learning with T_S development.

Essentially, the notion is advanced that acquisition of materials is related to the stage of T_S development whereas the memory or storage of the material is related to the strength of the T_S at the time of its occurrence. This point requires elaboration.

Again, viewing T_S development in terms of motor skill acquisition, acquisition of input is viewed as a function of the refinement or ease of execution of the skill. Storage, however, is considered to be a function of the strength of the T_S, viewing T_S strength as an amplitude type of concept. Thus, with practice, ease of acquistion is facilitated; however, retention is taken to be a function of T_S strength, and such strength may vary over training as a function of the parameters of habituation.

Task Responses and Task Systems

Our survey of motor processes has suggested that instead of having virtually no knowledge about the operation of the hypothesized T_R and T_S, we in fact may have some idea, even though vague, about the properties of such systems—provided, of course, that we are willing to accept certain speculations regarding the motorlike nature of such responses. In this section implications of such a position are discussed.

Acquisition: Single List

Let us inquire first as to how a T_S may develop as acquisition proceeds. Regarding the earliest stages of acquisition of a single list, it is quite probable that a substantial amount of the learning of T_S takes place via the instructions. On the one hand, the validity of this statement is not testable because the subject, having only been instructed, has not yet been presented the materials and cannot be tested on what he has "learned." On the other hand, if he is asked what he is to do, the subject typically is able to respond in some detail regarding the nature of the task and his role in it. In other words, he has "learned" quite a bit. It is strange that this latter aspect of the learning situation has received virtually no experimental study, at least insofar as I am aware.

An interesting example of task effects is illustrated in a serial learning experiment by Ahmed and Voss (1969). Prior to list presentation, subjects in one control condition were given a horizontal line which represented the serial list and they were asked to place each item on the line where they thought it may occur. Having never seen the actual list, the placements, as would be expected, were quite variable, and a measure of deviation from the correct point on the line (position) for the item yielded a nonsystematic relationship as a function of item position. Another control group was given complete information regarding each item, i.e., this is the fifth item, this is the third item, etc. In the placement of these items, a serial position curve was obtained for the deviation from correct position measure. Thus, even though in both conditions the subjects had not "learned" or even seen the actual serial list, information pertaining to the position of the item yielded the same general serial position function found with actual acquisition of the serial list. In other words, task information was of considerable importance even though no "learning" had taken place.

We have advocated that T_S development is quite important to the learning situation but have not offered any suggestions regarding how T_S development may be related to the material to be learned. If one reasons that an understanding of the task situation is a necessary condition for acquisition, then it would seem that the role of T_S development is to provide a type of fixing or stabilizing influence upon the input. In other words, the T_S development provides for a type of storage or perhaps consolidation of the input.

Speculating about this issue even more, it would seem possible that the influence of a particular T_S is inhibitory, i.e., inhibitory in the sense that input may be processed in a number of ways, but the operation of a T_S allows a specific input to be processed in a particular way, and alternative operations are inhibited. Indeed, it is a truly amazing fact that when subjects make overt errors, the intrusions are almost always intralist, i.e., subjects usually do not state words that are not on the list, even though the words usually have strong associates. What is suggested here is that the task instructions delineate the list to be learned and the subject's T_S of that particular situation acts to reduce any verbal interference. Again, the T_S serves as a type of "funnel" in which the input is processed in a precise way and interfering materials are inhibited.

With respect to the nature of interfering materials, it is of interest to note that there is evidence which suggests that interference during acquisition is produced more from weak items or pairs than from materials learned to a greater degree (Bloch & Voss, 1967; S. C. Brown, 1964; W. J. Thompson, 1967; Voss, 1967). Within the present framework, such findings suggest that interference occurs not from outside of the functioning T_S but from weak items within the task itself.

It is quite important to note that this interpretation is not a rewording of the term "set," for set usually is used to describe a predisposing or preoccurring condition; nor is this interpretation equivalent to the notion of "bins," i.e., that each T_S consititutes a bin and the input goes into it. Instead, the present interpretation is that T_S occurrence is an active process that occurs during learning, and that the items acquired and stored are processed as part of the entire system that is operating.

Returning to the issue of single-list acquisition, a satisfactory explanation of the typical learning curve has been elusive. Probably the most common viewpoint held today is that beyond a certain number of items or pairs of items there is a capacity problem in that individuals are not able to acquire more than some limited amount of information per trial. More trials are required, therefore, to process more information. Of course, intralist interference problems as well as the capacity problems may be involved.

Making the assumption that such presentation of a list item or list pair elicits task responses which develop into a T_S, it is not unreasonable to hypothesize that repeated presentations of a list produce habituation of the T_S, especially under conditions of massed practice and rapid presentation rate. Such habituation implies that over the course of acquisition, even though material is being acquired, the T_S being evoked is weakening. With this interpretation, the negatively accelerated learning curve that typically is obtained in the list learning situation is attributed, at least in part, to the habituation of T_S. Thus, as the material is repeatedly presented, the T_S, although becoming more refined and producing more efficient learning, is at the same time decreasing in strength with the likelihood that the strength of the input that is acquired decreases. Long-term retention, therefore, should decrease as a function of order in which the pairs or items are acquired.

Although the items or pairs acquired later in acquisition are considered to be weaker and retained to a lesser extent, their execution as well as their freedom from interference should be greater. Execution could be measured by use of latency, with the hypothesis generated that on the trial on which the first correct response is given, latency of response should decrease as a function of order in which the pairs are learned.

The notion that interference is lessened for items or pairs acquired later in acquisition is suggested by the following consideration. Since the number of items that have been acquired increases over trials and since, as previously mentioned, such items do not tend to produce interference, greater freedom of interference for items acquired later would be expected on a probability basis.

MULTIPLE LISTS

Transfer Effects

The present framework provides an interpretation regarding the acquisition of successive lists. The lists, in this discussion, refer primarily to the A-B, C-D paradigm. The positive transfer results, or learning-to-learn effects, that have been found in the multiple-list situation are attributed in the present framework to the development of T_S. As previously stated, with T_S development acquisition of new lists should occur more readily.

Two points of interest are raised by this interpretation. First, Meyer and Miles (1953) presented evidence which suggested that the capacity to learn increases with learning. This interpretation is of interest because it supports the "phantom asymptote" characteristic that was suggested for T_S. Similarly, Webb (1962) found that prolonged learning produced a type of "mechanization" of acquisition. The second point is that the boundary conditions of such effects have not been established. From our consideration of T_S operation as essentially a motor skill, one boundary condition that would be expected is that of timing (e.g., Poulton, 1952). Specifically, it may be hypothesized that a shift in the rate of presentation may reduce or eliminate learning-to-learn effects. Such a result has been obtained (Rogers, 1968), but the degree of learning was so minimal that support for the hypothesis must be regarded as quite tentative.

Proactive Inhibition

One of the more interesting aspects of the present formulation pertains to the phenomenon of proactive inhibition (PI). Essentially, the present notions lead to the view that PI is primarily a learning rather than a retention phenomenon.

When acquisition of a series of lists occurs under massed conditions, the present formulation indicates that although positive transfer may be occurring with successive list learning, retention should decrease as a function of ordinal position of the list. This hypothesis follows from the hypothesized habituation of the T_S. Such findings have been reported (e.g., Underwood, 1957). However, if acquisition of the lists is distributed, PI should be reduced or eliminated because the T_S has recovered. Such findings also have been reported (e.g., Underwood & Freund, 1968).

Of further interest in the realm of PI are findings which indicate that PI effects may be reduced or eliminated via instructions (Bjork, 1970). These results suggest that instructions may produce a change in the T_S, a notion that is in general agreement with the concepts discussed thus far, although a change in instructions should have a decreasing effect as a function of the number of lists learned, according to the present formulation.

The "PI release" work also has implications for the present formulation. This research has demonstrated that although PI tends to develop rapidly in the short-term memory situation (Keppel & Underwood, 1967; Scheirer & Voss, 1969), there is release from PI with a change in materials (Wickens, 1970). The interpretation offered here is derived from the habituation–sensitization findings previously discussed. Specifically, a change in the materials yields a sensitization which has a stronger effect than the habituation that is occurring and, as pointed out by Groves and Thompson (1970), the strength of the response should be taken as reflecting the summation of these two processes.

Retroactive Inhibition

The phenomenon of retroactive inhibition (RI) may be viewed in the present framework as follows: When lists are acquired under massed conditions, strength would be expected to decrease as a function of ordinal position of the list. In accordance with the previous discussion on the inverse relation of strength and interference, it would be expected that interference would be a function of ordinal position of the list. However, there is a problem, namely, the earlier lists already have been acquired, and it would be expected that interference could not occur retroactively, i.e., interference clearly would not influence the previous list acquisition. The question is, therefore: What happens to the first or earlier lists when a subsequent list is being acquired?

In accord with certain contemporary viewpoints, let us assume that acquisition of a subsequent list under essentially the same task conditions as acquisition of the prior list(s) involves suppression or inhibition of the preceding list or lists (cf. Postman, Stark, & Fraser, 1968). Furthermore, it would be expected that such a suppression does not produce any loss of strength per se because strength is a function of T_S strength at the time of input. Therefore, retroactive inhibition should be a transient phenomenon where recovery from suppression occurs. The only permanent RI effects that could possibly be expected to operate is that if there were a number of lists of the A-B, A-C, A-D type that were acquired, strength would not be expected to vary, but there may be a problem of discriminating which A was related to each list, i.e., the A with the B, with the C, etc. Essentially, then, RI is taken in the present framework to be a function of the suppression of materials under equivalent T_S conditions.

RETENTION

One of the primary outcomes of the present model is that retention is taken to be primarily a function of acquisition, i.e., no mechanisms other than suppression, which is taken to be of a transient nature, have been postulated to influence retention. Interference, in the present framework, is taken to influence acquisition, and perhaps more important, the strength of the particular T_S at the time of acquisition is taken to be of primary importance.

A second implication of the present formulation for the study of retention is that warm-up should be an important aspect of the retention process, although in verbal behavior, warm-up effects generally have not been substantial.

Rather than giving up on warm-up effects, an alternative view is that research in the area is not sufficiently plentiful to warrant any firm conclusions. Irion (1948, 1949) and Irion and Wham (1951) reported substantial warm-up effects in a retroactive inhibition paradigm, and Dinner and Duncan (1959) reported positive effects of warm-up upon retention, but other findings have yielded relatively small effects (Lazar, 1967; Postman, 1969).

One reason for the relatively poor effects of warm-up upon retention may be that in a number of studies the degree of learning of the original task was insufficient. It is clear from the present notions that warm-up should be particularly effective when the task is highly learned, where warm-up provides for reinstatement of the T_S.

RELATION OF RETENTION AND TRANSFER

Bunch and his colleagues (e.g., Bunch, 1936; Bunch & McCraven, 1938) published an interesting set of papers in the late 1930s and early 1940s which were designated to study the relation of retention and transfer. A variety of tasks was used, and the general paradigm was to have the subjects acquire one list or one maze, and then to compare subsequent retention and transfer effects over time. The result of interest in the present context was that whereas retention tended to decrease over time, transfer effects remained relatively constant.

This finding raises a number of interesting points with respect to the current formulation. First, these results suggest that transfer effects are not primarily due to the utilization of the content or material that has been learned but are attributable to the T_S acquired during original learning. In other words, transfer may have little to do with what specific material is learned; instead, it may be related to the T_S that are developed. This question clearly warrants more experimental attention. Second, these findings suggest that T_S tend to be retained quite well, a factor of no real surprise when T_S is viewed as a motor system. Indeed, it would seem to be reasonable to expect that a considerable amount of forgetting of T_S that does occur should be recovered by warm-up activity.

INDIVIDUAL DIFFERENCES

The present formulation raises some interesting questions about individual differences. First, in the variation that is found in learning abilities, the present notions suggest that acquisition would be highly influenced by the ability of the individual to develop a strong T_S. However, it is conceivable that there are neurological limitations in this capacity. If such differences do occur, then it would appear that poorer learning is related to a poorer ability to inhibit extraneous influences, one of the major roles assumed for the T_S.

Concluding Comments

The present chapter, speculative as it is, constitutes an attempt to provide a coherent framework to the issue of non-content aspects of learning, retention, and transfer. If the individual is viewed in terms of the systems he develops and utilizes in order to adjust and relate to his environment, then the problem of non-content learning must be viewed as critical. The present formulation offers a number of interpretations which are amenable to empirical test, although whether or not the interpretations offered here are shown to be correct is of far less importance than is the purpose of this chapter—to focus attention upon, and hopefully stimulate interest in, one of the most elusive and fundamental problems of behavior.

REFERENCES

Adams, J. A. The second facet of forgetting: A review of warm-up decrement. *Psychological Bulletin,* 1961, **58**, 257–273.

Adams, J. A. Some mechanisms of motor responding: An examination of attention. In E. A. Bilodeau (Ed.), *Acquisition of skill.* New York: Academic Press, 1966. Pp. 169–200.

Ahmed, M., & Voss, J. F. Serial acquisition as a function of stage of learning. *Journal of Experimental Psychology,* 1969, **82**, 398–400.

Anokhin, P. K. Features of the afferent apparatus of the conditioned reflex and their importance for psychology. In N. O'Connor (Ed.), *Recent Soviet psychology.* New York: Liveright, 1968. Pp. 75–103.

Bahrick, H. P., Noble, M. E., & Fitts, P. M. Extra-task performance as a measure of learning a primary task. *Journal of Experimental Psychology,* 1954, **48**, 298–302.

Bartlett, F. C. *Thinking.* New York: Basic Books, 1958.

Bilodeau, E. A., & Bilodeau, I. McD. Variable frequency of knowledge of results and the learning of a simple skill. *Journal of Experimental Psychology,* 1958, **55**, 379–383.

Bilodeau, I. McD. Accuracy of a simple positioning response with variation in the number of trials by which knowledge of results is delayed. *American Journal of Psychology,* 1956, **69**, 434–437.

Bilodeau, I. McD. Information feedback. In E. A. Bilodeau, (Ed.), *Acquisition of skill.* New York: Academic Press, 1966. Pp. 255–296.

Bjork, R. A. Positive forgetting: The noninterference of items intentionally forgotten. *Journal of Verbal Learning and Verbal Behavior,* 1970, **9**, 255–268.

Bloch, R., & Voss, J. F. Acquisition of paired associates as a function of associative strength of competing responses. *Journal of Experimental Psychology,* 1967, **74**, 14–19.

Brown, J. S. A proposed program of research on psychological feedback (knowledge of results) in the performance of psychomotor tasks. USAF Report, 1949.

Brown, S. C. Interpair interference as a function of level of practice in paired-associate learning. *Journal of Experimental Psychology,* 1964, **67**, 316–323.

Bruner, J. S., Goodnow, J. J., & Austin, G. A. *A study of thinking.* New York: Wiley, 1956.

Bunch, M. E. The amount of transfer in rational learning as a function of time. *Journal of Comparative Psychology,* 1936, **22**, 325–337.

Bunch, M. E., & McCraven, V. G. The temporal course of transfer in the learning of memory material. *Journal of Comparative Psychology,* 1938, **25**, 481–496.

Crossman, E. R. F. W. A theory of the acquisition of speed-skill. *Ergonomics,* 1959, **2**, 153–166.

Dinner, J. E., & Duncan, C. P. Warm-up retention as a function of degree of verbal learning. *Journal of Experimental Psychology,* 1959, **57**, 257–261.

Evarts, E. V. Feedback and corollary discharge: A merging of the concepts. *Neurosciences Research Program Bulletin,* 1971, **9**, 86–112.

Festinger, L., Ono, H., Burnham, C. A., & Bamber, D. Efference and the conscious experience of perception. *Journal of Experimental Psychology,* 1967, **74**, (4, whole No. 637).

Fitts, P. M. Skill training. In R. Glaser, (Ed.), *Training research and education.* Pittsburgh: University of Pittsburgh Press, 1962. Pp. 177–197.

Fitts, P. M. Perceptual-motor skill learning. In A. W. Melton, (Ed.), *Categories of human learning.* New York: Academic Press, 1964. Pp. 243–285.

Fitts, P. M., & Posner, M. I. *Human performance.* Belmont, Calif.: Brooks/Cole, 1967.

Fleischman, E. A. A comparative study of aptitude patterns in unskilled and skilled psychomotor performances. *Journal of Applied Psychology,* 1957, **41**, 263–272.

Fleischman, E. A. The description and prediction of perceptual-motor skill learning. In R. Glaser, (Ed.), *Training research and education.* Pittsburgh: University of Pittsburgh Press, 1962. Pp. 137–175.

Fleischman, E. A. Individual differences and motor learning. In R. M. Gagne, (Ed.), *Learning and individual differences.* Columbus, Ohio: Merrill, 1967. Pp. 165–191.

Fleischman, E. A., & Hempel, W. E. Jr. The relation between abilities and improvement with practice in a visual discrimination reaction task. *Journal of Experimental Psychology,* 1955, **49**, 301–312.

Gorska, T., & Jankowska, E. The effect of deafferentation on instrumental (Type II) conditioned reflexes in dogs. In G. A. Kimble, (Ed.), *Foundations on conditioning and learning.* New York: Appleton, 1967. Pp. 155–168.

Gould, J. D. Differential visual feedback of component motions. *Journal of Experimental Psychology,* 1965, **69**, 263–268.

Greenwald, A. G. Sensory feedback mechanisms in performance control: With special reference to the ideo-motor mechanism. *Psychological Review,* 1970, **77**, 73–99.

Groves, P. M., & Thompson, R. F. Habituation: A dual-process theory. *Psychological Review,* 1970, **77**, 419–450.

Harlow, H. F. The nature of learning sets. *Psychological Review,* 1949, **56**, 51–65.

Haygood, R. C., & Bourne, L. E. Jr., Attribute-and-rule-learning aspects of conceptual behavior. *Psychological Review,* 1965, **72**, 175–195.

Held, R. Exposure-history as a factor in maintaining stability of perception and coordination. *Journal of Nervous and Mental Disease,* 1961, **132**, 26–32.

Held, R. Plasticity in sensori-motor systems. *Scientific American,* 1965, **213**, 84–94.

Held, R. Plasticity in sensorimotor coordination. In S. J. Freedman, (Ed.), *The neuropsychology of spatially oriented behavior.* Homewood, Ill.: Dorsey Press, 1968. Pp. 57–62.

Held, R., & Bossom, J. Neonatal deprivation and adult rearrangement: Complementary techniques for analyzing plastic sensory-motor coordinations. *Journal of Comparative and Physiological Psychology,* 1961, **54**, 33–37.

Held, R., & Freedman, S. J. Plasticity in human sensorimotor control. *Science,* 1963, **142,** 455–462.

Held, R., & Hein, A. V. Adaptation of disarranged hand-eye coordination contingent upon re-afferent stimulation. *Perceptual and Motor Skills,* 1958, **8,** 87–90.

Held, R., & Hein, A. V. Movement-produced stimulation in the development of visually guided behavior. *Journal of Comparative and Physiological Psychology,* 1963, **56,** 872–876.

Higgins, J. R., & Angel, R. W. Correction of tracking errors without sensory feedback. *Journal of Experimental Psychology,* 1970, **84,** 412–416.

Hinde, R. A. Behavioural habituation. In G. Horn & R. A. Hinde, (Eds.), *Short-term changes in neural activity and behaviour.* London and New York: Cambridge University Press, 1970. Pp. 3–40.

Honzik, C. H. The sensory basis of maze learning in rats. *Comparative Psychological Monograph,* 1936, **13** (Whole No. 64).

Hunter, W. S. A kinesthetically controlled maze habit in the rat. *Science,* 1940, **91,** 267–269.

Irion, A. L. The relation of "set" to retention. *Psychological Review,* 1948, **55,** 336–341.

Irion, A. L. Retention and warming-up effects in paired-associate learning. *Journal of Experimental Psychology,* 1949, **39,** 669–675.

Irion, A. L., & Wham, D. S. Recovery from retention loss as a function of amount of pre-recall warning-up. *Journal of Experimental Psychology,* 1951, **41,** 242–246.

James, W. *The principles of psychology.* New York: Dover, 1950.

Keele, S. W. Movement control in skilled motor performance. *Psychological Bulletin,* 1968, **70,** 387–403.

Keele, S. W., & Posner, M. I. Processing of visual feedback in rapid movements. *Journal of Experimental Psychology,* 1968, **77,** 155–158.

Keller, F. S. The phantom plateau. *Journal of Experimental Analysis of Behavior,* 1958, **1,** 1–13.

Keppel, G., & Underwood, B. J. Reminiscence in the short-term retention in paired-associate lists. *Journal of Verbal Learning and Verbal Behavior,* 1967, **6,** 375–382.

Kling, J. W., & Stevenson, J. G. Habituation and extinction. In G. Horn, & R. A. Hinde, (Eds.), *Short-term changes in neural activity and behavior.* London and New York: Cambridge University Press, 1970. Pp. 41–61.

Konorski, J. *Integrative activity of the brain.* Chicago: University of Chicago Press, 1967.

Lashley, K. S. The problem of serial order in behavior. In L. A. Jeffress (Ed.), *Cerebral mechanisms in behavior.* New York: Wiley, 1951. Pp. 112–136.

Lashley, K. S., & Ball, J. Spinal conduction and kinaesthetic sensitivity in the maze habit. *Journal of Comparative Psychology,* 1929, **9,** 71–106.

Lashley, K. S., & McCarthy, D. A. The survival of the maze habit after cerebellar injuries. *Journal of Comparative Psychology,* 1926, **6,** 423–432.

Lassak, A. M. Inactivation of voluntary motor function following rhizotomy. *Journal of Neuropathology and Experimental Neurology,* 1953, **3,** 83–87.

Lavery, J. J., & Suddon, F. H. Retention of simple motor skills as a function of the number of trials by which KR is delayed. *Perceptual and Motor Skills,* 1962, **15,** 231–237.

Lazar, G. Warm-up before recall of paired adjectives. *Journal of Verbal Learning and Verbal Behavior,* 1967, **6,** 321–327.

Lenneberg, E. H. *Biological foundations of language.* New York: Wiley, 1967.

Liberman, A. M. The grammars of speech and language. *Cognitive Psychology,* 1970, **1**, 301–323.

Liberman, A. M., Cooper, F. S., Shankweiler, D. P., & Studdert-Kennedy, M. Perception of the speech code. *Psychological Review,* 1967, **74**, 431–461.

Lincoln, R. S. Learning a rate of movement. *Journal of Experimental Psychology,* 1954, **47**, 465–470.

Locke, E. A., Cartledge, N., & Koeppel, J. Motivational effects of knowledge of results: A goal-setting phenomenon? *Psychological Bulletin,* 1968, **70**, 474–485.

Lorge, I., & Thorndike, E. L. The influence of delay in the after-effect of a connection. *Journal of Experimental Psychology,* 1935, **18**, 186–194.

Mandler, G. Organization and memory. In K. W. Spence, & J. T. Spence, Eds.), *The psychology of learning and motivation:* Advances in research and theory. Vol. 1. New York: Academic Press, 1967. Pp. 327–372.

Mandler, G., & Pearlstone, Z. Free and constrained concept learning and subsequent recall. *Journal of Verbal Learning and Verbal Behavior,* 1966, **5**, 126–131.

Meyer, D. R., & Miles, R. C. Intralist-interlist relations in verbal learning. *Journal of Experimental Psychology,* 1953, **45**, 109–115.

Mott, F. W., & Sherrington, C. S. Experiments upon the influence of sensory nerves upon movement and nutrition of the limbs. *Proceedings of the Royal Society of London,* 1895, **57**, 481–488.

Munn, N. L. *Handbook of psychological research on the rat.* Boston, Mass.: Houghton, 1950.

Oscarsson, O. Functional organization of spinocerebellar paths. In A. Iggo, (Ed.), *Handbook of sensory physiology.* Vol. 2. Berlin and New York: Springer-Verlag, 1970. Pp. 121–127.

Paul, C., & Paul, H. Transfer-activated response sets in verbal learning and transfer. *Psychological Review,* 1968, **75**, 537–549.

Payne, R. B., & Hauty, G. T. Effect of psychological feedback upon work decrement. *Journal of Experimental Psychology,* 1955, **50**, 343–351.

Pew, R. W. Acquisition of hierarchical control over the temporal organization of a skill. *Journal of Experimental Psychology,* 1966, **71**, 764–771.

Postman, L. Experimental analysis of learning to learn. In G. Bower & J. T. Spence, (Eds.), *The psychology of learning and motivation:* Advances in research and theory. Vol. 3. New York: Academic Press, 1969. Pp. 241–297.

Postman, L., Stark, K., & Fraser, J. Temporal changes in interference. *Journal of Verbal Learning and Verbal Behavior,* 1968, **7**, 672–694.

Poulton, E. C. The basis of perceptual anticipation in tracking. *British Journal of Psychology,* 1952, **43**, 295–302.

Rogers, J. G. Input and output speed components of learning to learn. *Journal of Experimental Psychology,* 1968, **78**, 233–241.

Scheirer, C. J., & Voss, J. F. Reminiscence in short-term memory. *Journal of Experimental Psychology,* 1969, **80**, 262–270.

Smode, A. Learning and performance in a tracking task under two levels of achievement information feedback. *Journal of Experimental Psychology,* 1958, **56**, 297–304.

Sokolov, E. N. The modeling properties of the nervous system. In M. Cole, & I. Maltzman, (Eds.), *A handbook of contemporary Soviet psychology.* New York: Basic Books, 1969. Pp. 671–704.

Sperry, R. W. Neural basis of the spontaneous optokinetic response produced by visual inversion. *Journal of Comparative and Physiological Psychology,* 1950, **43**, 482–489.

Stratton, G. M. Vision without inversion of the retinal image. *Psychological Review,* 1897, **4**, 341–360 and 463–481.

Taub, E., & Berman, A. J. Movement and learning in the absence of sensory feedback. In S. J. Freedman, (Ed.), *The neurophysiology of spatially oriented behavior.* Homewood, Ill.: Dorsey, 1968. Pp. 173–192.

Teuber, H. L. Lacunae and research approaches to them. In F. L. Darley & C. H. Millikan, (Eds.), *Brain mechanisms underlying speech and language.* New York: Grun & Stratton, 1967. Pp. 204–216.

Thompson, R. F., & Spencer, W. A. Habituation: A model phenomenon for the study of neuronal substrates of behavior. *Psychological Review,* 1966, **73**, 16–43.

Thompson, W. J. Recall of paired-associate items as a function of interpolated pairs of different types. *Psychonomic Science,* 1967, **9**, 629–630.

Twitchell, T. E. Sensory factors in purposive movement. *Journal of Neurophysiology,* 1954, **17**, 239–254.

Underwood, B. J. Interference and forgetting. *Psychological Review,* 1957, **64**, 49–60.

Underwood, B. J., & Freund, J. S. Effect of temporal separation on two tasks on proactive inhibition. *Journal of Experimental Psychology,* 1968, **78**, 50–54.

von Helmholtz, H. *Handbuch der physiologischen optik.* Vol. 1. Leipzig: Voss, 1867. pp. 601–602.

von Holst, E. Relations between the central nervous system and the peripheral organs. *British Journal of Animal Behavior,* 1954, **2**, 89–94.

Voss, J. F. Intralist interference in associative learning. *Journal of Verbal Learning and Verbal Behavior,* 1967, **6**, 773–779.

Webb, W. B. The effects of prolonged learning on learning. *Journal of Verbal Learning and Verbal Behavior,* 1962, **1**, 173–182.

Wickens, D. D. Encoding categories of words: An empirical approach to meaning. *Psychological Review,* 1970, **77**, 1–15.

Woodworth, R. S. The accuracy of voluntary movement. *Psychological Monograph Review Supplements 1899,* **3**. (Whole No. 13).

CHAPTER 9

THE FUNCTIONAL STIMULUS IN SERIAL LEARNING

William L. Bewley

The problem of the functional stimulus in serial learning has been generating research at a fairly significant level for the past ten years. During this time, two literature reviews have been published (Jensen & Rohwer, 1965; Young, 1968), neither of which, based upon the available evidence, was able to identify the functional stimulus. The present review will also be unable to make the identification. As will be seen, data in this area are still quite confusing. There are at least two possible reasons for this confusion. First, it is possible that the functional stimulus methodology is inadequate. Second, it is possible that there is no single functional stimulus used in all situations by all subjects (*Ss*). In this chapter I will attempt to show that both of these possibilities may be correct.

The chapter begins with a description of the major hypotheses concerning the functional stimulus in serial learning. Following this is a discussion of the methodologies employed in testing the predictions of these hypotheses. Finally, a conception of serial learning which is not based on the idea of a functional stimulus will be presented.

The Major Hypotheses

Functional stimulus hypotheses can be divided into three categories according to the basic process thought to underlie the learning of a serial list. The three categories are chaining hypotheses, serial position hypotheses, and dual-process hypotheses.

CHAINING HYPOTHESES

The chaining hypotheses represent the application to serial learning of S-R theory as set forth by Lepley (1934). According to this view, contiguously occurring items become associated so that the stimulus for each item is the immediately preceding item. For example, in the serial list ABCDEFGHI, item A is the stimulus for item B, item B is the stimulus for item C, and so on. In addition to these associations between adjacent items, it is thought that associations are also formed between nonadjacent items, the strength of the association varying with the degree of remoteness of the items. An excellent summary of the remote association assumption of chaining hypotheses along with a critical examination of evidence for the existence of remote associations is presented by Slamecka (1964). First suggested by Ebbinghaus at the end of the nineteenth century (for a recent translation, see Ebbinghaus, 1964), the notion of a serial list learned as a chain of associations between successive items was generally accepted by students of verbal learning until the early 1960s. A variation of the basic chaining hypothesis is the cluster hypothesis (Horowitz & Izawa, 1963), which states that a cluster of preceding items serves as the functional stimulus. According to this hypothesis, in the list ABCDEFGHI, ABC or BC might be the stimulus for D. Both the basic chaining and cluster hypotheses have in common the idea that a serial list is learned by forming associations between items.

SERIAL POSITION HYPOTHESES

The serial position hypotheses represent the application of cognitive theory to serial learning. Cognitive theory is based primarily on the ideas of Gestalt psychology in that the organization and patterning of stimulus items is seen as the fundamental process in learning rather than the formation of associations between contiguous items. According to cognitive theory, serial learning involves organizing the list into an integrated whole according to perceived patterns of relationships among items. Woodworth (1938) and Lashley (1951) were among the first to suggest this general idea, but it was not until the early 1960s that it began to generate much research. This lag between the statement of the hypothesis and the testing of its validity was due in part to the general acceptance of the chaining hypotheses at that time, but probably the greatest cause of the apparent lack of interest was the vagueness of the hypothesis. It is difficult to test the predictions of a hypothesis which talks about organization according to patterns of relationships among items if the relationships are not defined.

The work of Asch, Hay, and Diamond (1960), which demonstrated the large influence of the spatial configuration of list items on serial learning, suggested that list organization may be based on the positions of the items within the list. That is, the relationships among items which are important in organizing the list are their relative serial positions. In learning a serial list, then, *S* learns that a particular item occurs first in the list, another is second, another is last, and so on. Although developed within the framework of cognitive theory, the idea of serial position serving as a cue in serial learning is easily incorporated into S-R theory by saying that associations are formed between the serial position of the item as the functional stimulus and the item itself as the response. Neisser (1967) and Asch (1968) object to this associative interpretation on the grounds that the serial position of an item is not really a stimulus as usually defined in S-R theory because it is a relational concept and does not have an existence out of the context of the serial list. Regardless of whether it is called the functional stimulus or a cue for list organization, it is clear that the serial position of an item plays an important role in serial learning according to both serial position hypotheses.

DUAL-PROCESS HYPOTHESES

According to the dual-process hypotheses, both chaining cues and serial position cues are important in serial learning, their relative importance depending upon certain parameter values of the experiment. The main parameter is thought to be serial position, and there are two views of the relation of serial position to the functional stimulus. The first, expressed by Young (1962) and Young, Patterson, and Benson (1963b), holds that serial position is the functional stimulus in the middle of the list, preceding items being the stimuli at the two ends of the list. Ebenholtz (1963a) suggests the opposite relation, i.e., serial position cues are functional stimuli at the list ends with preceding items being functional stimuli in the middle of the list. Another set of parameters thought to influence the relative importance of serial position cues and preceding items as functional stimuli are material and task variables. Battig, Brown, and Schild (1964), e.g., suggest that serial position cues are important with lists of relatively low task difficulty, such as with short lists and meaningful, low similarity items. Similarly, associations between adjacent items are thought to occur in lists of high difficulty, e.g., in long lists and with material of low meaningfulness and high similarity.

Methodologies

Research designed to test the predictions of the hypotheses just described can be divided into two general methodological categories: transfer designs and single-list designs. The general results found with each and possible difficulties in drawing conclusions from these results are discussed in this section.

TRANSFER DESIGNS

The reasoning behind the use of transfer designs is that if *S* learns something relevant to a second task during a first task, the learning of the second task ought to be facilitated. For example, if associations between items are important, then prior learning of relevant associations between adjacent items will produce faster learning. Similarly, if serial position cues are important, then prior association of an item with its serial position will produce faster learning. These predictions are tested through the use of three different transfer designs: transfer from a paired-associate list (PA) to a serial list (SL), transfer from SL to PA, and transfer from SL to SL. The PA to SL and SL to PA designs can be further subdivided into those testing predictions of the chaining hypotheses and those testing predictions of the serial position hypotheses. The SL-to-SL transfer design has generally been used to test predictions of the serial position or dual-process hypotheses.

PA-to-SL, Chaining Hypotheses

In this design, *S*s in the experimental group learn a PA requiring acquisition of associations between items which are adjacent in the subsequent SL. For example, the list ABCDEF would be preceded by either A-B, C-D, E-F, or A-B, B-C, C-D, D-E, E-F. The former is a single-function PA in that each item serves a single function (i.e., is either a stimulus or a response). The latter is a double-function PA since each item serves as both a stimulus and a response and therefore has two functions. The *Ss* in the control group would learn a PA composed of items different from those in the SL. If *Ss* learn a chain of associations between adjacent items in SL, positive transfer would be expected for the experimental group relative to the control group.

The general finding (e.g., Jensen, 1962; Young, 1959; Young, Milauckas, & Bryan, 1963a) is that there is slight but significant positive transfer. There is, however, a problem with this kind of design which makes it difficult to say with certainty that this is evidence for the chaining hypotheses. According to the stage analysis of learning (Underwood, Runquist, & Schulz, 1959), *Ss* learn both the response and the association between stimulus and response. Assuming that this is true, it follows that in the PA-to-SL design response learning, as well as the association learning predicted from the chaining hypotheses, will be transferred. That is, since the same items are used in both the SL and PA tasks, item or response learning taking place during the first task presented eliminates the necessity for response learning in the second task. Positive transfer thus might be expected even without the transfer of associations, especially in the early trials of task 2 where response learning is thought to be most important. It is interesting to note that the positive transfer in the PA-to-SL design observed by Young (1959) occurs mainly in the early trials of task 2, exactly as expected if response learning was being transferred. A suitable control for this possibility would be a PA constructed from the same items as the SL, but with different item pairings. For example, if the SL was ABCDE, the PA might be A-D, B-E, C-A, D-B, E-C. Transfer of response learning would produce positive transfer, but transfer of associative learning would produce negative transfer since the transfer paradigm would be A-B, A-Br. Young *et al.* (1963a) included this kind of group in their study and found that, as predicted by the chaining hypotheses, negative transfer did occur. The results of tests of the chaining hypotheses using a PA-to-SL transfer design suggest, therefore, that *Ss* form associations between adjacent items and that the functional stimulus for any list item as a response is the preceding item.

SL-to-PA, Chaining Hypotheses

The rationale behind the use of this design is identical to that for the PA-to-SL design. If *Ss* learn associations between adjacent items in SL, then transfer to PA which requires the acquisition of the same associations should be positive. It is generally found, however, that no transfer occurs in this situation (e.g., Young, 1959, 1961). This is true for both single-function and double-function PA (Erickson, Ingram, & Young, 1963; Young, 1962). When transfer is found, it is restricted to the early trials of PA (Young, 1962).

It is surprising that SL-to-PA transfer should be negligible while PA-to-SL transfer is positive. A possible explanation for this fact is found by noting that in a double-function PA list each item serves as both a stimulus and a response, e.g., A-B, B-C, C-D. If, as suggested by the principle of associative symmetry (Asch & Ebenholtz, 1962), B-A is learned at the same time as A-B, the combination of B-A and B-C is an A-B, A-C interference paradigm. If this is true, it is possible that this interference will make the double-function PA task so difficult that any SL-to-PA transfer is masked. The plausibility of this interpretation is suggested by Battig and Koppenaal (1965). These investigators presented *S*s with a 10-pair double function PA list for 10 trials, followed by 2 trials of S-R and R-S recall. For the S-R test, *S*s recalled 90.6 and 89.5% of the correct responses for S-R recall presented first and second, respectively. For the R-S test, *S*s recalled 84.0 and 73.3% of the correct stimuli for R-S recall presented first and second, respectively. Although S-R associations are apparently stronger than R-S associations, backward or R-S learning is clearly quite substantial.

Granting the existence of backward associations in a double-function PA list, Umemoto and Hilgard (1961) offer evidence for their interfering role in acquisition. Three groups of *S*s received 8-pair lists of nonsense syllables, the groups differing with respect to degree of double-functioning. Group 1 received a list in which each of 8 items served as both a stimulus and a response. Group-2 *S*s received a list in which each of 4 items served as both a stimulus and a response, the remaining 8 items serving as a stimulus or response, but not both. In group 3, no items had a double function, all 16 serving as a stimulus or response but not both. In terms of number of trials to criterion, difficulty increased from group 3 to group 2 to group 1. That is, the greater the degree of double-functioning (and thus the greater the number of interfering backward associations), the slower the learning. It is interesting to note that this relation holds despite the fact that the number of different items in the list varies inversely with degree of double-functioning. It appears that double-function PA lists are quite difficult to learn and thus could be masking any SL-to-PA transfer. Moreover, the results of Battig and Koppenaal (1965) suggest that the observed difficulty may be due to interference from backward associations.

It should be noted that the foregoing explanation of the lack of positive transfer in SL-to-PA designs would not apply to a single-function PA since backward associations acquired during PA learning cannot be elicited unless an item serves as both a stimulus and a response. As pointed out by Stark (1968), however, backward associations acquired in SL will be elicited in PA for the experimental condition. To the extent that these backward associations produce interference, the increased difficulty of the PA would tend to mask any positive transfer from SL to single-function PA. In addition to possible interference from these backward associations, Stark (1968) noted that studies finding no transfer in SL to single-function PA designs have used a mixed PA, both experimental and control pairs occurring in the same list. Johnson and Penney (1965) have found that this can reduce transfer as compared to an unmixed presentation of experimental and control pairs.

Another explanation for the failure to find positive SL-to-PA transfer has been suggested by Salafia (1969). Salafia points out that part of the functional stimulus of the preceding item may be saying the stimulus and getting auditory feedback since all items are pronounced in serial learning. With PA learning, however, *S*s are usually not required to pronounce the stimulus. To the extent that articulatory and auditory cues are part of the functional stimulus, then, the functional stimulus would not be totally reinstated in PA learning if the stimulus was not pronounced. In support of this idea, Salafia presents data showing positive SL-to-PA transfer only when the stimulus term was vocalized during PA learning. In a similar study, however, Stark (1968) failed to find any effect of pronunciation on SL-to-PA transfer. Significant positive transfer was found regardless of the presence or absence of vocalization of the stimulus term. One important difference between the two studies was that Stark (1968) informed *S*s of the relation between SL and PA. As will be seen later in this section, instructions of this kind have a very powerful effect on SL-to-PA transfer. It is possible that this effect was strong enough to mask the effects of vocalization in the Stark (1968) study.

Postman and Stark (1967) suggest that the lack of positive transfer in SL to PA might be explained as an artifact of the method of measurement of PA learning. As mentioned earlier, Young (1962) found positive transfer in early PA trials. In later trials, transfer was reduced and even became slightly negative. According to Postman and Stark (1967), the use of data from later PA trials provides a misleading measure of transfer because data from these later trials represent the acquisition of difficult list items in that they come from the middle of the serial list. These items are presumably more difficult because the interitem associations are weaker. One kind of evidence for this assumption is that SL-to-PA transfer, when it occurs, is usually greatest for items coming from the ends of the SL (e.g., Young, 1962), suggesting that associations between items are stronger at the list ends than at the middle. As Postman and Stark (1967) point out, however, this result can be explained by the fact that the end items in SL have a single function in a derived PA and would therefore be less affected by interference from backward associations.

Better evidence might come from studies investigating the effects of degree of prior SL learning. If transfer in later PA trials is reduced because weaker associations are involved, increasing the level of SL learning should produce greater transfer in these later trials by strengthening the SL associations. Stark (1968) presents evidence which supports this idea. In the second experiment which she describes, *S*s learned a 10-item SL in two segments. The first 5 items were learned to a criterion of one perfect trial, after which the second 5 items were added and practice continued until the entire list was learned to a criterion of one perfect trial. The effect of this procedure was to eliminate the usual bowed serial position curve and thus to ensure that the associations in the middle of the list were not weaker than those at the ends. The derived PA was learned to one perfect trial and significant positive transfer was found for all stages of learning. Transfer was also found for pairs taken from all serial positions of the SL. These data seem to support Postman and Stark (1967) regarding the insensitivity of measuring transfer in the later trials of PA learning. It is important to note, however, that *S*s were informed of the nature of the relationship between the SL and the PA.

Several studies have investigated the effect on SL-to-PA transfer of strengthening associations in SL by using the standard anticipation procedure but varying the learning criterion. The only study finding evidence for greater transfer with higher levels of SL learning was that reported by Crowder (1968). Data reported by R. L. Breckinridge and Dixon (1970), Horton and Turnage (1970), and Young (1961), however, find no evidence for an increase in SL-to-PA transfer as a function of degree of SL learning. While box-score methodology should be avoided (see Gardner, 1966), it is clear that this kind of evidence offers little support for the Postman and Stark (1967) explanation of why transfer is reduced in later PA trials.

In addition to increasing the SL learning criterion, the strength of interitem associations may also be varied by the use of normative associations among SL items. If transfer in later PA trials is reduced because of the acquisition of weakly associated items, increasing the strength of normative associations should increase transfer. This prediction is tested in a study by Rosner (1970). Positive transfer was found using both overall PA data and data from the first 10 PA trials. Degree of transfer did not vary, however, as a function of associative structure in SL. As in the study by Stark (1968), who also found significant transfer at all stages of PA, *S*s were informed of the relation between the SL and PA.

The foregoing discussion casts some doubt on the idea that the negative or zero transfer usually found in later trials of PA is due to the acquisition of difficult items. This discussion has also suggested that a variable of great importance in determining the degree of SL-to-PA transfer is the instruction given to *S*. In two of the studies just described (Rosner, 1970; Stark, 1968) which found significant SL-to-PA transfer, *S*s were informed of the relation between SL and PA. The importance of instruction is also indicated by Postman and Stark (1967). This study looked at SL-to-PA transfer as a function of instructions. In one experimental group, group E, the items and pairings in SL and PA were the same. The second experimental group, group Er, was really a control for response learning, the same items appearing in the two lists but with different pairings (an A-B, A-Br transfer paradigm). Group C, the control group, was a control for learning-to-learn effects, the SL and PA being composed of different items. The chaining hypotheses would predict positive transfer for group E and negative transfer for group Er relative to group C. One-half of the *S*s in each group received instructions describing the relation between SL and PA. Each group received three sets of SL-PA list pairs. Each SL was learned to a criterion of one perfect trial, and each PA was presented for 10 trials. Looking first at the results for the first SL-PA set, significant positive transfer for both the first PA trial and all 10 PA trials was found only for the instructed group E. The predicted negative transfer for group Er relative to group C was found only in the data from all 10 PA trials. The amount of negative transfer was not affected by the instruction variable. The results for the second and third SL-PA sets revealed essentially the same relations: more positive transfer for instructed group E than for uninstructed group E and negative transfer for group Er not varying as a function of instructions.

Postman and Stark (1967) see the effect of instructions as allowing more efficient utilization of SL learning in PA learning by increasing the likelihood of Ss rehearsing the serial associations during PA. The effect of this rehearsal is to reduce the interference from backward associations in a double-function PA. If this is true, transfer should be facilitated by increasing the anticipation interval in PA, i.e., if instructed Ss show greater transfer because they are rehearsing serial associations, then increasing the time available for such rehearsal should increase the amount of transfer. The results of studies attempting to demonstrate this have been somewhat inconsistent. Erickson *et al.* (1963), using a mixed PA list, decreased the PA presentation rate from the usual 2:2 (2 sec for the stimulus term, 2 sec for the pairing of stimulus and response) to 4:4 but found no increase in transfer. As pointed out by Stark (1968), however, the use of a mixed PA list may mask any transfer effects. Stark (1968), using unmixed PA, increased anticipation time by using a 3:2 rate and also found no increase in transfer. The only study finding an effect of anticipation time on SL-to-PA transfer is that of Heaps, Greene, and Cheney (1968), who found significant positive transfer with a 6:6 rate. With unmixed PA and anticipation times at least as long as 6 sec, then, there appears to be some evidence that SL-to-PA transfer is increased when Ss are able to rehearse serial associations during PA. The ability to rehearse serial associations is presumably enhanced by instructions describing the relation between SL and PA or by providing ample time for such rehearsal.

The idea that positive SL-to-PA transfer can be attributed to efficient utilization of SL learning in PA learning has recently been used by Lesgold and Bower (1970) to explain the fact that positive transfer usually occurs only in the early PA trials. As in Postman and Stark (1967), Ss were either instructed (group I) or uninstructed (group U) about the relation between SL and PA. Compared to a learning-to-learn control group, groups I and U both show positive transfer on the first two PA trials with group I showing more transfer than group U. As PA learning proceeds, however, transfer for groups I and U is reduced, with the performance of group U becoming virtually identical to that of the control group and the performance of group I actually becoming worse than that of the control group. Lesgold and Bower (1970) explain these results by saying that instructed Ss try to use what they have learned in SL throughout PA learning while uninstructed Ss use SL learning only in the first trials of PA if at all. Evidence for this idea comes from an analysis of the pattern of errors in PA learning. The SL was a 15-item list chunked by temporal grouping into five triplets. In PA learning, errors tended to be greater for pairs crossing the SL chunks than for pairs which were within SL chunks. For example, if SL was composed of three 3-item chunks such as ABC DEF GHI, pairs like C-D and F-G would produce more errors than pairs like B-C, E-F, or H-I. This tendency for more PA errors for between-chunk pairs was most pronounced for group I, there being no difference between group U and the control group. These results clearly suggest the use of serial knowledge by instructed *S*s but not by uninstructed *S*s. The reason that uninstructed *S*s stop using SL learning and that instructed *S*s, who presumably continue using it throughout PA learning, show eventual negative transfer may be that utilization of what is learned in SL learning is an inefficient strategy for PA learning. The strategy would be inefficient if the processes involved in SL learning and PA learning were different.

In summary, in this section it has been shown that the absence of SL-to-PA transfer can be explained in at least four ways. First, the interference from backward associations in double-function PA learning may be masking transfer. Second, as suggested by Salafia (1969), positive transfer may be reduced because the articulatory and auditory cues present in SL are usually not present in PA. The third explanation, suggested by Postman and Stark (1967), is that the lack of transfer is an artifact associated with the practice of including data from later PA trials (representing the acquisition of difficult items) in the measure of transfer. The fourth explanation is that positive transfer is produced by the efficient utilization of what is learned in SL learning during PA learning. The evidence presented has favored the first and fourth explanations over the second and third. That these two are not necessarily incompatible has been shown by Postman and Stark (1967), who suggest that the efficient utilization of serial knowledge reduces interference from backward associations in double-function PA learning. Regardless of whether one or both of these explanations are accepted, it is clear that the SL-to-PA design is not well suited to determining the functional stimulus in serial learning. Either transfer effects are masked by interference from backward associations or, if transfer occurs, it can be interpreted as indicating that *S*s are utilizing serial associations. Utilization does not necessarily mean that these associations were important in the acquisition of the SL. This point will be discussed in more detail at the end of the discussion of transfer designs.

PA-to-SL, Serial Position Hypotheses

In this design, transfer is made from PA to SL with some representation of the serial position of an item in SL as the stimulus for the item in PA. A good example of this kind of design is a condition in the study reported by Ebenholtz (1963a). The *S*s first learned a set of items presented at different spatial locations in a vertical array of windows. Each item always appeared at a particular window. There was no constant temporal order of appearance. The anticipation cue for each item was a red patch appearing in the appropriate window. This was, therefore, essentially a PA with spatial position as the stimulus term. Following acquisition to a criterion of one errorless trial, *S*s were assigned to 1 of 3 groups for SL learning. In group C, items appeared in temporal positions corresponding to the spatial positions in PA. For example, the temporally first item in SL had appeared at the top of the vertical array in PA and the temporally last item in SL had appeared at the bottom of the vertical array in PA. In group D, the items in SL held temporal positions different from their spatial positions in PA. In group R, the SL items held absolute temporal positions different from the PA spatial locations, but the relative positions were the same, e.g., items which had appeared in spatial positions 1 through 10 in PA might appear in temporal positions 8, 9, 10, 1, 2, 3, 4, 5, 6, and 7, respectively, in SL. If absolute or relative serial position serves as a cue in SL learning, positive transfer would be expected for groups C and R, respectively. The results showed that performance in group C was in fact better than that in groups D and R in terms of both trials to criterion and errors per trial. In addition, performance in group R was better than that in group D in terms of errors per trial. While these data are suggestive of the importance of both absolute and relative serial position as a cue in SL learning, it is impossible to come to a definite conclusion because of the absence of an appropriate control group. Since group D should produce negative transfer according to serial position hypotheses (the transfer paradigm is A-B, A-Br), it is impossible to say whether groups C and R showed positive transfer or simply less negative transfer than group D.

Winnick and Dornbush (1968) report a study similar to Ebenholtz (1963a) except that a control group was added. In 3 of the 4 groups stimuli in the PA were numbers. Group A was similar to Ebenholtz' group C in that the numbers used as stimuli in PA corresponded to the temporal positions of the items in SL. Group B was like Ebenholtz' group R in that the stimuli in PA had only sequential correspondence to the temporal positions in SL. For example, items which had the numbers 9 through 20 in PA occurred in temporal positions 1 through 12, respectively, in SL. Group C was the same as Ebenholtz' group D, position and item pairings in PA being changed in SL. The control group, group D, used words instead of numbers as stimuli in PA. Assuming that serial positions are stimuli in SL learning, the control group followed an A-B, C-B transfer paradigm, a paradigm which has been shown in some studies (e.g., Kausler & Kanoti, 1963; Twedt & Underwood, 1959) to produce negative transfer relative to the usual A-B, C-D control. The results reported by Winnick and Dornbush (1968) agree quite well with those of Ebenholtz (1963a), group A showing better performance than group B, and group B showing better performance than group C. As with Ebenholtz (1963a), however, interpretation is made difficult by the absence of an appropriate control group, group D showing performance equal to negative-transfer group C.

SL-to-PA, Serial Position Hypotheses

This design is SL to PA with some representation of the serial position of the item in SL as the stimulus for the appropriate item in PA. One of the conditions in the study by Ebenholtz (1963a) uses this kind of design with spatial position as the stimulus in PA. The experimental groups in this condition correspond to those of Ebenboltz (1963a) discussed in the preceding section. The results showed that PA learning in group C was superior to that in groups D and R in terms of both trials to criterion and errors per trial. There were no differences between groups D and R. As mentioned in the preceding section, however, this study suffers from the absence of an appropriate control group. It is not possible to say whether group C showed the predicted positive transfer or merely showed less negative transfer than groups D and R.

Studies using the same sort of design have been reported by Jensen and Rohwer (1965), Mueller (1970), and Young, Hakes, and Hicks (1967). The results are essentially the same as those of Ebenholtz (1963a) and so are the difficulties in interpretation.

SL-to-SL, Serial Position Hypotheses

One kind of design which has been used quite often to test the predictions of the serial position hypotheses is SL-to-SL transfer in which items hold the same or different serial positions in the two lists. If *S*s use serial position as a cue in SL learning, then transfer should be positive for those items occupying the same positions in the two lists. A good example of this approach is the second experiment reported by Ebenholtz (1963b). There were 3 groups, each learning two SLs in succession. The groups differed with respect to the relation between the two SLs.

In group 1, the second SL was constructed such that every other item from the first list was repeated in the same serial position. All other items in the second serial list were new. Group 2 also learned a second SL in which every other item was repeated, but for this group the items were not repeated in the same absolute serial position. The items were repeated in the same relative positions, however, the position of each repeated item being shifted to the left by four positions relative to their positions in the first SL. In group 3, no items from the first SL were repeated in the second SL. Considering only the repeated items, the results showed better performance for group 1 than for groups 2 and 3, which did not differ. As predicted by the serial position hypotheses, when position is held constant from one SL to a second SL, there is more transfer than when position is changed in the second list. Jensen and Rohwer (1965) and Young (1968) criticize this study on the grounds that *S*s may learn the rule that every other item in the first SL is repeated in the second SL and respond to repeated items in the second SL by simply skipping every other item learned in the first SL. If this were true, however, group 2, in which every other item was repeated in the same relative but different absolute positions, should show performance equal to group 1. Another criticism is that, as in the studies described in the previous section, there was no adequate control group. Group 3, which learned two SLs composed of different items, received the A-B, A-C negative-transfer paradigm according to the serial position hypotheses.

Keppel and Saufley (1964) describe a study which is in many respects similar to that of Ebenholtz (1963b). The design was SL-to-SL transfer in which items held the same or different serial positions in the two lists. Unlike Ebenholtz (1963b), they repeated all items in the two lists in all groups except a learning-to-learn control group. Since items repeated in different positions follow the A-B, A-Br negative-transfer paradigm, overall negative transfer was expected for all groups relative to the control group which is, as has been shown, also a negative-transfer group according to the serial position hypotheses. The predicted overall negative transfer did occur, and, in agreement with Ebenholtz (1963b), items occupying the same positions were anticipated correctly in the second SL more often than items occupying different positions. Whether items occupying the same positions show positive transfer as predicted by the serial position hypotheses or less negative transfer than items occupying different serial positions is not clear.

Another kind of SL-to-SL design which has been used to test the predictions of the serial position hypotheses is based on the assumption that serial position cues are eliminated by varying the starting position of the SL on each trial. Since the serial positions of the items change with each trial, it would be impossible to learn with serial position as the functional stimulus. The sequence of the items is the same on each trial, however, suggesting that the preceding item could be the stimulus when an SL is presented with a varied starting position. When an SL is presented with a constant starting position, either the serial position or the preceding item could be the functional stimulus. On the strength of these assumptions, Keppel (1964) has tested the serial position hypotheses through the use of a retroactive inhibition design. The experimental group learned two SLs composed of different items. The first SL was learned with either a varied or a constant starting position to one errorless trial. The second SL was then practiced under the same starting-position condition as the first for 10 trials, after which the items from both SLs were recalled. The control group learned a single SL with either a varied or constant starting position. Instead of practicing the second SL, however, control *S*s worked a puzzle before recalling the SL items. If it is assumed that the preceding item is the functional stimulus, the two SLs form the A-B, C-D zero-transfer paradigm, the stimuli and responses in the two lists being different. If serial position is the functional stimulus, however, the two SLs form the A-B, A-C negative-transfer paradigm since the same stimulus, serial position, is associated with two different responses. Assuming that the preceding item is the functional stimulus with a varied starting position, there should be slight positive learning-to-learn transfer in the acquisition of the second SL and very little retroactive inhibition in first-list recall. To the extent that serial position is the functional stimulus with a constant starting position, there should be negative transfer in the acquisition of the second SL and significant retroactive inhibition in recall of the first SL. The results are in good agreement with these predictions: There was greater second-list transfer and better first-list recall with varied starting positions.

SL-to-SL, Dual-Process Hypotheses

The SL-to-SL design has been used to test predictions of the dual-process hypotheses by the use of a procedure in which items appear in the same or different list loci in two successive SLs. The loci referred to are the beginning, middle, and end serial positions. According to the dual-process hypotheses, different functional stimuli are used in these different loci. An example of this kind of design is the study of Battig, Brown, and Schild (1964). Battig *et al.* had *S*s learn a serial list of 12 bigrams to one of two criteria: one (1R) or three (3R) consecutive correct anticipations of a 3-item cluster which was present in list 2 as well as in list 1. The 3 bigrams were transferred from list 1 to list 2 in one of three arrangements: same-position, changed-position, or nonadjacent positions. The transferred bigrams came from either the beginning of the list (positions 2, 3, and 4) or the middle of the list (positions 6, 7, and 8). In the same-position arrangement, the 3 items had the same positions in both list 1 and list 2. If the changed-position arrangement came from the beginning of list 1, they appeared in the middle of list 2. Similarly, if they came from the middle of list 1, they appeared in the beginning of list 2. The nonadjacent position condition transferred 3 nonadjacent bigrams (positions 3, 7, and 10) to their same respective positions in list 2. The results indicated that: (a) more mean total errors were made in the nonadjacent condition than in either the same or changed conditions; (b) mean total errors for the same and changed conditions were not significantly different; (c) mean percent errors increased over the three beginning positions of list 2 for all conditions with no significant differences between conditions; (d) there was improvement over the middle cluster positions of list 2 for both the same and changed conditions with the 3R list 1 criterion but not for the other conditions. On the basis of these results, Battig *et al.* (1964) suggest that a dual-process operates in a serial learning task, with either a chaining or serial position process at the beginning and a complex chaining process at the middle of the serial list.

Young *et al.* (1963b) also find evidence for a dual-process hypothesis, but their hypothesis is different from that of Battig *et al.* (1964). When Ss learned the reverse of list 1 as list 2, the serial position curve was flatter at the center, indicating better performance, than when a list of different items was learned as list 2. Since the positions of the items in list 2 were more nearly the same as the positions of the items in list 1 at the center of list 2 for the experimental group, it seems that serial position is more important as a cue in the center of the list. These data can be explained in nonassociative terms, however, by noting that the middle of the list has relatively more to gain from positive transfer than the list ends. That is, the list ends will be learned rapidly even without positive transfer and will therefore be less benefited by such transfer than the middle of the list.

Conclusions

The evidence from experiments using transfer designs would seem to suggest that all the major functional stimulus hypotheses are correct. The validity of this conclusion, however, is severely limited by the large number of methodological problems associated with these experiments. Some of these problems have already been mentioned: the interference in a double-function PA, the possibility of the transfer of response learning rather than associations, and negative-transfer control groups.

Another criticism of these studies has been made by Battig and Lawrence (1967), who claim that the anticipation procedure used by virtually all of the experiments testing functional stimulus hypotheses is not sensitive to the effects of the important variables. They suggest that the recall procedure, in which learning and performance measurement are separated in time, would provide a better indication of the processes involved in SL learning. As evidence for this idea, they report data showing that, as compared to the anticipation procedure, the recall procedure produced greater differences in the effects of varied and constant starting positions and greater second-SL facilitation in the backward serial-learning design of Young *et al.* (1963b). As pointed out by Battig and Lawrence (1967), however, these results could be taken to imply the operation of different learning processes in the two procedures rather than a difference in the sensitivity of two procedures applied to the same learning process. A choice between these two alternatives can be made only after further research comparing the two procedures in many different experimental situations.

Perhaps the most serious criticism of the studies reviewed thus far was suggested earlier as a criticism of the SL-to-PA design as applied to testing the chaining hypotheses. Evidence was presented which indicated that the basic process involved in PA learning in that design was the utilization of serial associations from the learned SL. As was pointed out, this utilization does not necessarily imply that the SL was learned as a chain of serial associations. The only implication is that *S*s are able to obtain information about interitem associations from a learned SL. The same idea can be applied as a criticism of the use of all transfer designs in functional stimulus research by noting that both serial position and interitem associations are available to *S* in a learned SL. Taking a telephone number as an example of a learned SL, it is clear that both the approximate serial position of all numbers and the number following any given number can be identified. In other words, a transfer design tests the end result rather than the process of SL learning. A similar criticism has been made by Postman (1968) and Battig and Young (1969).

SINGLE-LIST DESIGNS

Single-list experiments avoid all of the methodological problems of transfer experiments. Since only one list is learned, there are clearly no problems of interference in the double-function PA, negative transfer in the control group, or obtaining results biased by the possibility of transfer of response learning. Moreover, a single-list design allows the examination of the process of serial learning rather than the associations available at the end of serial learning.

The predictions of the functional stimulus hypotheses are tested in this kind of design by means of the disruption or facilitation of interitem or serial position associations during the acquisition of the SL. One method of disrupting serial position associations is to vary the starting position of the SL from trial to trial. Keppel (1964) found that this procedure retarded SL learning relative to a condition in which the starting point was constant. Several other studies (e.g., Bowman & Thurlow, 1963; Ebenholtz, 1963b; McManis, 1965; Saufley, 1967; Winnick & Dornbush, 1963) used a similar procedure and obtained similar results. Acquisition is also found to be retarded when serial position associations are disrupted by elimination of the intertrial interval (e.g., K. Breckinridge, Hakes, & Young, 1965; Glanzer & Peters, 1962; Lippman & Denny, 1964). These results clearly indicate the importance of the serial position cue in serial learning.

Facilitation of sequential associations has been accomplished by the use of normative word association data. In one condition described by Horowitz and Izawa (1963), *S*s learned one of four different SLs. The lists were composed of 21 words selected from the Minnesota norms of the Kent-Rosanoff Word Association Test and were constructed so that list F had strong forward associations, list B contained strong backward associations, list R contained only remote associations so that there was no forward or backward association between adjacent items, and list I contained no associations at all. The results show that list F was learned in fewer trials than list B or list I, which did not differ. The results indicate the importance of interitem associations in serial learning.

Diethorn and Voss (1967) use the same general method in a test of the dual-process hypothesis. *S*s learned a 12-word SL with a 4-word segment of chained association (taken from the Minnesota norms) inserted at serial positions 1–4, 5–8, or 9–12. In three additional experimental conditions, a reverse chain was placed at each of the three list loci. A control group learned a list containing no chained associations. The results showed that in terms of number of correct responses, forward chaining was facilitative at all loci, while reverse chaining was facilitative only at serial positions 5–8. These results suggest that, contrary to the dual-process hypotheses, interitem associations are important at all sections of the list.

Voss (1968) reports an experiment in which the degree of disruption on interitem associations was manipulated by varying the number of successively occurring list items. Lists were constructed such that there were 1, 2, 4, 8, or 16 successively occurring items. This was done by alternating two different forms of the list on successive trials with the letter "x" representing items not shown on a particular trial. For example, in the list with 1 successively occurring item, the first trial might appear as follows: item, x, item, x, item, x, etc. The second trial would then be: x, item, x, item, etc. Similarly, in the list with 16 successively occurring items, trial 1 might be: item, item, item, item, etc. Trial 2 would be: x, x, x, x, etc. Each *S* received 40 trials of practice on a list, 20 with each list form. They were instructed to attempt to anticipate each of the 16 items on each trial. Since only interitem associations were disrupted, serial position hypotheses would predict no differences among conditions. The chaining hypotheses would predict slower acquisition with greater disruption, i.e., slower acquisition with fewer successively occurring items. In general, the results support the chaining hypotheses, the number of correct responses increasing with the number of successively occurring items.

Some of the other data which Voss (1968) describes, however, suggest that something other than simple chaining is occurring. First, the shapes of the serial position curves for the various conditions indicate the existence of subcurves corresponding to the locations of successively occuring list items. With 8 successively occurring items, e.g., there were subcurves for positions 1–8 and positions 9–16. Similarly, with 4 successively occurring items, subcurves were found for positions 9–12 and 13–16. Second, the conditional probability of a correct response at position $i + 1$, given a correct response at position i, for lists with 2, 4, and 8 successively occurring items, was unusually low at positions at which a break occurred in the chain. As an example, the lowest probabilities in the list with 4 successively occurring items were found at positions 5, 9, and 13. Finally, the intrusion data indicate that, in the lists with 2, 4, and 8 successively occurring items, the most frequent intrusions were items from the same relative serial position of other subchains. For example, in the list with 4 successively occurring items, errors at serial position 3 tended to be intrusions from serial positions 7 and 11. These three kinds of data all seem to suggest that *S*s organized the lists into units corresponding to groups of successively occurring items. In addition, the intrusion data suggest that intraunit organization is related in some way to relative serial position. This is clearly something quite different from simple chaining.

Evidence for organizational processes has also been found by Battig and Young (1969). As in the Voss (1968) study, two different forms of the same list were presented on alternate trials. All items appeared on each trial, however, the difference in list forms being in the serial order of items. There were nine conditions defined in terms of the degree of relationship between the two serial orders. Degrees of relationship ranged from identity to no relationship. Intermediate degrees were obtained by treating the 11 items in the list as two subsets, one of 3 items and one of 8 items. The 3-item subset was composed of either adjacent items (items at serial positions 5, 6, and 7) or nonadjacent items (items at serial positions 3, 6, and 9). In each case, the 8-item subset was composed of the remaining items. Items in each subset appeared at either the same or different serial positions in the two list forms for the 3-item subset, variation of serial position being achieved by shifting each item to the following and preceding serial positions for the subset on successive trials. For example, if adjacent items appear in the order E-F-G in trial i, they would appear in the order G-E-F in trial $i + 1$. Similarly, if nonadjacent items appear in the order C-F-I (at serial positions 3, 6, and 9, respectively) in trial i, they would appear in the order I-C-F (at serial positions 3, 6, and 9) in trial $i + 1$. Variation of serial position for the 8-item subset was achieved either by reversing the positions within successive pairs (e.g., with an adjacent 3-item subset holding constant positions, A-B-C-D-E-F-G-H-I-J-K in trial i would become B-A-D-C-E-F-G-I-H-K-J in trial $i + 1$) or by using a random or unsystematic rearrangement of order. The effect of these procedures is to produce different levels of disruption of both serial position and interitem associations with either systematic or unsystematic relationships between the two list forms. Each list was practiced by the recall method for 24 trials, 12 study-test trials for each order, or to a criterion of two successive errorless trials. The *S*s were instructed to recall the items in the order most recently presented.

In regard to the major hypotheses discussed at the beginning of this chapter, the results suggest the greater importance of serial position cues as compared to interitem associations. Specifically, it was found that performance was equally facilitated in the adjacent and nonadjacent 3-item subset when serial position was the same in both list forms. If interitem associations were important, the nonadjacent subset should have shown poorer performance than the adjacent subset. Other data, however, are not easily explained in terms of serial position or interitem associations. It was found, e.g., that in lists with the serial positions of one of the two subsets varied, performance was almost equally as good in both subsets. In other words, disruption of serial position or interitem associations in either subset seemed to have little effect as long as there was constancy in the other subset. In fact, performance was even better on the varied 3-item subset with a constant 8-item subset as compared to the condition in which the positions in both subsets were varied. Battig and Young (1969) explain these results in terms of an organizational process in which *S*s learn a rule describing the relationship between the two serial orders. This rule is then used to generate responses for each list order. As an example, the rule describing the relationship between list orders for the 3-item subset is a backward or forward shift of list items on successive trials. For systematic variation of the 8-item subset, the rule would be the pairwise reversal of list items. The importance of constancy in one subset would presumably be due to the greater ease with which the two subsets could be identified and isolated for rule learning.

As Battig and Young (1969) point out, the detection of a relationship and subsequent rule learning in their experiment can be done only after some preliminary learning of serial order. The question of the processes involved in this preliminary learning still remains. To the extent that the learning of rules depends upon the existence of systematic relationships between list forms, the use of a procedure for disrupting serial position and interitem associations in which such relationships are absent should reveal the relative importance of these associations when rule learning is not possible. A procedure of this kind has been used by Voss (1966). Voss disrupted serial position and interitem associations by varying item probability (*IP*) and conditional probability (*CP*) within the same list. *IP* is the probability that a particular item will occur in a particular serial position. For example, if items A, B, C, and D occur in positions 1, 2, 3, and 4, respectively, 75% of the time, *IP* = .75. *CP* is the probability that, given item A, item B will follow it. For example, if after item A appears, item B appears 75% of the time, *CP* = .75. A list of four or eight adjectives was presented for 80 trials. Within each list length there were six experimental conditions: 1.00–1.00, .75–1.00, .50–1.00, .75–.75, .50–.75, and .50–.50, where the first number refers to *IP* and the second refers to *CP*. The data were analyzed for the first 20 trials, the first 40 trials, and all 80 trials. The results indicate that (a) *CP* was not a significant variable for the 4-item list; (b *IP* was significant for the 4-item list if *CP* = 1.00; (c) for the 8-item list, if *IP* = .75, *CP* was significant for all stages of learning, but if *IP* = .50, *CP* was significant only in the 80-trial analysis; (d) for the 8-item list, if *CP* = 1.00, *IP* was significant, but if *CP* = .75, *IP* was not significant. In all cases the significant differences are in the expected direction: better performance with higher *IP* or *CP*. It is evident from the results that both serial position and interitem associations are important in *SL* learning. The extent of the contribution of each cannot be readily determined, however, due to two characteristics of the lists employed in this study. First, *IP* and *CP* were not varied independently. *CP* was always equal to or greater than *IP*. Second, the range of variation was not equal for all comparisons. For example, with *CP* = 1.00, *IP* varied through a range of .50. With *IP* = .75, however, *CP* varied over a range of .25.

Bewley (1966) reports a study using a method similar to that of Voss (1966) but in which *IP* and *CP* were made to vary independently and the range of variation of the two was equal. Each *S* received 48 anticipation trials on one of five 8-item lists. The lists were constructed so that both *IP* and *CP* had values of .25, .50, and .75. These probabilities were combined to form the following five lists: .50–.25, .50–.50, .50–.75, .25–.50, and .75–.50, where the first and second numbers refer to *IP* and *CP*, respectively. The results showed that in terms of overall number of correct anticipations both *IP* and *CP* had significant effects, performance improving with higher probabilities. Furthermore, the amount of this improvement was the same for both *IP* and *CP*. *IP* and *CP* did have a differential effect, however, on performance at particular serial positions. With high *IP*, performance was facilitated chiefly at the ends of the list, while with high *CP*, facilitation was found at the middle of the list. These results suggest that both serial position and sequential associations are important in SL learning, with serial position associations occurring at the list ends and interitem associations occurring at the middle of the list. This supports the dual-process hypothesis of Ebenholtz (1963a).

Further support for this hypothesis comes from Bewley (1969). In this experiment, serial position associations were disrupted at the beginning, middle, or end of an SL. This disruption was achieved by varying the starting position of a 4-item segment located at positions 1–4, 5–8, or 9–12 in a 12-item list. Disruption of interitem associations was minimized by maintaining the same sequence of items within the segment. As an example of disruption at the middle of the list, if item order in trial i was A-B-C-D-E-F-G-H-I-J-K-L, the order on trial $i + 1$ would be A-B-C-D-F-G-H-E-I-J-K-L. As predicted by the dual-process hypothesis of Ebenholtz (1963a), the results showed that, relative to a control list in which there were no disruptions, disruption of serial position associations had its greatest effect at the beginning and end of the SL.

Conclusions

The single-list studies which have been reviewed suggest that (a) the chaining hypotheses are correct (Diethorn & Voss, 1967; Horowitz & Izawa, 1963), (b) the serial position hypotheses are correct (Keppel, 1964), and (c) the Ebenholtz (1963a) dual-process hypothesis is correct (Bewley, 1966; 1969). Thus, although single-list designs have been shown to be more methodologically sound than transfer designs, the conclusion to be drawn from each is the same: All the major functional stimulus hypotheses are correct. To complicate matters further, the studies of Voss (1968) and Battig and Young (1969) suggest still another process: list organization according to nonassociative relationships among items in list segments.

Serial Learning as Strategy Selection

The conflicting evidence regarding the functional stimulus in serial learning can be explained by viewing the learning task as a problem in strategy selection rather than stimulus selection. Given a set of items, the *S* is asked to learn in such a way that the items can be recalled in a particular order. There seem to be at least three ways in which this can be done. First, as suggested by the chaining hypotheses, each item could serve as a cue for the recall of the following item. Second, as suggested by the serial position hypotheses, some aspect of the temporal position of an item in the series could serve as a cue for recall. Third, as suggested by the results of Battig and Young (1969) and Voss (1968), described in the preceding section, acquisition could involve the organization of list items according to cues provided by relationships among the list items. Each of these can be called a learning strategy and each can be used by *S*. The choice of a strategy depends upon the set of *S* and upon the nature of the list.

The set of *S* depends upon such things as instructions and prior experience. One source of evidence for the effects of instructions comes from the SL-to-PA transfer designs already discussed. As was shown by Lesgold and Bower (1970) and Postman and Stark (1967), special instructions regarding chained associations tend to cause *S* to choose a chaining strategy despite the fact that, as shown by Lesgold and Bower (1970), this strategy may be inefficient. Other evidence for the influence of instructions on strategy selection is presented by Wing (1964). Wing showed that typographical differentiation of items in the first half of a list from those in the second half produced a greater reduction of error at the middle of the list if *S*s were instructed to learn the list as if it were two lists. The effect of prior experience on strategy selection was also demonstrated by Postman and Stark (1967). As described earlier, when *S*s learned three SL-PA list pairs, there was no effect of instructions in the later PA trials of the first pair or at any stage of PA learning for the second and third pairs. One possible interpretation of this finding is that with prior experience *S*s essentially instruct themselves.

The nature of the list can be defined either in terms of how the list is presented or in terms of relationships among list items. The influence of the presentation method has been shown in studies comparing the effects of varied and constant starting positions. In the study of Keppel (1964), which was discussed earlier, it was found that retroactive inhibition was reduced when both the first and second SL were learned with varied starting positions. This result suggested that *S*s used a chaining strategy with varied starting position and a serial position strategy with constant starting position. The same conclusion is suggested by the results of Saufley (1967). In that study, *S*s learned an SL with either varied or constant starting position to a criterion of one errorless trial, after which practice on the list continued under either the same starting-position condition or the alternate condition. The results showed that going from the varied starting position method of presentation to the constant starting position method was much easier than the reverse. This is the effect which would be expected if a chaining strategy is used with the varied starting-positin method and a serial position strategy is used with the constant starting-position method (since the chaining strategy can be used under both presentation methods while the serial position strategy can be used only with the constant starting position method).

The influence of the presentation method on strategy selection has also been shown in two studies investigating the effects of temporal grouping of items in list presentation (Lesgold & Bower, 1970; McLean & Gregg, 1967). Both find that temporal grouping produces grouping in recall, a result which suggests the use of an organizational strategy based on cues provided by relationships among list items. In these studies, the relationships were the temporal groupings. Another kind of relationship among items, grouping according to sets of successively occurring items, has already been seen to produce grouping in recall (Voss, 1968).

Relationships among items which are not dependent upon the presentation method are normative associations among items, conceptual relationships among items, and the existence of sequences within the list which can be described by a rule. The influence of normative associations has already been seen in the work of Diethorn and Voss (1967) and Horowitz and Izawa (1963). The effect of conceptual relationships among items is shown by the study of Wright and Bernstein (1965), in which there was an indication that the presence of a conceptually related cluster of items altered the usual order of learning in an SL in that the cluster was always learned first. Battig and Young (1969) have shown that the existence of patterns among list items which can be described by a rule will cause the list to be organized according to that rule. Restle and Brown (1970) find similar results using patterned sequences of lights.

There seems to be evidence, then, for the idea that *S*s can learn a serial list by the use of any one of several alternate strategies, the choice of strategies being determined by the set of *S* and the characteristics of the task. This conception of serial learning suggests that there is no single functional stimulus used by all *S*s in all situations. In fact, with some tasks there is no functional stimulus at all, the use of rules allowing the generation of list items with no specific cues or stimuli. The research which has been reviewed here seems to indicate that naive (uninstructed) *S*s may choose strategies in a particular order. Keppel (1964) and Saufley (1967), e.g., have shown that *S*s prefer to use a serial position strategy unless this strategy is made impossible by the elimination of serial position cues. The strategy employed when serial position cues are eliminated is the chaining strategy. The results of Bewley (1966, 1969) might be explained by saying that *S*s attempt to use the serial position strategy over the entire list but are forced to use the chaining strategy in the middle of the list due to a lack of distinctiveness of the middle serial position cues (see Murdock, 1960). This is essentially the view expressed by Ebenholtz (1963a). The serial position and/or chaining strategies provide for the preliminary learning mentioned by Battig and Young (1969) as being necessary for the recognition of patterns among stimuli which is necessary for the use of the organizational strategy.

REFERENCES

Asch, S. E. The doctrinal tyranny of associationism: Or what is wrong with rote learning. In T. R. Dixon and D. L. Horton (Eds.), *Verbal behavior and general behavior theory*. Englewood Cliffs, N.J.: Prentice-Hall, 1968. Pp. 214–228.

Asch, S. E., & Ebenholtz, S. M. The principle of associative symmetry. *Proceedings of the American Philosophical Society*, 1962, **106**, 135–163.

Asch, S. E., Hay, J. C., & Diamond, R. M. Perceptual organization in serial rote-learning. *American Journal of Psychology*, 1960, **73**, 177–198.

Battig, W. F., Brown, S. C., & Schild, M. E. Serial position and sequential associations in serial learning. *Journal of Experimental Psychology*, 1964, **67**, 449–457.

Battig, W. F., & Koppenaal, R. S. Associative asymmetry in S-R and R-S recall of double function lists. *Psychological Reports*, 1965, **16**, 287–293.

Battig, W. F., & Lawrence, P. S. The greater sensitivity of the serial recall than anticipation procedure to variations in serial order. *Journal of Experimental Psychology*, 1967, **73**, 172–178.

Battig, W. F., & Young, R. K. Simultaneous serial-recall learning of two serial orders of the same list. *Journal of Verbal Learning and Verbal Behavior*, 1969, **8**, 393–402.

Bewley, W. L. The effect of varying probability of association and position of items on acquisition and transfer of serial learning. Unpublished M.A. thesis, University of Wisconsin, 1966.

Bewley, W. L. The effect of locus and degree of associative disruption on the acquisition of a serial list. Unpublished doctoral dissertation, University of Wisconsin, 1969.

Bowman, R. E., & Thurlow, W. R. Determinants of the effect of position in serial learning. *American Journal of Psychology*, 1963, **76**, 436–445.

Breckenridge, K., Hakes, D. T., & Young, R. K. Serial learning in a continuous serial list. *Psychonomic Science,* 1965, **3**, 139–140.

Breckenridge, R. L. & Dixon, T. R. Problem of the stimulus in serial learning. *Journal of Experimental Psychology,* 1970, **83**, 126–130.

Crowder, R. G. Evidence for the chaining hypothesis of serial verbal learning. *Journal of Experimental Psychology,* 1968, **76**, 497–500.

Diethorn, J. A., & Voss, J. F. Serial learning as a function of locus of chained associations. *Journal of Experimental Psychology,* 1967, **73**, 411–418.

Ebbinghaus, H. *Memory: A contribution to experimental psychology.* New York: Dover, 1964.

Ebenholtz, S. M. Position mediated transfer between serial learning and a spatial discrimination task. *Journal of Experimental Psychology,* 1963, **65**, 603–608. (a)

Ebenholtz, S. M. Serial learning; position learning and sequential associations. *Journal of Experimental Psychology,* 1963, **66**, 353–362. (b)

Erickson, C. C., Ingram, R. D., & Young, R. K. Paired associate learning as a function of rate of presentation and prior serial learning. *American Journal of Psychology,* 1963, **76**, 458–463.

Gardner, R. A. On box score methodology as illustrated by three reviews of overtraining reversal effects. *Psychological Bulletin,* 1966, **66**, 416–418.

Glanzer, M., & Peters, S. C. Re-examination of the serial position effect. *Journal of Experimental Psychology,* 1962, **64**, 258–266.

Heaps, R. S., Greene, W. A., & Cheney, C. D. Transfer from serial to paired-associate learning with two paired-associate rates. *Journal of Verbal Learning and Verbal Behavior,* 1968, **7**, 840–841.

Horowitz, L. M., & Izawa, C. Comparison of serial and paired-associate learning. *Journal of Experimental Psychology,* 1963, **65**, 352–361.

Horton, D. L., and Turnage, T. W. Serial to paired-associate learning: Utilization of serial information. *Journal of Experimental Psychology,* 1970, **84**, 88–95.

Jensen, A. R. Transfer between paired-associate and serial learning. *Journal of Verbal Learning and Verbal Behavior,* 1962, **1**, 269–280.

Jensen, A. R., & Rohwer, W. D. What is learned in serial learning? *Journal of Verbal Learning and Verbal Behavior,* 1965, **4**, 62–72.

Johnson, G. J., & Penney, R. K. Transfer effects of mixed and unmixed list designs in paired-associate learning of children. *Psychonomic Science,* 1965, **2**, 171–172.

Kausler, D. H., & Kanoti, G. A. R-S learning and negative transfer effects with a mixed list. *Journal of Experimental Psychology,* 1963, **65**, 201–205.

Keppel, G. Retroactive inhibition of serial lists as a function of presence or absence of positional cues. *Journal of Verbal Learning and Verbal Behavior,* 1964, **3**, 511–517.

Keppel, G., & Saufley, W. H., Jr. Serial position as a stimulus in serial learning. *Journal of Verbal Learning and Verbal Behavior,* 1964, **3**, 335–343.

Lashley, K. S. The problem of serial order in behavior. In L. A. Jefress (Ed.), *Cerebral mechanisms in behavior.* New York: Wiley, 1951. Pp. 112–136.

Lepley, W. M. Serial reactions considered as conditioned reactions. *Psychological Monographs,* 1934, **46**, 1.

Lesgold, A. M., & Bower, G. H. Inefficiency of serial knowledge for association responding. *Journal of Verbal Learning and Verbal Behavior,* 1970, **9**, 456–466.

Lippman, L. G., & Denny, M. R. Serial position effect as a function of intertrial interval. *Journal of Verbal Learning and Verbal Behavior,* 1964, **3**, 496–501.

McLean, R. S., & Gregg, L. W. Effects of induced cheenking on temporal aspects of serial recitation. *Journal of Experimental Psychology,* 1967, **74**, 455–459.

McManis, D. L. Position-cues in serial learning. *American Journal of Psychology,* 1965, **78**, 668–671.

Mueller, J. H. Response properties of the position indicant in serial learning. *Journal of Experimental Psychology,* 1970, **84**, 35–39.

Murdock, B. B., Jr. The distinctiveness of stimuli. *Psychological Review,* 1960, **67**, 16–31.

Neisser, U. *Cognitive psychology*. New York: Appleton, 1967.

Postman, L. Association and performance in the analysis of verbal learning. In T. R. Dixon and D. L. Horton, (Eds.), *Verbal behavior and general behavior theory.* Englewood Cliffs, N.J.: Prentice-Hall, 1968. Pp. 550–571.

Postman, L., & Stark, K. Studies of learning to learn. IV. Transfer from serial to paired-associate learning. *Journal of Verbal Learning and Verbal Behavior,* 1967, **6**, 339–353.

Restle, F., & Brown, E. R. Serial pattern learning. *Journal of Experimental Psychology,* 1970, **83**, 120–125.

Rosner, S. R. Serial mediation: Effects of associative strength and structure on serial learning and transfer. *Journal of Experimental Psychology,* 1970, **84**, 370–372.

Salafia, W. R. Response made as a determinant of transfer from serial to paired-associate learning. *Psychonomic Science,* 1969, **15**, 197–199.

Saufley, W. H., Jr. An analysis of cues in serial learning. *Journal of Experimental Psychology,* 1967, **74**, 414–419.

Slamecka, N. J. An inquiry into the doctrine of remote associations. *Psychological Review,* 1964, **71**, 61–76.

Stark, K. Transfer from serial to paired-associate learning: A reappraisal. *Journal of Verbal Learning and Verbal Behavior,* 1968, **7**, 20–30.

Twedt, H. M., & Underwood, B. J. Mixed vs. unmixed lists in transfer studies. *Journal of Experimental Psychology,* 1959, **58**, 111–116.

Umemoto, T., & Hilgard, E. R. Paired-associate learning as a function of similarity: Common stimulus and response items within the list. *Journal of Experimental Psychology,* 1961, **62**, 97–104.

Underwood, B. J., Runquist, W. N., & Schulz, R. W. Response learning in paired-associate lists as a function of intralist similarity. *Journal of Experimental Psychology,* 1959, **58**, 70–78.

Voss, J. F. Serial acquisition as a function of item probability and sequential probability. *Journal of Experimental Psychology,* 1966, **71**, 304–313.

Voss, J. F. Serial acquisition as a function of number of successively occurring list items. *Journal of Experimental Psychology,* 1968, **78**, 456–462.

Wing, J. F. Effects of set on the serial position curve for typographically differentiated lists. *Perceptual and Motor Skills,* 1964, **19**, 515–519.

Winnick, W. A., & Dornbush, R. L. Role of positional cues in serial rote learning. *Journal of Experimental Psychology,* 1963, **66**, 419–421.

Winnick, W. A., & Dornbush, R. L. Ordinal position in serial learning. *Journal of Experimental Psychology,* 1968, **78**, 536–538.

Woodworth, R. S. *Experimental psychology*. New York: Holt, 1938.

Wright, J. H., & Bernstein, D. A. Effects of conceptual grouping of adjacent items on serial learning. *Psychological Reports,* 1965, **17**, 187–190.

Young, R. K. A comparison of two methods of learning serial associations. *American Journal of Psychology,* 1959, **72**, 554–559.

Young, R. K., The stimulus in serial verbal learning. *American Journal of Psychology,* 1961, **74**, 517–528.

Young, R. K. Tests of three hypotheses about the effective stimulus in serial learning. *Journal of Experimental Psychology,* 1962, **63**, 307–313.

Young, R. K. Serial learning. In T. R. Dixon and D. L. Horton (Eds.), *Verbal behavior and general behavior theory.* Englewood Cliffs, N.J. Prentice-Hall, 1968. Pp. 122–148.

Young, R. K., Hakes, D. T., & Hicks, R. Y. Ordinal position number as a cue in serial learning. *Journal of Experimental Psychology,* 1967, **73**, 427–438.

Young, R. K., Milauckas, E. W., & Bryan, J. D. Serial learning as a function of prior paired-associate training. *American Journal of Psychology,* 1963, **76**, 82–88. (a)

Young, R. K., Patterson, J., & Benson, W. M. Backward serial learning. *Journal of Verbal Learning and Verbal Behavior,* 1963, **1**, 335–338. (b)

CHAPTER 10

WORDS AS SETS OF FEATURES: THE ROLE OF PHONOLOGICAL ATTRIBUTES[1]

Douglas L. Nelson

The Ordinal Position Effect

Initial and, to a lesser extent, terminal portions of words are more influential determinants of their processing than are their medial portions. Evidence consistent with this generalization comes from several sources

[1] The research reported in this chapter has been supported by Grant MH-16360 from the National Institute of Mental Health.

using diverse methodologies. Bruner and O'Dowd (1958) presented nouns containing typographical reversals of letters at various ordinal positions. Disruption of tachistoscopic word identification was greatest with a reversal in the initial part of the word and next greatest at the end of the word. The least disruption was found when the error was localized in the middle of the word. In order to precipitate a "tip of the tongue" state, Brown and McNeill (1966) read definitions of infrequently occurring English words and required identification of the word associated with each of the definitions. While in this state, identification of the beginnings and ends of the target word was superior to middle-letter identification. Following the presentation of lists of six- or nine-letter words, Horowitz, White, and Atwood (1968) showed fragments of these words on a recall test. Regeneration of the words was highest when beginning fragments were shown, next highest when end fragments were shown, and lowest when middle fragments were shown. One implication of these findings is that, in addition to unique semantic, associative, and imaginal properties, words have a characteristic organizational structure which may influence the manner in which they are perceived and processed for subsequent retrieval.

Data collected in the University of South Florida laboratory over the past four years have corroborated this apparent first-last-middle processing pattern, and have related this finding to the involvement of phonological attributes of words in various coding tasks. In all of these tasks the variable of principle concern has been the ordinal position of identical letters shared by a set of words coded for subsequent recognition or recall. Interest in this variable was aroused by the findng (Nelson, 1968) that difficulty of acquisiton of a word–number paired-associate task was greater when the first letters of the stimulus words were identical (e.g., SAG, SET, SOW, SIP, etc.) than when the last letters were identical (e.g., BAN, HEN, WON, DIN, etc.). Both of these conditions were more difficult than a control in which stimulus words did not share consonants in any position. These data represent one of the first demonstrations that formal similarity among *words* disrupts acquisition, and they were the first to identify the importance of the *locus* of the letter sharing.

To ascertain the reliability of this locus effect, Nelson and Rowe (1969) systematically varied the position of identical letters throughout all possible locations within the three-letter word stimuli of paired-associate lists. Each list consisted of two subsets of four words each. Within each subset there were identical letters in only specified ordinal positions: first (F), middle (M), last (L), or F & M, F & L, or M & L. Responses were the single digit numbers 1–8. For example, for condition F the pairs

TABLE 1
Mean Errors as a Function of Number and Location of Identical Letters within Paired-Associate Stimuli (N = 16) [a]

	Location of identical letters					
Zero	F	M	L	F and L	F and M	M and L
34.06	58.60	33.37	48.12	78.37	73.00	50.43

[a] From Nelson and Rowe (1969). Copyright (1969) by The American Psychological Association, and reproduced by permission.

were BAT-7, BEN-1, BID-4, BUM-6, SOB-2, SHE-5, SLY-8, and SKI-3. Pairs were presented visually, practice was paced (2:2 sec), there was no intertrial interval between successive list presentations, the stimulus words were pronounced aloud upon presentation, and response guessing was required. Each subject *(S)* acquired only a single list. Mean errors to the 20-trial acquisition criterion for each locus condition are shown in Table 1. Difficulty of acquisition was greatest when the beginnings of the stimulus words were identical and next greatest when the ends shared letters; the least difficulty was encountered when the letters within the medial position were identical. This ordinal position effect was obtained regardless of whether sharing was within a single position or within two positions.

The successful replication of the effect attested to its reliability and suggested additional experimentation designed to test its generality. Nelson (1969) constructed three-letter word stimulus sets with the same variations in locus and number of identical letters. However, half of the *S*s within each identity conditon practiced the list by the method of free recall and half practiced by the method of serial recall. Mean errors to the 10 trials acquisition criterion are shown in Table 2. When recall was free,

TABLE 2
Mean Errors under Conditions of Free and Serial Recall as a Function of Number and Location of Identical Letters (N = 12) [a]

Recall method	Zero	Location of identical letters: F	M	L	F and L	F and M	M and L
Free	33.25	24.33	34.42	29.67	27.92	31.42	34.50
Serial	51.33	57.67	53.82	54.58	83.42	59.84	57.78

[a] From Nelson (1969). Copyright (1969) by the American Psychological Association, and reproduced by permission.

TABLE 3
Mean Errors as a Function of Number and Location of Letters Shared by Stimuli and Their Responses (N = 20) [a]

	Location of stimulus–response overlap					
Zero	F	M	L	F and L	F and M	M and L
23.40	11.75	19.80	17.10	7.35	6.90	5.45

[a] From Nelson and Garland (1969). Copyright (1969) by the American Psychological Association, and reproduced by permission.

difficulty of acquisition (and degree of clustering) *increased* in the order beginning-end-middle. That is, identity within the beginning portions of words produced the fastest acquisition and greatest degree of organization. When recall was serial, difficulty of acquisition *decreased* in the order beginning-end-middle. In a related experiment, Nelson and Garland (1969) demonstrated that the facilitation effect also occurs in paired-associate tasks if stimuli overlap with their responses. As shown in Table 3, paired-associate word pairs were learned fastest if the beginnings portions overlapped (e.g., JAY-JOB), next fastest when terminal letters overlapped (e.g., CUB-JOB), and slowest if sharing was within medial positions (e.g., COW-JOB). These findings demonstrated that the locus of identical letters within words could produce differential facilitation or interference, depending upon the task requirements. When discriminations between stimuli are required, difficulty of acquisition *decreased* as identity was shifted in a first-last-middle pattern. When words related by letter sharing could be grouped together, difficulty of acquisiton *increased* in a first-last-middle pattern.

Explanations for the Ordinal Position Effect

The initial explanation for the ordinal position effect was referred to as the informational structure hypothesis because of its association with the application of information theory to the study of English words. This application indicated that the amount of information provided by a letter within a word depended upon its ordinal position within that word. Beginnings and ends of words apparently carried more information than middle letters, and beginnings carried more than end letters. This conclusion was based upon the employment of Shannon's (1951) guessing-game technique in which *S*s were provided with words containing missing letters. The *S*s were required to guess these missing letters until they were correct. From the distributions of letters guessed at various positions, estimates of the amount of information transmitted by particular positions could be calculated (e.g., Carson, 1961). As a check on the assumption that speakers of the language possessed detailed knowledge of its statistical properties, all the three-letter words found in the *American College Dictionary* were selected and the distributional uncertainty at all positions was calculated. For positions F, M, L, F & M, F & L, and M & L *bits* of information were, respectively, 4.46, 3.35, 4.21, 7.06, 8.10, and 6.89 (Nelson & Rowe, 1969). The results of this actual count corroborated the findings obtained using estimation techniques: Information provided by a letter in a word varied in a beginning-end-middle pattern.

The major assumption of the informational structure hypothesis is that word processing mechanisms are sensitive to word structure so that words are coded in terms of their informational content. For example, since initial letters typically carry the greatest amount of information for discriminating words, and initial portions of words play a differentially important role in storing and retrieving words. Therefore, identity of first letters in a task requiring discriminations between stimuli should produce greater difficulty of acquisiton relative to other identity locations. The normally most informative position within the words would provide no information for discriminating the words within the set. Similarily, in a task involving overlapping stimulus–response pairs, identity of first letters should differentially facilitate rate of acquisition. In this case, the stimulus provides more information about its response than overlap in other less informative positions.

The correspondence between the ordinal position effect obtained in various coding tasks and the apparent informational structure of three-letter words was close enough to warrant its serious consideration. However, the data have not been in complete accord with expectations. Because the information transmitted by first and by last letters is nearly equal, the hypothesis would predict that the difference between first *versus* last locations should be *less* than that between middle *versus* last locations. However, the former difference has always been greater (Nelson, 1969; Nelson & Garland, 1969; Nelson & Rowe, 1969). Even more compelling evidence for rejecting this hypothesis stems from locus effects obtained within six-letter words. An informational analysis of the sequential constraint and distributional uncertainty of the 2999 six-letter words obtained from the G count of the Thorndike–Lorge (1944) norms indicated that medial provided nearly as much information as initial letters, with terminal letters being the least informative. According to the informational structure hypothesis, when the six-letter word stimuli of paired-associate lists share letters, or when these stimuli share letters with their responses, the pattern of acquisition performance should be first-middle *versus* last. However, as with three-letter words, acquisition has been related to ordinal locus of identity in the first-last-middle pattern (Nelson, Fosselman & Peebles, 1971c; Nelson, Peebles, & Pancotto, 1970e).

These and other considerations indicated that this hypothesis was inadequate as a viable explanation for the ordinal position effect. Two alternative interpretations have been appraised. The major assumption of the first is that words in these tasks are coded by pronunciation, rendering them subject to acoustic-articulatory interference or facilitation (cf. Runquist, 1968). To account for the effect, this hypothesis must simply assume that words sharing initial letters are more acoustically similar than words sharing terminal or medial letters, and that words overlapping in terminal letters are more similar than words sharing medial letters. To test this assumption, pairs of words overlapping in various positions (e.g., PAN-PIT) were rated in terms of their phonological similarity (Nelson & Nelson, 1970). The results of this scaling were at variance with expectations derived from the pronunciation code hypothesis. No differences in rated similarity were found between pairs sharing medial *versus* terminal letters, even though there has been a consistent locus difference between these conditions in various acquisition tasks. More importantly, however, pairs sharing M & L letters were given significantly higher similarity ratings (they rhyme) than words sharing F & M or F & L letters. Therefore, identity within M & L loci should produce the greatest interference or the strongest facilitatory effects relative to F & M or F & L. However, it does not (Nelson, 1969; Nelson *et al.,* 1971c, Experiment II; Nelson & Rowe, 1969). One way to reconcile the rating and acquisition data would be to assume that different processes are involved in the two tasks. Rhyming may have been a prepotent response in the rating task, resulting in higher similarity ratings for word pairs agreeing in terminal sounds. However, it seems unlikely that rhyming would operate in the rating task but not in the acquisition task, especially a task in which stimuli overlapped with their respective responses (Nelson *et al.,* 1971c; Nelson & Garland, 1969).

The principal assumption of the second alternative explanation for the effect is that, in these tasks, words are processed, at least in part, as phonological *sequences,* analogous to miniature serial lists (Nelson *et al.,* 1970e, 1971c, Nelson & Garland, 1969). Most generally stated, this hypothesis assumes that words are comprised of sets of distinctive features, attributes, or dimensions (cf. Anisfeld & Knapp, 1968; Wickens, 1970). When a word is presented, it is assumed that a feature or some combination of features is recoded into memory and that the attributes decoded at retrieval will depend upon the characteristics of the task. Thus, when words within a to-be-coded set share letters, their phonological features become salient. To the extent that processes involved in stimulus recall are based upon the retrieval of these acoustic-articulatory features, acquisition will be impaired or facilitated, depending upon the task. As phonological codes, words appear to have a characteristic beginning-end-middle structure. Thus, the words-as-features hypothesis is similar to the pronunciation code hypothesis in that it assumes that phonological attributes can represent significant components of stored words but it differs from that hypothesis in that it also specifies the serial structure of these codes. This specification is necessary to account for the ordinal position effect.

The words-as-features hypothesis does not represent a unique contribution of this program of research. In fact, the notion that complex cognitive representations, words in this case, are capable of analysis into more simple elements antedates the study of psychology as a separate discipline. For Locke (Boring, 1957), complex ideas were composites of simple ideas bonded together through association. Thus, comprehension of the mind could be achieved by the analysis of compound ideas into their more simple elements. Variations of this viewpoint have persisted in various forms to the present day and, recently, have been given explicit expression in theories of pattern perception (e.g., Neisser, 1966), in conceptualizations of phoneme structure (Jakobsen, Fant, & Halle, 1961), and in models of word constituency (e.g., Deese, 1965; Johnson, 1970; Osgood, 1968). In the latter case, word forms are conceived of as bundles of distinctive semantic (Osgood, 1968) or associative (Deese, 1965) features. These theoretical models are capable of extension so as to incorporate other word features such as their imagery-evoking capability (e.g., Paivio, 1969), their physical or orthographic characteristics (e.g., Brown & McNeill, 1966), their phonological attributes (e.g., Nelson *et al.,* 1970e), and, perhaps, information about stress or emphasis. Furthermore, the distinctive feature analysis is amenable to the notion that significant environmental information, such as position in series, modality, context, etc., may be coded along with specific word features so that this information may represent an important distinguishing characteristic of a stored word (cf. Underwood, 1969; Wickens, 1970). The ultimate representation of a word in memory may therefore consist of a rich store of information about its characteristics and about the characteristics of the situation in which it is recoded. This assumption has been given explicit expression in the theory of the structure of long-term storage proposed by Atkinson and Shiffrin (1968), and has served as the principal theoretical framework for guiding current research on the ordinal position effect in the University of South Florida laboratory.

ORDINAL POSITION EFFECT WITHIN PAIRED-ASSOCIATE STIMULI

The first-last-middle processing pattern occurs when either three-letter or six-letter words serve as the paired-associate stimuli (Nelson *et al.*, 1970e; Nelson & Rowe, 1969) but not when these stimuli are low association value nonsense syllables sharing letters within a single locus (Nelson, 1968; Runquist, 1968; Runquist & Blackmore, 1971). This finding suggests that the effect is dependent upon the stimuli being processed as integrated sequences. The null effect within low-meaningfulness syllables may have occurred because responses were associated to distinct letters within the stimuli so that stimuli were coded in terms of their constituent letters and not as sequences. If presented aurally, however, the syllables would be coded as phonetic sequences, which should enhance the likelihood of obtaining the effect with these stimuli. To test this hypothesis, Nelson, Brooks, and Fosselman (in press, Experiment I) varied the location of letters shared by low association value CVC's serving as paired-associate stimuli and presented items either visually or auditorily. In ad-

TABLE 4
Pairs for List Set I [a]

	Location of identical letters					
	F		M		L	
High meaningfulness	TAG	6	BAG	9	MAT	9
	TEA	5	HAM	4	PET	6
	TIN	8	LAX	7	BIT	7
	TOW	4	MAD	5	DOT	4
	TUB	7	SAP	6	NUT	8
	TRY	9	VAT	8	ART	5
Low meaningfulness	TAZ	5	GAQ	5	XAT	8
	TIJ	7	FAJ	8	QET	7
	TEF	9	BAV	9	YIT	4
	TOV	6	YAF	7	ZOT	5
	TUQ	3	DAX	4	VUT	6
	TYB	4	ZAL	6	JYT	9

[a] Note that initial-final letters were equated (i.e., in list set I stimuli in F and in L began or ended with the letter T. The letter P was used in list set II).

TABLE 5

Mean Errors as a Function of Meaningfulness, Location of Identical Letters, and Modality (N = 12) [a]

	High meaningfulness			Low meaningfulness		
Modality	F	M	L	F	M	L
Visual	32.58	22.75	25.00	49.33	44.08	37.83
Auditory	37.08	30.08	32.16	54.75	49.33	52.40

[a] From Nelson *et al.* (in press). Copyright (1971) by the American Psychological Association, and reproduced by permission.

dition, similar manipulations were made within relatively common CVC words. With words as stimuli it was assumed that, regardless of presentation modality, stimulus recognition would be at least partially based upon the retrieval of phonological features. Thus it was expected that the ordinal position effect would emerge under conditions of both visual and auditory presentation.

Each *S* acquired a single list of six paired associates, with the digits 4–9 serving as responses. Examples of pairs used in one of the list sets are shown in Table 4. Practice was by the method of anticipation (1.5:1.5-sec rate) for a total of 14 trials following the study trial. On all trials test stimuli were pronounced aloud as they were shown and response guessing was required. To make the tapes for the auditory conditions, the materials in each condition were projected via a Kodak Carousel projector, using the conditions for visual presentation, and a male *E* read aloud each stimulus and each stimulus–response pair as it appeared. His readings for each condition were taped, and these recordings were later played to each *S* over a speaker. In all conditions the intertrial interval was eliminated.

Mean errors to the acquisition criterion are shown in Table 5. Acquisition is relatively more difficult when meaningfulness is low, when identical letters are within the initial position, and when presentation is within the auditory modality. When stimuli are words, difficulty varies in the usual first-last-middle pattern. This effect is independent of presentation modality. A similar locus effect appears when low-meaningfulness stimuli are presented auditorily, but, consistent with previous findings (e.g., Nelson, 1968), errors decline as identity is moved from first to second and third positions when these stimuli are shown visually. These findings are consistent with the hypothesis that the ordinal position effect is dependent upon the stimuli being processed as integrated sequences.

This dependency suggests an explanation for the results of an experiment reported by Nelson, Bercov, and Leslie (1970a). They constructed an 8-item word list using all combinations of two different first, middle, and last letters: BAD, BAG, BED, BEG, LAD, LAG, LED, LEG. The number of possible single-digit responses (2, 4, or 8) and locus of response assignment were varied. Location was manipulated by assigning identical responses to stimuli sharing letters within given ordinal positions. For example, with first-letter assignment, all words beginning with B had the same digit response, and all those beginning with L shared the other response. For middle-letter assignment, identical middle letters had the same response, etc. In the four-response conditions, identical digits were assigned to words sharing identical bigrams. In the eight-response condition, the control, the digits 1–8 were randomly assigned to stimuli so that each response was paired with only a single stimulus.

Each of the paired-associate lists was practiced by different groups of *S*s for 25 trials using procedures identical to those employed by Nelson and Rowe (1969). The instructions explicitly stated the nature of the pairing, i.e., that each response was paired with four words, etc. Contrary to expectation, errors increased in the order F (10.44), M (21.75), and L (25.30) for the two-response conditions and in the order F & M (51.62), F & L (55.25), and M & L (84.87) for the four-response conditions. All means were reliably different from each other. A second experiment indicated that these findings were not a result of the confounding of consonant–vowel alternation pattern with locus (i.e., since all stimuli were CVC's, the critical bigrams for F & M, F & L, and M & L were, respectively, CV, CC, and VC).

This relative ordering indicates that the stimulus words in this task were processed in a left-to-right rather than in a first-last-middle pattern. The reason for this difference may lie in the concept formation aspect of this task. For example, with first-letter position assignment, the concept would be "words with the same first letter have the same response." The information that each response was paired with more than a single stimulus may have led to attempts to identify a rule relating stimuli and their responses. Thus the systematic application of a left-to-right rule would account for these patterns of acquisition difficulty. This hypothesis is predicated on the assumption that words were being decoded in terms of their constituent letters and not as phonetic sequences. This analysis suggests that elimination of the concept formation aspect should enhance the likelihood of obtaining the more typical beginning-end-middle pattern. An analysis of the confusion errors in the eight-response control condition indicated that such was the case. If this interpretation is correct, it suggests that the ordinal position effect will occur only when words are decoded as well-integrated phonetic sequences. In addition, it suggests that the same set of stimulus words may be processed in terms of their contituent letters or on the basis of their phonological features, depending upon the task characteristics.

Up to this point the potential contribution of the unique semanic, associative, and imaginal features of the words has been deemphasized. In fact, the occurrence of the ordinal position effect suggests that responses were not being solely related to these features. If they were, then no locus effect would be expected since each stimulus in each locus condition was uniquely distinctive in terms of these attributes. However, it seemed reasonable to suppose that the overriding influence of the phonological features might be eliminated if the characteristics of the task enhanced the saliency of the unique semantic or of the unique associative features of the stimulus words. To test this possibility, Nelson, Brooks, and Fosselman (in press, Experiment V) constructed lists of words sharing either first, middle, or last letters. Within each condition of locus the relationship between individual stimuli and their word responses was varied. In the Compatible conditions each response word was semantically or associatively related to its respective stimulus (e.g., in one of the lists in condition First the pairs were BAR-TAVERN, BET-GAMBLE, BIN-COAL, BUG-INSECT, SOD-DIRT, SHE-WOMAN, SKI-MOUNTAIN, SLY-CRAFTY). In the Incompatible conditions the responses were assigned to inappropriate stimuli (e.g., BAR-COAL, BET-INSECT, BIN-GAMBLE, BUG-TAVERN, SOD-WOMAN, SHE-MOUNTAIN, SKI-CRAFTY, SLY-DIRT). Note that responses were incompatible with respect to stimuli *within* a subset. In the Unrelated conditions the response words were unrelated to their respective stimuli.

It was expected that locus would have no reliable effect within the Compatible conditions if only semantic-associative features were coded. Performance on the Incompatible lists was expected to be dependent upon the degree to which both phonological and semantic-associative features were processed. If phonological characteristics were coded, then a locus effect should occur, and it should be on the same order of magnitude as that obtained in the Unrelated lists. To the extent that both types of features were processed, then acquisition of the Incompatible lists should be more difficult than that for the Unrelated lists since "meaning features are mispaired in the former and neutral in the latter conditions.

The procedures, apparatus, and timing arrangements were identical to those used for the visual presentation conditions of the experiment in which modality was varied. However, practice was continued for 20 trials following the study trial or for 4 consecutive trials without error, which-

TABLE 6
Mean Errors as a Function of Location of Identical Letters and Stimulus–Response Relationship ($N = 16$)[a]

S–R relationship	Location of identical letters		
	F	M	L
Compatible	6.19	4.82	5.31
Incompatible	100.12	57.06	94.62
Unrelated	58.87	46.43	64.50

[a] From Nelson *et al.* (in press). Copyright (1971) by the American Psychological Association, and reproduced by permission.

ever came first. Although test words were overtly articulated, guessing was no longer required. The findings are shown in Table 6. Fewest errors occurred when pairs were compatible and next fewest when unrelated; the greatest difficulty was encountered when pairs were incompatible. The effect of locus was statistically dependent upon stimulus–response relationship. Within the Compatible conditions there were no reliable differences as a function of locus. For the Incompatible treatments errors significantly increased in a first-last-middle pattern. Within the Unrelated conditions, however, the pattern was last-first-middle. The large number of errors found in the terminal position appeared to be the result of the difficulty experienced by 3 *S*s in learning one of the lists. The suggestion that this result is atypical is corroborated by recently collected data. As part of a similar experiment currently in progress, unrelated lists were acquired under similar procedural conditions, except that there were only six pairs in each list. Mean errors for first, middle, and last locations were, respectively, 46.66, 27.66, and 35.22, with 18 *S*s per condition.

The attenuation of locus effects in the Compatible conditions suggests that decoding may have been primarily accomplished on the basis of the retrieval of semantic-associative features. This result is consistent with findings reported by Bobrow (1970), who found that, in sentence contexts, "meaning," as compared to phonological features, plays the predominant role in processing words. However, it should be noted that a minimal first-last-middle pattern did emerge within this condition. Thus the possibility remains that, because of the relative ease of acquisition of the compatible lists, no reliable locus effects were obtained. Until this possibility can be tested, it seems most appropriate to characterize this result as representing an attenuation, but not as representing an elimination of the locus effect.

Both phonological and semantic-associative features were apparently being processed within the incompatible conditions. The ordinal position effect obtained in these conditions suggests that relatively nondiscriminating phonological features were being retrieved, and the differential difficulty of these relative to the unrelated conditions suggests that semantic-associative characteristics were being decoded as well. Thus, when context is minimal, decoding may be on the basis of more than a single feature. Alternatively, some of the words in the list may have been decoded phonetically while others were decoded solely in terms of their semantic-associative features. Although the multiple-feature interpretation is perferred, the data of this experiment would not permit my clear rejection of the single-feature explanation.

Despite the interpretative ambiguity inherent in the last experiment, the results of this series suggest that the ordinal position effect is dependent upon processing the stimuli as well-intergrated phonetic sequences. When poorly integrated, low-meaningfulness CVC's serve as stimuli, the effect does not occur if materials are presented visually. Similarly, the effect is attenuated if the nature of the task encourages processing words in terms of their constituent letters. Furthermore, the locus effect is considerably reduced if the task enhances the likelihood that the stimuli are processed in terms of their semantic-associative features. However, the effect does appear to be independent of word length and of presentation modality. Other experiments suggest that it is also independent of whether or not the test stimuli are overtly articulated or not, and whether presentation rate is fast or slow. Nelson, Brooks, and Fosselman (in press, Experiment II) used the high-meaningfulness–locus lists employed in the experiment on modality (cf. Table 4). All items were presented visually, using the same procedures as in the initial experiment except that *S*s were instructed to not pronounce the stimulus words but to read them silently without lip or tongue movement. Mean errors to the acquisition criterion were 34.79, 23.57, and 31.29, respectively, for F, M, and L loci. An analysis of these data which included the comparable conditions of the initial experiment indicated that only locus was significant. Articulation and Locus X Articulation sources were less than unity. In Experiment III of the same series these lists were acquired under one of two rates, 1.5: 1.5 or 3.0: 3.0 sec. Items were again presented visually, and test stimuli were overtly articulated, but acquisition was carried out for 20 trials or for 4 consecutive errorless trials, whichever came first. Mean errors are shown in Table 7. The statistical analysis indicated that rate and locus, but not their interaction, were significant. Thus, fewer er-

TABLE 7
Mean Errors as a Function of Location of Identical Letters and Rate of Presentation (N = 18) [a]

Rate	Locus of identical letters		
	F	M	L
Fast	36.39	24.05	28.22
Slow	21.22	17.88	18.00
Average	28.80	20.97	23.11

[a] From Nelson *et al.* (in press). Copyright (1971) by the American Psychological Association, and reproduced by permission.

rors were obtained at the slower rate, and errors decreased in the typical first-last-middle pattern. Although the locus effect appeared to be attenuated at the slower rate, this reduction was not great enough to produce a reliable interaction between these factors.

ORDINAL POSITION EFFECT WHEN STIMULI OVERLAP WITH THEIR RESPONSES

Nelson and Garland (1969) systematically varied the degree and locus of sharing between three-letter word stimuli and their responses. Paired-associate word pairs were learned fastest if the beginnings of the items overlapped, next fastest if the ends overlapped, with slowest acquisition occurring if sharing was within medial positions (cf. Table 3). The effect was obtained when the sharing was within either one (e.g., CUP-COB) or two positions (e.g., COW-COB). Bower and Bolton (1969) manipulated the locus of sharing within two positions (e.g., F & M, F & L, M & L) and obtained a similar pattern of results. Parenthetically, it is interesting to note that in each of these studies difficulty of acquisition was greater for "rhyming" pairs (i.e., M & L) than for pairs overlapping the remaining bigram positions, each of which involves sharing in initial letters. This finding is clearly at variance with the pronunciation code hypothesis (Runquist, 1968), which predicts fastest acquisition for pairs sharing M & L letters since they are given the highest phonetic similarity ratings (Nelson & Nelson, 1970).

The stimulus words of the Nelson and Garland (1969) experiment provided cues for response retrieval, with cue effectiveness depending upon the locus of overlap. This differential cue effectiveness might have worked in at least two different ways. If the response retrieval process is analogous to a search through memory for the correct alternative, the more information the stimulus provides about the response, the more likely the search is to terminate with the correct response (Atkinson & Shiffrin, 1968; Bower & Bolton, 1969). Thus, amount and location of overlap may serve to vary the size of the relevant response set which must be searched in order to locate the correct alternative. The smaller the set of alternatives through which the search must be conducted, the greater the likelihood of retrieving the correct response. Alternatively, the acquisition of each pair might be considered as analogous to the simultaneous practice of two overlapping serial lists (Bewley, Nelson, & Brogden, 1969), one "list" represented by the stimulus and one by the response word. In this view, words are coded primarily as phonetic sequences having definite beginnings and ends.

Nelson *et al.* (1971c) attempted to test some of the implications of each of these hypotheses. Paired-associate lists were constructed in which six-letter words served as stimuli and as responses. These pairs shared either initial, medial, or terminal bigrams. In addition, on the assumption that response retrieval is analogous to a search process, the size of the potentially relevant response set was also varied. Three of the pairs within each overlap condition were selected so that there were a large number of words sharing that bigram within the given positions, and three pairs were selected so that there were a small number of words sharing a particular bigram within that locus. For example, for INSTEP-INFLUX there were 51 six-letter words beginning with the letters IN listed in Thorndike–Lorge (1944), whereas for TYPHUS-TYRANT there were only 5 words listed beginning with the letters TY. Since it seemed unlikely that words in memory are stored in sets differentiated by length, it was assumed that the distributions of bigrams in terms of initial, medial, and terminal positions for six-letter words were representative of words of all lengths. The reasonableness of this assumption was supported by a count of all words beginning with particular bigrams within the large and small set size categories. For example, Thorndike–Lorge list 577 words beginning with IN and 17 beginning with TY. Obviously, it was impossible to specify exact set size for any given *S*. Instead, a direct relationship between the size of the existing set and the size of the set in memory was assumed. Because of this assumption, set size was manipulated as a within-*S* factor.

The procedures were similar to those used by Nelson and Garland (1969). Items were presented at a 1.5:1.5-sec rate, there was no intertrial interval, test stimuli were overtly articulated, and practice was continued for 15 trials after the study trial. There were two completely

TABLE 8

Mean Errors (and Mean-Rated Similarity) as a Function of Location of Stimulus-Response Overlap and Size of Set (N = 20) [a]

Set size	Location of Bigram overlap F	M	L
Large	6.85 (3.56)	14.10 (2.27)	11.10 (3.72)
Small	4.25 (3.85)	13.60 (2.54)	6.25 (4.59)

[a] From Nelson *et al.* (1971). Copyright (1971) by the American Psychological Association, and reproduced by permission.

different list sets within each condition of locus. Means of errors to the acquisition criterion are shown in Table 8. Comparison of these values indicates that ease of acquisition significantly increases as locus of overlap is moved from middle to terminal to initial bigram locations. This pattern is consistent with that found for overlapping three-letter words. In addition, significantly fewer errors were obtained when set size was small than when large, but only if words shared initial or terminal bigrams. However, data collected after the paired-associate experiment suggested that these differences were a result of a confounding. Ratings of all pairs in terms of their mutual phonological similarity were gathered, using a different intact group of *S*s. These *S*s assigned numerical values from 1 to 7 to each pair, a value of 1 indicating "completely dissimilar" and a value of 7 indicates "completely similar." As shown in Table 8, these ratings indicated that set size and degree of acoustic similarity had been inadvertently confounded: Items within the small set size category were phonetically more similar. In view of this problem, similarity ratings for 150 pairs of words were obtained and the results of this scaling were used to construct pairs assigned equal similarity values, but which differed in terms of size of set. It was also possible to equate the initial and terminal overlap conditions in terms of their rated similarity, but pairs sharing medial bigrams were invariably rated lower. Table 9 presents the means of errors to the acquisition criterion along with specific numerical phonetic similarity ratings for each condition. As in previous experiments, the typical first-last-middle error pattern is evident. However, there are no effects of set size. The results of the second experiment suggest that the apparent set-size effect obtained initially was a result of the confounding of this variable with degree of phonological similarity.

The facilitating effects of locus do not appear to be a result of variations in the size of the search set (Bower & Bolton, 1969; Nelson & Garland, 1969). Three lines of evidence support this conclusion. First, an in-

TABLE 9

Mean Errors (and Mean-Rated Similarity) as a Function of Location of Stimulus–Response Overlap and Size of Set ($N = 20$) [a]

	Location of Bigram overlap		
Set size	F	M	L
Large	7.44 (3.60)	12.81 (2.36)	11.94 (3.61)
Small	6.06 (3.64)	12.19 (2.37)	11.94 (3.56)

[a] From Nelson *et al.* (in press). Copyright (1971) by the American Psychological Association, and reproduced by permission.

formational analysis of six-letter words indicates that distributional uncertainty, a measure of number of alternatives, is approximately equal for initial and medial bigrams and is less for the terminal bigram position. Therefore, since the size of the relevant set increased in the order terminal, initial-medial, difficulty of acquisition should have followed this pattern. It did not. Second, if response retrieval in this task is analogous to search, it seems reasonable to suppose that there might be some proportion of misretrievals sharing letters with the correct response. Although Nelson and Garland (1969) found such intrusions when stimuli and responses were three-letter words, no such intrusions were obtained in these experiments. Third, and most importantly, when pairs in the differing set-size categories were equated for phonetic similarity, set size was no longer a reliable source of variation. Furthermore, as an additional check on set-size effects, eight pairs of three-letter words were chosen which overlapped in first letters only. Four of the pairs were chosen from large sets (e.g., BAR-BUS) and four were selected from small sets (e.g., ZIP-ZOO), with degree of phonetic similarity equated. Twenty *S*s practiced the list for 15 trials. Mean errors for large and small set size were identical, 13.70. Thus, although the evidence is largely indirect, differential locus effects do not appear to result from constraints produced by the stimulus on the size of the relevant response set.

The hypothesis that words can be decoded as phonetic serial sequences would appear to provide the most adequate general explanation for the effects of locus obtained within both three- and six-letter words. This interpretation requires the assumption that providing initial portions renders greater retrieval access to a sequence than terminal or medial portions. Evidence consistent with this premise has been provided by Horowitz *et al.* (1968) for the regeneration of words from their initial, medial, or terminal fragments after a single presentation. In another experiment in this series Nelson *et al.* (1971c) attempted to test this assumption within the constraints of a paired-associate task by using overlapping word triads instead of overlapping letter triads. Lists were constructed so that pairs consisted of three stimulus and three response words. In different lists either the first, middle, or last word of each pair in the stimulus set was identical to the corresponding word in the response set. For example, in the first condition one of the pairs was VEX FRY MOP-VEX HUG SKI. Thus, each paired-associated pair consisted of two three-word serial lists which overlapped in either initial, medial, or terminal positions. This method of construction produced "pairs" which were analogous to the word pairs used by Nelson and Garland (1969). All lists were practiced by the anticipation method (4:4-sec rate) for a total of 20 trials following the study trial. Pairs were presented horizontally in the window of a memory drum, there was no intertrial interval, and *S*s were not informed about sharing.

Within each of the three conditions of locus of overlap there were three possible positions within the triad, the position containing the overlapping word and the remaining two nonoverlapping positions. Table 10 presents the mean number of errors for the between-*S* effect of locus of overlap and the within-*S* effect of position within the triad. Comparison of the means along the diagonal indicated that errors within the overlapping position significantly decreased as they were shifted from the middle to the terminal and to the initial position within the sequence. A similar pattern was also obtained for errors within nonoverlapping positions. Thus these findings are consistent with the hypothesis that providing the initial word in a sequence renders greater retrieval access to that sequence than either medial or terminal words. To a lesser extent, terminal words render greater access than medial elements. These conclusions were also supported by a tabulation of the number of totally correct triads within each locus condition, these means being 50.83, 35.72, and

TABLE 10

Mean Errors as a Function of Location of Overlap (between-S) and Position in the Triad (within-S) [a]

	Position of word within the triad		
Location of overlap	F	M	L
F	4.67	44.72	46.11
M	57.00	22.67	53.50
L	54.83	49.89	14.17

[a] From Nelson *et al.* (1971). Copyright (1971) by the American Psychological Association, and reproduced by permission.

41.39, respectively, for first, middle, and last locations. These findings were completely replicated in a subsequent experiment involving a minor procedural alteration.

The findings of this series of experiments are consistent with the hypothesis that the words in this task were coded, at least in part, as phonological sequences, analogous to miniature serial lists. Providing initial and, to a lesser extent, terminal portions of a sequence renders greater retrieval access to that sequence than cuing with medial elements. This effect appears to have some generality in that it occurs for sequences of words and for sequences of letters within three- and six-letter words.

ORDINAL POSITION EFFECT IN FREE RECALL

In the first experiment concerned with the effects of locus of overlap on the free recall of words, Nelson (1969) found that acquisition was fastest when identical letters were located in F & L positions, next in F & M positions; poorest performance was obtained when identity was within M & L positions (cf. Table 2). Consistent with previous findings, word beginnings and ends appeared to be more influential determinants of their processing then their middles. However, in a subsequent experiment this particular pattern was not obtained (Nelson, Garland, & Crank, 1970d). As part of a larger experiment, lists of words were constructed so that, within each list, there were three subsets of three words each. Sharing within a subset was within F & M, F & L, or M & L positions. The list for F & M, e.g., was BAG, BAN, BAT, PEG, PEN, PET, RUG, RUN, RUT. Using standard free-recall procedures, practice was continued for 12 trials, with items being presented at a 2-sec rate. Mean errors were 31.90, 31.00, and 23.90, respectively, for locations F & M, F & L, and M & L. Contrary to previous findings, fastest acquisition was found when sharing was within M & L positions, when the words rhymed. However, there were differences between these experiments in procedures and in list construction which might have produced the apparently inconsistent results. In the first experiment each of 12 items were pronounced on presentation, while in the second experiment each of the 9 items of the last were spelled as they were presented. Furthermore, in the first experiment, when identity was localized in any given positions (e.g., F & M), the letters in the remaining position (e.g., L) were all different. In contrast, in the second experiment, there was high similarity within this position.

The purpose of the third experiment in this series was to resolve the apparently conflicting effects of locus within the free-recall task. Six 9-

TABLE 11

Mean Errors as a Function of Location of Letter Sharing and Similarity within the Position of the Uncorrelated Letter

Similarity of uncorrelated letters	Location of sharing		
	F and L	F and M	M and L
High	32.59	45.59	22.59
Zero	16.17	25.92	21.50

item lists were constructed which differed in locus of overlap and in whether there was high or zero similarity within the position of the uncorrelated letters. The procedures were identical to those used in the second experiment, except that all words were pronounced upon presentation. Mean errors to the acquisition criterion are shown in Table 11. Statistical analysis indicated that locus, similarity, and Locus × Similarity were significant. The findings of both previous experiments were replicated. When all letters within the position of the uncorrelated letter were different, significantly fewer errors were obtained for the F & L than for the M & L locus. When similarity within this position was high, the reverse was found. Thus, in free recall, words appear to be processed as rhymes only when the distinctiveness of initial phonemes within the stimulus set is low. Otherwise, as in other tasks, the initial portion of the word is critical.

Conclusions and Implications

When words serve as paired-associate stimuli, identity of initial letters impairs acquisition to a greater extent than identity of terminal letters, which in turn produces greater difficulty than identity of medial letters. This ordinal position effect appears to be independent of word length, presentation modality, overt articulation, and presentation rate. A similar first-last-middle processing pattern has been obtained when paired-associate stimuli share letters with their responses, and when words are coded for free recall. These findings suggest that the locus effect is reliable and has considerable generality in that it occurs independently of several procedural variations and within several different word coding tasks. However, the effect is not invariant. Under comparable conditions of paired-associate stimulus similarity, it is attenuated when the responses of the list are associatively related to their respective stimuli, or when the task or materials enhance the likelihood of processing stimuli in terms of their constituent letters. Furthermore, when similarity of initial phonemes is high, the free recall of words is differentially facilitated if they also rhyme.

One implication of these findings is that the context in which words are processed determines or at least influences what features are stored, retrieved, or both stored and retrieved. Context in this case refers to relationships between words within the last, characteristics of the response, task requirements, etc. Thus within certain contexts words appear to be processed, at least in part, as phonological sequences having a characteristic beginning-end-middle structure. Accordingly, words seem to be processed in these tasks as miniature serial lists and not in terms of their informational structure or as simple pronunciation codes. Within other contexts processing may be based upon constituent letters, semantic-associative properties, imaginal features, or, perhaps, on the basis of combinations of features. In still other situations, environmental features may be coded along with specific word attributes. For example, Nelson, Wheeler, and Bercov (1970f) manipulated high and low meaningfulness and formal similarity within a serial anticipation task under conditions in which the temporal constancy cues were or were not eliminated. In the Constant conditions item sequence and the temporal position of the items were confounded as in the standard procedure. In the Varied conditions item sequence was maintained, but each trial was started on a different item in the list. The findings indicated that varying starting position significantly interfered with recall, even when the stimuli were highly distinctive words. Changes in position from trial to trial produced an A-B, A-C, A-D, etc., interference paradigm since the item in position *a* is changed on each trial. Thus position information may represent an important distinguishing characteristic of a coded item. Consistent with this interpretation, the findings indicated that as distinctive semantic-associative and phonological cues decrease, there is a proportionally greater reliance upon positional cues. When meaningfulness is low and similarity is high, 75% of the *S*s show little or no progress in learning the list if these cues are eliminated, even after 100 trials.

These considerations suggest that words and other verbal stimuli are not processed as invariant units but as sets of distinctive features. In this view, word coding is a dynamic process with the processing of specific features controlled, at least in part, by the context in which the coding is taking place. Of all of the explanations for the ordinal position effect which have been considered, only the words-as-features hypothesis, and its related assumptions, appears to be sufficiently flexible to account for the coding diversity which has been observed. Thus words may be stored as complexes of features and, as a result of particular task characteristics or demands, stimulus recognition or retrieval is based on only certain of these features. This hypothesis assumes that retrieval may be based upon any attributes within this complex. For example, in a recent exploratory experiment an attempt was made to test the hypothesis that phonological features are processed even when words are presented under conditions of minimal letter sharing. With few exceptions (e.g., Lawrence, (1970), nearly all of the studies demonstrating the importance of phonological cues in word-coding tasks involve high levels of formal similarity. This high degree of sharing may enhance the saliency of acoustic-articulatory cues which may not serve as distinctive features for controlling word processing in more usual tasks (e.g., reading textual material), except under special circumstances (e.g., reading a poem). However, if words are processed as complexes of features, phonetic and semantic-associative information should be processed even under conditions of minimal sharing and minimal semantic constraint.

The recognition memory task (e.g., Anisfeld & Knapp, 1968; Kimble, 1968; Underwood, 1965) seemed to provide an ideal methodology. In individual sessions 200 words were presented, one at a time for 3 sec each. The *S*s were instructed to read each word aloud as it appeared, and to try to remember as many words as possible. Following the single study presentation, 172 test words were shown. These test words could be subdivided into four categories of 43 words each, depending upon the relationship between given test words and particular words appearing in the study phase. In the New Homophone category, test words were homophones of particular study-phase words so that if "BEAR" appeared as a study phase word, "BARE" appeared as the test word. Each of the New Homophone words appearing in the test phase had a control word matched to it on the basis of frequency of occurrence, length, and first letter. These words were New Controls and did not appear in the study phase. In the Old Homophones category, words having a homophone appeared in both study and test phases. Thus, if "CEREAL" appeared as a study word it also appeared as a test word. Matched to each of these words were the Old Control words which appeared in both phases but which had no homophone pairmate. During the test phase a 5-sec rate was used and *S* pronounced aloud each word as it appeared, then indicated whether it was "OLD" or "NEW." There were 48 *S*s, 12 assigned to each of four different lists generated in counterbalancing the appearance of homophones as study or test words. The order of words within each phase was independently and unsystematically randomized for each *S*.

The comparison of false recognition errors made on New Control words relative to New Homophones was of particular interest. If, in the study phase, the homophone pairmate was coded solely in terms of its sematic-associative properties (i.e. "BEAR" as "furry animal"), then false recognitions should be no greater on New Homophones (i.e., "BARE") than on New Control words (i.e., BUSH). However, if phonological features were also coded, then false recognitions should be significantly greater for New Homophones which share phonetic identities to study-phase words than for New Control words which bear no such relation. Consistent with this expectation, nearly twice as many false recognition errors were found for New Homophones (11.32) than for New Control words (6.30). This difference was statistically reliable. Mean errors on Old Homophones and Old Controls were 12.62 and 14.42, respectively, and these values were not reliably different, suggesting that failing to detect an old word as old was not affected by whether or not it had a homophone. Although half the items in the test were old and half were new, the probability that "New" was reported was .56. Thus there was a slight false positive bias. This bias, however, should have operated equally for all new items. Furthermore, this bias would decrease the number of errors on New Homophones relative to Old Homophones and Old Controls.

The results of this pilot experiment are consistent with the hypothesis that phonological attributes are processed when single words are presented with the general instruction to remember them, and when semantic constraint and phonetic similarities within the to-be-coded stimuli are minimal. To the extent that these findings are replicable and free of the influence of confounded variables, they would seem to be consistent with the hypothesis that words are coded as complexes of features so that, at the point of decoding, recognition may be based upon the retrieval of misleading phonological attributes. At least it seems reasonable to assume that such a process might occur, although it might not occur inevitably for all subjects and for all words.

REFERENCES

Anisfeld, M., & Knapp, M. Association, synonymity, and directionality in false recognition. *Journal of Experimental Psychology*, 1968, **77**, 171–179.

Atkinson, R. C., & Shiffrin, R. M. Human memory: A proposed system and its control processes. In K. W. Spence and J. T. Spence (Eds.), *The psychology of learning and motivation: Advances in research and theory*. Vol. 2. New York: Academic Press, 1968. Pp. 89–195.

Bewley, W. L., Nelson, D. L., & Brogden, W. J. Effect of cue alternation for ordinal position on acquisition and serial position curve form. *Journal of Experimental Psychology,* 1969, **79**, 445–451.

Bobrow, S. A. Memory for words in sentences. *Journal of Verbal Learning and Verbal Behavior,* 1970, **9**, 363–372.

Boring, E. G. *A history of experimental psychology.* New York: Appleton, 1957.

Bower, G. H., & Bolton, L. S. Why are rhymes easy to learn? *Journal of Experimental Psychology,* 1969, **82**, 453–461.

Brown, R., & McNeill, D. The "tip-of-the-tongue" phenomenon. *Journal of Verbal Learning and Verbal Behavior,* 1966, **5**, 325–337.

Bruner, R. W., & O'Dowd, D. A note on the informativeness of parts of words *Language and Speech,* 1958, **1**, 98–101.

Carson, D. H. Letter constraints within words in printed English. *Kybernetic,* 1961, **1**, 46–54.

Deese, J. *The structure of association in language and thought.* Baltimore, Md.: Johns Hopkins University Press, 1965.

Horowitz, L. M., White, M. A., & Atwood, D. W. Word fragments as aids to recall: The organization of a word. *Journal of Experimental Psychology,* 1968, **76**, 219–226.

Jakobsen, R., Fant, C. G. M., & Halle, M. *Preliminaries to speech analysis.* Cambridge, Mass.: MIT Press, 1961.

Johnson, M. G. A cognitive feature model of compound free associations. *Psychological Review,* 1970, **77**, 282–293.

Kimble, G. A. Mediating associations. *Journal of Experimental Psychology,* 1968, **76**, 263–266.

Lawrence, M. U. Role of homophones in transfer learning. *Journal of Experimental Psychology,* 1970, **86**, 1–7.

Neisser, U. *Cognitive psychology.* New York: Appleton, 1966.

Nelson, D. L. Paired-associate acquisition as a function of association value, degree and location of similarity. *Journal of Experimental Psychology,* 1968, **77**, 364–369.

Nelson, D. L. Information theory and stimulus encoding in free and serial recall: Ordinal position of formal similarity. *Journal of Experimental Psychology,* 1969, **80**, 537–541.

Nelson, D. L., Bercov, S., & Leslie, L. Ordinal positions of letters within words as concepts: Effect of assigning identical responses to words sharing letters in various ordinal positions. *Psychonomic Science,* 1970, **18**, 201–202. (a)

Nelson, D. L., Brooks, D. H., & Fosselman, J. R. Words as sets of features: Processing phenological cues. *Journal of Experimental Psychology,* 1971, in press. (b)

Nelson, D. L., Fosselman, J., & Peebles, J. Words as phonological sequences. *Journal of Experimental Psychology,* 1971, **87**, 361–366. (c)

Nelson, D. L., & Garland, R. M. Amount and locus of stimulus-response overlap in paired-associate acquisition. *Journal of Experimental Psychology,* 1969, **82**, 297–300.

Nelson, D. L., Garland, R. M., & Crank, D. Free recall as a function of meaningfulness, formal similarity, form and amount of internal structure, and locus of contingency. *Journal of Verbal Learning and Verbal Behavior,* 1970, **9**, 417–424. (d)

Nelson, D. L., & Nelson, L. Rated acoustic (articulatory) similarity for word pairs varying in number and ordinal position of common letters. *Psychonomic Science,* 1970, **19**, 81–82.

Nelson, D. L., Peebles, J., & Pancotto, F. Phonetic similarity as opposed to informational structure as a determinant of word encoding. *Journal of Experimental Psychology,* 1970, **86**, 117–119. (e)

Nelson, D. L., & Rowe, F. A. Information theory and stimulus encoding in paired-associate acquisition: Ordinal position of formal similarity. *Journal of Experimental Psychology,* 1969, **79**, 342–346.

Nelson, D. L., Wheeler, J., & Bercov, S. Variations in item availability and the role of temporal constancy cues in serial anticipation. *Journal of Experimental Psychology,* 1970, **86**, 463–464 (f)

Osgood, C. E. Toward a wedding of insufficiencies. In T. R. Dixon and D. L. Horton (Eds.), *Verbal behavior and general behavior theory.* Englewood Cliffs, N.J.: Prentice-Hall, 1968. Pp. 495–519.

Paivio, A. Mental imagery in associative learning and memory. *Psychological Review,* 1969, **76**, 241–263.

Runquist, W. N. Formal intralist similarity in paired-associate learning. *Journal of Experimental Psychology,* 1968, **78**, 634–641.

Runquist, W. N., & Blackmore, D. Individual differences of interference from stimulus similarity. *Journal of Experimental Psychology,* 1971, **87**, 141–143.

Shannon, C. E. Prediction and entropy of printed English. *Bell System Technical Journal,* 1951, **30**, 50–64.

Thorndike, E. L., & Lorge, I. *The teachers word book of 30,000 words.* New York: Columbia University Press, 1944.

Underwood, B. J. False recognitions by implicit verbal responses. *Journal of Experimental Psychology,* 1965, **70**, 122–129.

Underwood, B. J. Attributes of memory. *Psychology Review,* 1969, **76**, 559–573.

Wickens, D. D. Encoding categories of words: An empirical approach to meaning. *Psychological Review,* 1970, **77**, 1–15.

CHAPTER 11

ORGANIZATION IN MEMORY: MULTITRIAL FREE RECALL OF CATEGORIZED WORD LISTS[1]

Charles P. Thompson

During the past decade, there has been an extremely vigorous experimental attack on the role of organizational processes in human long-term memory. Much of the research in this attack has used free recall since

[1] I owe a debt to many colleagues and student-colleagues for aid in the research reported in this chapter. Dan Roenker, Valerie Hamlin, and, in particular, Velma Handlin were deeply involved in most of the research reported here. Sam Brown, Thad Cowan, and John Uhlarik offered comments and constructive criticism at several points along the route. This chapter has been improved by their help, and I am grateful for

that procedure is relatively unstructured and thus maximizes opportunities for organization to occur. Any summary of the information gleaned from these free-recall studies would include these important points: (1) Subjects organize material presented to them for recall. This organization is what Tulving (1968) has termed secondary organization—i.e., it is based on characteristics other than input order. What is most interesting is that such organization occurs even when *S* is dealing with what is presumed to be a list of unrelated words. (2) Organization of the material aids recall. Perhaps the two most dramatic demonstrations of the effectiveness of organization have been the category-recall relationship demonstrated with the Mandler procedure (e.g., Mandler & Pearlstone, 1966) and the demonstration by Bower, Clark, Lesgold, and Winzenz (1969) of the effectiveness of hierarchical retrieval schemes. (3) Organization increases with practice. Clearly, the degree of organization *could* remain stable over trials. However, since *both* degree of organization and number of words recalled increase with practice, some investigators have hypothesized that increases in recall over trials must be attributable to increases in organization over trials. (4) Research dealing with cued recall suggests the potential importance of search processes in memory. Tulving puts the problem most succinctly when he notes that words may be *available* in memory but are not *accessible*—presumably because the cues necessary to locate the words in memory are lacking (Tulving & Pearlstone, 1966).

The latter statement—that memory involves a search process—is one that has generated considerable controversy. Many theories of memory (e.g., Shiffrin, 1970) incorporate such a notion as a central part of the theory, but there is no strong evidence to favor such an interpretation over many alternative possibilities. It was the search for evidence which would either support or reject the memory-search hypothesis that led to the work to be reported in this chapter. This "search for the search" has taken most of our research group's efforts for what is now a little over two years. Along the way we have learned a great deal about how *S*s behave when they receive multiple trials on several categorized word lists, but we have, as yet, garnered relatively little information about the hypothetical and elusive search process. In short, the present chapter describes a line of research which is far from finished at the time of this writing.

---

it. This research was supported in part by a predoctoral fellowship in experimental psychology to Dan Roenker from NIMH Experimental Training Grant MH-08359-06, and in part by a research grant from the United States Office of Education, Department of Health, Education, and Welfare. The opinions expressed herein, however, do not necessarily reflect the position or policy of the United States Office of Education, and no official endorsement by the United States Office of Education should be inferred.

The Basic Assumptions and Strategy

The research was undertaken assuming that there is some sort of search process involved in recall from long-term memory and that organization of the to-be-remembered material facilitates that search process. This point of view was adopted because, although the memory-search hypothesis is controversial, there is increasing suggestive support for that hypothesis. For example, most advocates of a memory-search hypothesis would probably agree in predicting that recall would be facilitated if the set of items to be searched could be defined so that the search could proceed in a systematic fashion. The demonstration of the great efficacy of hierarchical organization for recall (Bower *et al.*, 1969) is consistent with this prediction. Further, most systematic search notions would predict that, given hierarchical organization, superordinate items should be recalled before subordinate items. Thus the finding that category names are usually recalled before category exemplars when both are included in the list (Segal, 1969) lends considerable support to the hypothesis. Still another prediction from this theoretical framework would be that probability of recall would increase as the size of the search set decreased. The evidence indicating that recall increases as category size decreases (Craik, 1968; Thompson & Poling, 1969) certainly suggests a search process in memory.

The objective of the research program is, primarily, to shed some light on the nature of this hypothesized search process and, secondarily, on the memory structure through which the search takes place. The major strategy has been to produce interference with recall with the notion that the conditions necessary to overcome this interference would be informative about the search in memory and/or about the structure of memory. Thus far, we have produced interference with recall by repeating categories in successive categorized word lists. As several investigators (e.g., Shuell, 1969; Thompson & Poling, 1969; Winograd, 1968) have shown, repeating categories (but not specific category exemplars) in successive lists produces substantial proactive interference. In this report, general effects found in single and/or successive categorized lists will be discussed first, followed by a discussion of the proactive interference effects observed when categories are repeated in successive lists.

The Experimental Paradigm and Procedure

To avoid unnecessary repetition in the body of the chapter, the general paradigm and experimental procedure are described here with the appropriate modifications noted during the discussion of individual experiments.

PARADIGM

In the basic paradigm, *S*s received three successive trials on each of two or four categorized lists. Some or all of the categories in the last list had occurred in previous lists. Excluding the last list in the sequence, there were no repeated categories. Whenever possible, within-*S* designs were used with each *S* receiving all the experimental treatments.

MATERIALS

As is customary, multiple lists were generated and used so that the results would not be list specific. Similar precautions were taken so that the results would not be category specific. Unless otherwise noted, the lists contained 4 categories with 12 exemplars from each category. The categories and category exemplars were taken from the Battig and Montague (1969) norms with the normative frequency of occurrence of the words matched as closely as possible across categories both within and between lists.

PROCEDURE

During the study portion of each trial, the words were presented at a 2-sec rate with a Kodak Carousel projector. The order of presentation of the words was varied randomly from trial to trial. During presentation of each word, *S* identified the category membership of the word by writing the category initial in an answer booklet. This procedure assured that *S*s attended to each word and, presumably, also assured that category membership was a salient characteristic of each word.

The final word in each list was followed by a 3-digit number. The *S*s filled a 30-sec interval between presentation and recall by counting backwards by 3's from that number at a 1-sec rate. This task presumably eliminates the short-term memory component in recall (Glanzer & Cunitz, 1966).

The *S*s were instructed to write down the words in recall in whatever order the words occurred to them. Two minutes were allowed for the recall portion of each trial. Each study and recall protocol was recorded on a separate sheet in the answer booklet. There was a 30-sec interval between trials and a 3-min interval between lists.[2]

The Measurement of Clustering

The choice of a paradigm using categorized word lists to pursue the research objectives dictated that clustering [the tendency for words from the same category to appear together in the recall protocol (Bousfield, 1953)] would be the major measure of organization in recall. Naturally, it was imperative that we have a clustering measure that would allow comparison between *S*s, between experiments, and within *S*s over trials or conditions. Unfortunately, previous measures of clustering can be shown to vary with characteristics of recall (such as number of categories recalled or the distribution of total items recalled across categories) in ways that make such comparisons extremely difficult. More specifically, previous clustering measures are such that the value representing chance clustering is free to vary and/or the value representing perfect clustering is free to vary. Thus, e.g., the same "clustering score" might represent chance clustering for *S* on one trial and clustering at, below, or above chance for that *S* on the next trial.

To counter this measurement problem, Dan Roenker, Sam Brown, and I developed the adjusted ratio of clustering (ARC) score in which chance clustering is set at zero and perfect clustering at one (Roenker, Thompson, & Brown, 1971). The ARC score represents the proportion of actual category repetitions above chance to the total possible category repetitions above chance for any given recall protocol. Hence, the ARC score is invariant with respect to factors unrelated to relative amount of clustering. The computational formula for the ARC score is as follows:

$$\text{ARC} = \frac{R - E(R)}{\max R - E(R)} \tag{1}$$

where R = total number of observed category repetitions (i.e., the number of times a category word follows a word from the same category); max R = maximum possible number of category repetitions; $E(R)$ = expected (chance) number of category repetitions. It should be noted that

$$\max R = N - k \tag{2}$$

[2] The 3-min interval between lists includes an additional 2 min of recall allowed for the terminal trial on each list. These data were tabulated and evaluated separately. Since these data have not produced any useful additional information, they are not presented in the present chapter.

where N = total number of words recalled; k = number of categories represented in the recall protocol; and (from A.K. Bousfield & Bousfield, 1966)

$$E(R) = \frac{\sum_i n_i^2}{N} - 1 \qquad (3)$$

where n_i = number of words recalled from category i and N is as before.

It should be noted that we have adopted the convention of disregarding intrusions and words appearing previously in the recall protocol when computing ARC. Intrusion data are tabulated and reported separately.

Finally, we recognize that organization other than the categorical organization imposed by the experimenter takes place in the recall of categorized word lists. However, there is convincing evidence that the dominant form of output organization in recall of categorized word lists is clustering (Puff, 1970b), and we have restricted our evaluation of organization in these studies to the measurement of clustering.

PERFORMANCE ON SINGLE AND/OR SUCCESSIVE CATEGORIZED LISTS

The Role of Clustering in Free Recall

Changes in clustering tend to be associated with changes in recall. This covariation can be viewed in three ways. One might suggest that clustering determines recall, that clustering aids recall, or that clustering is an epiphenomenon. The strong statement that clustering determines recall cannot be made for categorized word lists. In this discussion, e.g., the reader will note several instances in which degree of clustering increases but recall does not change. These data obviously suggest a nondeterminant role for clustering in recall.

The question remains whether clustering aids recall or is an epiphenomenon. There are scattered reports in the literature (e.g., Puff, 1970a) which suggest that clustering does not aid recall. These reports compare the performance of good and poor clusterers. If clustering aids recall, then *S*s showing a high degree of clustering should demonstrate better recall than *S*s showing a low degree of clustering. However, a recent study by Puff (1970a) shows no reliable differences in recall between *S*s with high and low degrees of clustering.

If ability to cluster is not related to amount recalled, then the impact of the rather large body of research on clustering (including a considerable portion of our research program) is considerably lessened. This rather di-

TABLE 1

Mean Recall for Ss Showing High and Low Degrees of Clustering

Group	List 1			List 2			List 3		
	Trial			Trial			Trial		
	1	2	3	1	2	3	1	2	3
High clusterers	16.6	23.2	25.9	18.8	25.7	28.2	18.6	24.6	28.5
Low clusterers	13.2	18.7	20.3	14.9	20.4	22.3	15.6	19.9	22.4

rect challenge to our research program inspired Valerie Hamlin, Dan Roenker, and me to attempt to verify Puff's results on our data (Thompson, Hamlin, & Roenker, 1971). For that purpose, we used data from Experiment A—the first in a series of three experiments in which *S*s received three successive trials on each of four lists. (Data from Experiments B and C will be presented during discussion of proactive interference effects.) The fourth list contained repeated categories and is not included here. Sixty *S*s, divided into six subgroups receiving different list sequences, were used in the experiment. To maximize differences in clustering ability, the three best and three poorest clusterers were selected from each of the six subgroups in the experiment. The mean recall for those *S*s is presented in Table 1. As can be seen, the difference was clear, consistent, and reliable.[3] Good clusterers recall more than poor clusterers.

There are several differences in procedure and subsequent data analysis between Experiment A and Puff's experiment, which may account for the failure to find differences in recall between good and poor clusterers in the latter experiment. First, the procedure for defining tendency to cluster in Experiment A was to compare mean clustering scores derived from the three trials of the first list. This multitrial base, because it provides a larger sample of clustering behavior, should provide a more sensitive estimation of tendency to cluster than the single-trial base used in the other experiment. Second, examination of the data for only those *S*s with the best and poorest clustering scores should maximize chances for detecting differences in recall related to clustering. In contrast, the data from all *S*s were used for the comparison in the Puff experiment. Third,

[3] Virtually all statements about the data in this chapter are based on interpretation of significant (i.e., .05 level or better) interactions or main effects in analyses of variance. Exceptions to this general rule are explicitly noted.

Puff's lists were shorter (30 words) than our lists. Short, easily learned lists would be insensitive instruments for measuring differences in recall. Thus, list difficulty may also have been a factor which operated to produce the differing results in the two experiments.

In summary, our data were consistent with the notion that clustering aids recall. In fact, the data presented here suggest that the role of clustering in free recall may be substantial. Organization by category membership is apparently no exception to the rule that organization of the to-be-remembered material greatly facilitates recall.

Learning to Cluster

Organization of the material to be learned apparently aids recall, and intralist organization increases with practice. If organization does aid recall, it seems reasonable to hypothesize that so-called learning-to-learn effects may reflect the increasing ability of *S* to organize the material for recall. With that hypothesis in mind, we examined clustering during the learning of successive lists.

The illustrative data described here come from Experiment A, and the mean clustering scores are presented in Fig. 1a. There was a clear and dramatic increase from the first list to the second list in first-trial clustering. Thus the evidence that *S*s learn to organize the material is clear, and the hypothesis that learning-to-learn effects reflect the increasing ability of *S*s to organize the material was supported. In accord with previous investigations, intralist organization tended to increase systematically from trial to trial. (The puzzling discrepancy in the second list has not occurred in any other experiment in the series.)

A direct comparison of recall and clustering scores is of some interest. Therefore, the recall data for the first three lists of Experiment A are presented in Fig. 1b. The increase in recall from the first to the second list with no change in performance thereafter reflected a consistent pattern found in these experiments (e.g., Thompson & Poling, 1969). As can be seen, the clustering data essentially mimic the recall data with the major exception being that clustering scores show a much more dramatic increase from the first to the second list. (The apparent increase from the second list to the third list is not reliable.)

Category Size as a Factor in Recall

The demonstration that clustering facilitates recall leads rather naturally to speculation about the process that might be underlying this ef-

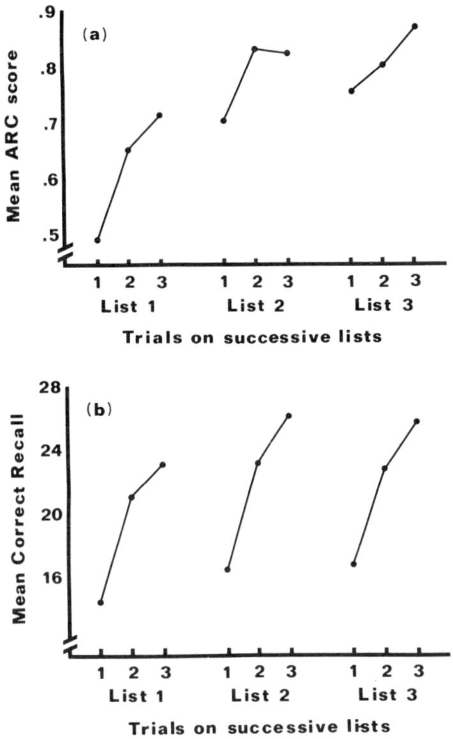

Fig. 1. (a) Mean adjusted ratio of clustering (ARC) scores for each trial for each of three lists. (b) Mean correct recall for each trial for each of three lists.

fect. Many investigators, including ourselves, have adopted the assumption that recall involves some sort of search process and that organization of the to-be-remembered material will facilitate that search process. The memory search is not assumed to be random. When attempting to recall a word, e.g., all items in memory (of which words are a subset) are not included in the search to locate the appropriate response. Indeed, all *words* in memory are not included in this search. What is included is a subset of words defined by the recall task. For a specific example, the fact that extracategory intrusions are virtually never made in the recall of categorized word lists strongly suggests that the categories presented to *S* define the subset of words searched in that task.

The restricted-search view leads to the prediction that the probability of recall of an item would be higher when it is contained in a small subset of items than when it is contained in a large subset of items. To investigate whether recall for individual words varies as a function of the size of the category in which the word is located, an experiment (Experiment

TABLE 2

Mean Recall and Total Intrusions for Each Condition [a]

	Condition			
	0	1	3	5
Mean recall	4.6	4.3	4.0	4.0
Total intrusions	15	32	28	30
major	12	24	21	
minor	2	4	7	

[a] The 0, 1, 3, and 5 conditions represent combinations of 0 and 10, 1 and 9, 3 and 7, and 5 and 5 words, respectively, from the 2 subcategories. The recall data are pooled over the two lists, and the intrusion data are pooled over *S*s and trials on the first list.

D) was performed in which all *S*s received the same set of words but the size of the categories to which the words belonged was varied.

The 40 *S*s in Experiment D learned two 4-category lists. The same 4 categories were used in both lists, but the 20 words in each category (10 words per list) could be divided into 2 subcategories (e.g., wild and domestic animals). Each of the categories presented in the first list represented a combination of items from the subcategories. The first-list combinations ranged from a set in which both subcategories were equally represented to a set in which only one subcategory appeared. Specifically, the four combinations represented in the first list contained 0 and 10, 1 and 9, 3 and 7, and 5 and 5 items from the 2 subcategories, respectively (hereafter designated as the 0, 1, 3, and 5 conditions, respectively). The remaining items from each category were presented in the second list. Over all *S*s, each category appeared equally often in each condition. The normative frequency of the category exemplars (Battig & Montague, 1969) was matched as closely as possible, both between and within *S*s, over all conditions for the two lists.

The mean correct per-category recall for each condition is presented in the top portion of Table 2. Since the conditions by lists interaction did not approach significance, the recall data was pooled across lists and the recall scores given in Table 2 were derived from these pooled data. As can be seen, performance was best when a single subcategory (condition 0) was represented in the set of words to be learned and performance deteriorated as words from a second subcategory were included in the set. These data are consistent with the restricted-search hypothesis proposed at the outset of the experiment.

Although intrusion errors are few in number, their distribution and frequency are theoretically important. A restricted-search hypothesis predicts that more intrusions should be made when both subcategories are represented in the set of items to be learned than when only 1 subcategory is represented. The data for total intrusions are presented in the bottom portion of Table 2, and it is evident that they lend support to the hypothesis. Here it must be noted that, in contrast to the correct-recall data, there was a reliable list × conditions interaction for the intrusion data. Therefore, the intrusion data in Table 2 were taken from first-list presentation only.

Intrusions increased sharply when more than 1 subcategory was represented in the set of words to be recalled. Further, the increase in intrusions appeared to be an all-or-none effect. That is, inclusion of one word from a second subcategory increased intrusions as much as having an equal number of words from the 2 subcategories. These data fit nicely with a restricted-search hypothesis. However, when the intrusions are examined to determine from which subcategory they originate, the neat fit evaporates. In Table 2 the intrusions have been divided into "major" and "minor" classes, referring to intrusions from subcategories having the most and least words, respectively, in the set to be learned. (Note that no division is given for condition 5 since the major and minor distinction makes no sense for that condition. Also note that intrusions which could not be clearly identified as major or minor were omitted from classification. Finally, note that each subcategory appeared equally often as the major or minor class.)

As the major–minor division makes clear, including a second subcategory increased intrusion errors from *both* subcategories. In addition, these data suggest that the proportion of intrusion errors from each subcategory was roughly equivalent to the proportion of words included from each category in the set to be learned. In contrast, the restricted-search hypothesis implies that the increment in intrusion errors should be *entirely* attributable to intrusions from the second ("minor") subcategory. Thus the intrusion data strongly suggest that the restricted-search hypothesis, at least as originally formulated, is incorrect.

To summarize, correct recall decreased and intrusions increased when a second subcategory was included in the set of words to be recalled. These data are consistent with the hypothesis that recall is dependent upon the size of the set of items included in the memory search. However, classification of intrusion errors suggested that the restricted-search hypothesis must be modified to account for the distribution of intrusion errors.

Exemplar Frequency Effects: A Measurement Artifact?

Before turning to the data on proactive interference in categorized word lists, a few comments should be made about the presumed relationship between exemplar frequency as defined by cultural norms (e.g., Battig & Montague, 1969) and the degree of clustering in the categories represented by those exemplars. In a comprehensive review of the clustering literature, Shuell (1969) noted that several studies have shown better clustering and better recall for categorized lists comprised of high-frequency words than for categorized lists comprised of low-frequency words. An examination of these studies shows that the authors used either the number of category repetitions, R [see Eq. (1)] or Bousfield's (1953) ratio of repetition *(RR)* as the index of clustering in recall. RR is computed as follows:

$$RR = \frac{R}{N - 1} \tag{4}$$

where R [Eq. (1)] and N [Eq. (2)] are as before.

Both R and RR can easily be shown to be inadequate for estimating degree of clustering when the total number of items recalled is systematically varying. Consider, e.g., a series of recall protocols which show perfect clustering and also show steadily increasing recall. With regard to category repetitions, these obviously increase with an increase in recall. With regard to RR, Eq. (4) shows that RR will increase and approach 1 as the number of items recalled increases. Further, using Eq. (2), it can be demonstrated that the disparity between maximum RR's for short and long protocols increases as the number of categories recalled increases. Cofer and his colleagues (Cofer, Bruce, & Reicher, 1966) add empirical weight to this argument by their demonstration of an overall positive relationship between number recalled and RR, although it must be noted that the relationship was not very high.

Given the characteristics of the clustering measures used in previous investigations, the obtained differences in clustering between high-frequency and low-frequency exemplars may be entirely due to differences in recall for these two types of words. If the frequency–clustering relationship is a measurement artifact, it should not be obtained using the ARC measure. With that possibility in mind, we examined the data from one of our studies (Experiment E) which manipulated exemplar frequency. The 64 *S*s in that experiment learned two 4-category lists. The same 4 categories were used in both lists with individual categories represented within a list by all high-frequency (H) or all low-frequency (L) exemplars. The categories in the two lists were arranged so that all *S*s received the four possible interlist within-category sequences of word frequency (i.e., HH, HL, LH, LL). The *Ss* had either 1 or 3 trials of practice on the first list, and they recalled either by the standard written free-recall procedure or by writing the words for each category in a separate unlabeled column.

The major point of interest here is that the *Ss* in Experiment E showed large and highly reliable differences in recall as a function of word frequency but no comparable differences in clustering. Taking the *Ss* which had 3 trials on the first list for illustrative purposes, the mean recall per category on the first list was 4.9 and 3.8 for the high-frequency and low-frequency items, respectively, whereas the mean clustering was .58 and .58 for the same items. The clear replication of the effect of exemplar frequency upon recall would seem to rule out the possibility that the experiment was not sensitive to the exemplar frequency manipulation. A very likely alternative explanation for the differences in results between our experiment and the others noted previously is that the differences are a function of the clustering indexes used in the experiments. The measure of clustering used in Experiment E was the ARC score which, as noted before, does not vary with characteristics of recall which are unrelated to the degree of clustering per se. In short, the results from Experiment E, together with an examination of the clustering measures used in other relevant experiments, strongly suggest that the proposed relationship between exemplar frequency and degree of clustering may be artifactual.

PERFORMANCE ON SUCCESSIVE LISTS CONTAINING REPEATED CATEGORIES

Proactive Interference

One of the most interesting findings in the research using categorized word lists has been the demonstration that repeating categories, but not category exemplars, in successive lists produces marked proactive interference. This phenomenon has been demonstrated in a number of experiments (e.g., Shuell, 1969; Winograd, 1968), including a series of six experiments from our laboratory. Our repeated-category experiments will now be discussed.

RECALL

The recall data from our six experiments are summarized in Table 3. Before discussing these data, several points must be made. First, only the

TABLE 3

Mean Recall per Category for Each List for Each of 6 Experiments in Which Ss Received Multiple Trials on Two or Four Successive Lists [a]

	List			
	1	2	3	4
Experiment A				
NR	4.9	5.5	5.4	5.8
R				4.0
Experiment B				
NR	5.0	5.5	5.6	5.8
R				4.1
Experiment C				
NR	3.6	4.0	3.9	3.8
R				3.0
Experiment D				
NR	4.2			
R		4.3		
Experiment E				
NR	4.3			
R		4.5		
Thompson and Poling (1969)				
NR	6.2	7.1	7.2	7.2
R	5.1	5.1	4.7	4.9

[a] Per-category recall is presented separately for categories which occurred in previous lists (R) and categories which have not occurred in previous lists (NR).

data from the 32 *S*s receiving 3 trials on the first list were used for Experiment E. Thus the procedure was identical for all *S*s represented in Experiments A through E in the table. Second, note that for those 5 experiments, categories were repeated only in the last list the subject received. In the Thompson and Poling study, some categories were repeated in all four lists. Third, first-list performance differed reliably for to-be-repeated and not-to-be-repeated categories in the Thompson and Poling study, thus necessitating two baseline entries for first-list recall in that instance.

The first fact to note in Table 3 is that when categories are not repeated in successive lists, the typical recall pattern is an increase in performance from the first to the second list with essentially stable performance thereafter. Note that this statement holds for nonrepeated categories when other categories in the list were repeated (e.g., Thompson and Poling data, 1969) and when there were no repeated categories (e.g., data from the first three lists in Experiments A, B, and C). In short, Table 3 verifies in three additional experiments the data presented for Experiment A in Fig. 1b.

The next fact to note is that when categories are repeated in successive lists, the inevitable result is proactive interference. Proactive interference was clearly demonstrated by the differential performance for repeated and nonrepeated categories in Experiments A, B, and C. It was also demonstrated by the interaction in the Thompson and Poling experiment which shows learning-to-learn effects for the nonrepeated, but not the repeated, categories. Finally, it is argued here that the failure to show learning-to-learn effects in Experiments D and E (in which all second-list categories were repeated categories), given the inevitable occurrence of such effects in lists without repeated categories, constituted presumptive evidence for proactive interference.

Given that Experiments D and E demonstrated proactive interference, the data clearly suggest that the past history of *S* has a major influence on the magnitude of the proactive interference. In those experiments in which repeated categories appeared immediately (i.e., in the second list), proactive interference was demonstrated as a failure to show learning-to-learn effects. Specifically, performance neither increased nor decreased over successive lists. However, when repeated categories were introduced after *S* had practiced on several lists containing no repeated categories, the effect of introducing them bordered on the catastrophic. As can be seen in Experiments A, B, and C, performance on the repeated categories plummeted to a level reliably *below* performance on the initial list. There are very few instances in the verbal learning literature of effects powerful enough to produce recall inferior to that shown on the first, practice, list. It is unlikely that this effect can be attributed to some sort of selective attending to the items from categories that were not repeated. Such selective attention would result in superior retention of items from those categories, and the data show that this was not the case.

Finally, it is perhaps worthy of mention that the data suggest that recall per category is dependent upon the number of words presented per category. Experiments A through D all used high-frequency exemplars with the number of words presented per category being 12, 12, 7, and 10 for the 4 experiments, respectively. (Note that, considering only categories consisting of high-frequency exemplars, the per-category recall in Experiment E was 4.9 with the number of words presented per category being 12.) Thus, with 12 words presented per category, per-category recall was 4.9; with 10 words presented, recall was 4.2; and with 7 words presented, recall was 3.6. There were 4 categories per list in all the lettered experiments except Experiment C, which used 6 categories per list.

Thus the data suggest (but, of course, do not establish) that the critical factor determining recall per category was not length of list or number of categories but number of words within categories.

CLUSTERING

The clustering data for Experiments A through E is summarized in Table 4. The data for the Thompson and Poling study were not available at the time this was written so they are not included. Note that the data presented were derived from the same sources as the data in Table 3.

The first fact to note in Table 4 is that clustering increased from the first to the second list and remains at a fairly stable level thereafter. As can be seen, this statement held for all 5 experiments.

The second fact to note is that the rather massive disruption of recall observed in these experiments had no concomitant effect in degree of organization. The degree of organization did not differ for repeated and nonrepeated categories in the fourth list of Experiments A through C,

TABLE 4

Mean Adjusted Ratio of Clustering (ARC) Scores for Each List for Each of 5 Experiments in which Ss Received Multiple Trials on Two or Four Successive Lists [a]

	List			
	1	2	3	4
Experiment A				
NR	.62	.78	.81	.82
R				.81
Experiment B				
NR	.63	.76	.80	.78
R				.76
Experiment C				
NR	.58	.77	.76	.81
R				.76
Experiment D				
NR	.63			
R		.75		
Experiment E				
NR	.56			
R		.64		

[a] Separate ARC scores are presented for categories which occurred in previous lists (R) and categories which did not occur in previous lists (NR).

nor did the interlist increment in degree of organization expected in the first two lists appear to have been appreciably truncated in Experiments D and E. Thus, whatever the proactive interference effect might involve, it apparently does not involve disruption of the organization of the remembered material.

Reduction of Proactive Interference

We began this line of research by establishing that we could readily produce substantial proactive interference by repeating categories in successive lists (Thompson & Poling, 1969). Having verified that fact, we directed our research efforts toward manipulations which might overcome or minimize repeated-category interference. To date, the manipulations used have sprung from the notion that memory involves a search process.

TEMPORAL PROXIMITY OF REPEATED CATEGORIES

Often, of course, manipulations to minimize repeated-category interference which are suggested by a memory-search hypothesis would also be suggested by many alternative theories. For example, most theories of memory would hold that the potential for common words from one list to interfere with common words from another list is, in part, a function of how close together in time the two lists occur. The closer together in time the lists, the greater the potential for interference. This prediction might be based on a notion involving "time tags," or a notion involving "decay of response strength," or some other hypothetical mechanism, but the expected effect is the same. In fact, such a prediction was made in Experiments A through C—and it failed. Some of the repeated categories in the fourth list in those experiments came from the third list and some came from the second list. Obviously, more time intervened between the second and fourth lists than intervened between the third and fourth lists. It is difficult to imagine that a list interpolated between two lists with repeated categories would increase repeated-category interference, although it is possible that the interpolated list would reduce such interference. (In fact, in a subsequent study which is not reported in this chapter there were no differences in performance between *S*s who did and did not learn an interpolated list.) Thus both factors led to the prediction that less interference should be generated by second-list categories than by third-list categories, but there were no consistent differences. Our speculation, which awaits a laboratory test, is that the expected results would occur if the time interval separating the lists were increased. The four lists might, e.g., be presented on successive days rather than all in one 2-hr session.

SUBCATEGORIZATION BY EXEMPLAR FREQUENCY

It is the usual practice to use common (i.e., high-frequency) words in free-recall tasks. It may be that *S*s use this fact to restrict their search set. In our experiments, e.g., *S*s might only include the common examples of each category in the search set. If such restriction occurs, the memory-search point of view makes straightforward predictions concerning the magnitude of proactive interference under several conditions. Proactive interference should be maximum when a repeated category is represented in both lists by common, or in both by uncommon, examples of the category. However, if common items are used to represent the category in one list and uncommon items are used for that purpose in the other list, proactive interference should be sharply reduced.

These predictions are of particular interest because this is one of those instances in which they stand in sharp contrast to the predictions that would be made by one of the major alternatives to the memory-search hypothesis. The alternative in this case is the notion that items in recall are retrieved via an interitem associative network (e.g., Deese, 1959). In brief, the associative network hypothesis states that the stronger the associations among the items in the list, the better the recall. Similarly, the stronger the extralist associates of list members, the greater the interference with correct recall. Together with that brief description of the associative network theory, note the following: (1) Bousfield, Steward, and Cowan (1964) have demonstrated that categorized lists composed of high-frequency words show many more interitem associations than do lists composed of low-frequency words. (2) Thompson (1970) has shown that *S*s generate more category associates for high-frequency words than for low-frequency words. (3) Categorical intrusions given to both high-frequency and low-frequency lists tend to be high-frequency words (Cofer *et al.*, 1966). The first two statements suggest that repeated categories would produce more proactive interference when the categories are represented in both lists by high-frequency words than when they are represented in both lists by low-frequency words. The third statement suggests that associations and, hence, interference may be "one-way." Specifically, low-frequency words are not likely to interfere with the recall of high-frequency words, but high-frequency words may interfere with the recall of low-frequency words. Thus an HL sequence (i.e., high-frequency first list, low-frequency second list) should produce more proactive interference than an LH sequence.

In summary, the memory-search hypothesis predicts the most (and equivalent) proactive interference for the HH and LL sequences and the least (and equivalent) proactive interference for the HL and LH sequences. However, the associative network theory also predicts the most interference for the HH sequence but predicts successively decreasing interference in the HL, LH, and LL sequences—in that order.

Experiment E was run to evaluate these contrasting predictions. As noted before, the categories in the two successive lists in Experiment E were arranged so that each *S* received the four possible interlist within-category sequences of word frequency (i.e., HH, HL, LH, LL). The *S*s had either 1 or 3 trials of practice on the first list.

The mean per-category recall for the second list is presented in Table 5, separately for *S*s having 1 and 3 practice trials on the first list. First-list recall for high-frequency and low-frequency words is also presented for comparison. Since second-list performance was averaged over 3 trials, only data from *S*s having 3 trials on the first list is presented for comparison.

There are several comparisons of interest in Table 5. First, performance on second-list high-frequency words (conditions HH and LH) was clearly superior to performance on low-frequency words (conditions LL and HL). Second, increased practice on first-list members had no effect on second-list recall if the members were high-frequency words (conditions HH and HL) but had a facilitatory effect on second-list recall if the members were low-frequency members (reliable only in condition LL).

TABLE 5

Mean per-Category Recall for the Four Interlist within-Category Sequences of Word Frequency [a]

	List 1		List 2			
Condition	H	L	HH	LH	LL	HL
One practice trial			4.8	4.8	3.3	4.3
Three practice trials	4.9	3.8	4.6	5.2	3.9	4.1

[a] Four sequences (i.e., high-high, high-low, low-high, and low-low, which are designated as conditions HH, HL, LH, and LL, respectively) are represented in the second list. The data for *S*s receiving 1 and 3 trials of practice on the first list are presented separately. For comparative purposes, the mean per-category recall for high- (H) and low- (L) frequency words in the first list is presented for those *S*s receiving 3 trials of practice on the first list.

Third, proactive interference produced an apparent decrement in second-list recall (relative to comparable first-list recall) in condition LL with 1 first-list trial. No comparable effect occurred for condition HH. The point is that, when the first list was not well-learned, the LL condition actually appeared to produce *more* interference than the HH condition. Fourth, the recall data show that conditions HL and LH tended to produce "release from proactive interference" (Wickens, 1970) with condition HL possibly more effective in that respect than condition LH.

These data clearly contradict the predictions that would be made from an associative-network hypothesis. That hypothesis predicts more interference in condition HH than in condition LL. In fact, amount of interference in the two conditions was indistinguishable when *S*s had 3 trials on the first list and the LL condition produced more interference than the HH condition when *S*s had 1 trial on the first list. The associative-network hypothesis also predicts more interference to be generated in condition HL than in condition LL and, of course, just the opposite occurred.

The memory-search hypothesis fares much better with these data, but the fit of theory to data is far from perfect. The search hypothesis would predict, on the one hand, that recall performance in the HL and LH conditions would be superior to performance in the LL and HH conditions, respectively—and such was the case. On the other hand, the prediction would be made that the magnitude of proactive interference should be about the same in the HH and LL conditions and also roughly equivalent in the HL and LH conditions. The data suggest that such was not the case for the HL and LH conditions, and the data clearly show that the magnitude of proactive interference was greater for the LL than the HH condition with 1 trial of practice on the first list. These deviations from the predicted results were sufficient to demonstrate that the simple version of the restricted-search hypothesis, which we have used to generate much of the research reported in this chapter, must be modified.

SUBCATEGORIZATION BY KIND

If the category being repeated in successive lists is animals, then it seems reasonable to assume that proactive interference could be reduced by presenting one kind of animal (e.g., wild) in the first list and another kind (e.g., domestic) in the second. Separation into subsets of this sort should have the same beneficial effect on proactive interference as the separation into common and uncommon words had in Experiment E. Substantial reduction in proactive interference should result from com-

TABLE 6
Mean Recall for Each Condition for Each List [a]

	Condition			
	0	1	3	5
First list	4.4	4.2	4.1	4.1
Second list	4.8	4.3	3.9	4.0
Difference	+.4	+.1	−.2	−.1

[a] The difference in mean recall for the two lists is also presented for each condition. The 0, 1, 3, and 5 conditions represent combinations of 0 and 10, 1 and 9, 3 and 7, and 5 and 5 words, respectively, from the 2 subcategories.

plete separation by kind with the magnitude of the reduction dropping sharply as some words from both subsets are included in both lists.

Experiment D (described on p. 250) was performed to test this hypothesis. The mean recall for each condition for each of the two lists is presented in Table 6, together with the differences in recall between the two lists. As can be seen, the results were in the expected direction with the condition with complete separation of the two subsets (condition 0) having shown the best second-list performance and the condition with complete overlap of the two subsets (condition 5) having shown the worst second-list performance. The conditions by list interaction was not significant, however, and the data can only be viewed as suggestive. A recommendation has been made that the study be replicated using a between-*S*s design since such a design might tend to magnify the differences shown in Table 6. We have not yet explored this possibility in the laboratory.

Concluding Remarks

The major results of our efforts thus far can be summarized as follows: (1) *S*s showing a high degree of clustering recall more than *S*s showing a low degree of clustering. (2) *S*s learn how to cluster just as they learn how to learn. The learning-to-cluster function roughly parallels the learning-to-learn function. (3) Recall for an item becomes better as the size of the set to which that item and related list items can be restricted (e.g., wild animals versus all animals) decreases. (4) Substantial proactive interference can be produced by repeating categories, but not specific category exemplars, in successive lists. The magnitude of this proactive interference is substantially increased when *S* has previous practice on several categorized lists which do not contain repeated categories. (5) The magnitude of this proactive interference can be substantially reduced by using common words to represent the category in one list and uncommon words to represent the category in the other list.

Our research was originally predicated on four general statements: that *S*s organize material presented to them for recall, that organization aids recall, that organization increases with practice, and that recall involves a search process. Our data, as well as the data of many other investigators, shows that there can be no questioning the fact that *S*s organize the material presented to them for recall or the fact that such organization increases with practice. However, we began this research with the firm conviction that organization invariably aids recall, but consideration of all our results leaves our belief somewhat shaken. While there can be no doubt about the fact that good clusterers recall more words than poor clusterers, the repeated-category data shows just as clearly that substantial changes can occur for clustering without comparable changes in recall. The first fact is consistent with the notion that clustering aids recall; the second fact casts doubt on that hypothesis. We are of the opinion that clustering has facilitatory effects which are overshadowed by the powerful proactive interference effects produced by category repetition but that possibility has not yet been tested in the laboratory. Finally, the memory-search hypothesis has had strong heuristic value. At the same time, the simple search model with which we have been working underestimates the robustness of the proactive interference effect. For example, we hypothesized, on the one hand, that presentation of different subcategories in successive lists should virtually eliminate proactive interference and, in the case of subcategorization by kind, no such effect is produced. On the other hand, the finding that recall becomes better as set size becomes smaller, and the pattern of results in the study using combinations of common and uncommon words to represent the categories in successive lists, seems particularly to support the search notion. In sum, the memory-search hypothesis has been useful for generating predictions, but the fit of data to theory has been far from perfect. Nonetheless, our "search for the search" has been enjoyable and instructive. We hope it continues to be both.

REFERENCES

Battig, W. F., & Montague, W. E. Category norms for verbal items in 56 categories: A replication and extension of the Connecticut Category Norms. *Journal of Experimental Psychology*, 1969, **80** (Monogr., No. 3, Part 2).

Bousfield, A. K., & Bousfield, W. A. Measurement of clustering and of sequential constancies in repeated free recall. *Psychological Reports,* 1966, **19**, 935–942.

Bousfield, W. A. The occurrence of clustering in the recall of randomly arranged associates. *Journal of General Psychology,* 1953, **49**, 229–240.

Bousfield, W. A., Steward, J. R., & Cowan, T. M. The use of free associational norms for the prediction of clustering. *Journal of General Psychology,* 1964, **70**, 205–214.

Bower, G. H., Clark, M. C., Lesgold, A. M., & Winzenz, D. Hierarchical retrieval schemes in recall of categorized word lists. *Journal of Verbal Learning and Verbal Behavior,* 1969, **8**, 323–343.

Cofer, C. N., Bruce, D. R., & Reicher, G. M. Clustering in free recall as a function of certain methodological variation. *Journal of Experimental Psychology,* 1966, **71**, 858–866.

Craik, F. I. M. Two components in free recall. *Journal of Verbal Learning and Verbal Behavior,* 1968, **7**, 996–1004.

Deese, J. Influence of inter-item associative strength upon immediate free recall. *Psychological Reports,* 1959, **5**, 305–312.

Glanzer, M., & Cunitz, A. R. Two storage mechanisms in free recall. *Journal of Verbal Learning and Verbal Behavior,* 1966, **5**, 351–360.

Mandler, G., & Pearlstone, Z. Free and constrained concept learning and subsequent recall. *Journal of Verbal Learning and Verbal Behavior,* 1966, **5**, 126–131.

Puff, C. R. Role of clustering in free recall. *Journal of Experimental Psychology,* 1970, **86**, 384–386. (a)

Puff, C. R. An investigation of two forms of organization in free recall. *Journal of Verbal Learning and Verbal Behavior,* 1970, **9**, 720–724. (b)

Roenker, D. L., Thompson, C. P., & Brown, S. C. A comparison of measures for the estimation of clustering in free recall. *Psychological Bulletin,* 1971, **76**, 45–48.

Segal, E. M. Hierarchical structure in free recall. *Journal of Experimental Psychology,* 1969, **80**, 59–63.

Shiffrin, R. M. Memory search. In D. A. Norman (Ed.), *Models of human memory.* New York: Academic Press, 1970. Pp. 375–450.

Shuell, T. J. Clustering and organization in free recall. *Psychological Bulletin,* 1969, **72**, 353–374.

Thompson, C. P. Note on word frequency as a factor in perception of category size. *Perceptual and Motor Skills,* 1970, **30**, 301–302.

Thompson, C. P., Hamlin, V. J., & Roenker, D. L. A comment on the role of clustering in free recall. *Journal of Experimental Psychology,* 1971, in press.

Thompson, C. P., & Poling, D. R. Free recall of successive lists: Effect of category size and category repetition. *Psychonomic Science,* 1969, **16**, 201–202.

Tulving, E. Theoretical issues in free recall. In T. R. Dixon & D. L. Horton (Eds.), *Verbal behavior and general behavior theory.* Englewood Cliffs, N.J.: Prentice-Hall, 1968. Pp. 2–36.

Tulving, E., & Pearlstone, Z. Availability versus accessibility of information in memory for words. *Journal of Verbal Learning and Verbal Behavior,* 1966, **5**, 381–391.

Wickens, D. D. Encoding categories of words: An empirical approach to meaning. *Psychological Review,* 1970, **77**, 1–15.

Winograd, E. List differentiation, recall, and category similarity. *Journal of Experimental Psychology,* 1968, **78**, 510–515.

AUTHOR INDEX

Numbers in italics refer to the pages on which the complete references are listed.

SUBJECT INDEX